Thailand's Reproductive Revolution

Social Demography

Series Editors   Doris P. Slesinger
James A. Sweet
Karl E. Taeuber

Center for Demography and Ecology
University of Wisconsin-Madison

Thailand's Reproductive Revolution

Rapid Fertility Decline in a Third-World Setting

John Knodel

Aphichat Chamratrithirong

Nibhon Debavalya

THE UNIVERSITY OF WISCONSIN PRESS

Published 1987

The University of Wisconsin Press
114 North Murray Street
Madison, Wisconsin 53715

The University of Wisconsin Press, Ltd.
1 Gower Street
London WC1E 6HA, England

First printing

Printed in the United States of America

For LC CIP information see the colophon

ISBN 0-299-11050-8 cloth
ISBN 0-299-11054-0 paper

Contents

Tables and Figures

Tables

Figures

Acknowledgments

The research on which this study is based was supported by grants from the Rockefeller Foundation and the Population Council's International Research Awards Program on the Determinants of Fertility. We are particularly grateful to Napaporn Chayovan, Napaporn Havanon, Peerasit Kamnuansilpa, and Anthony Pramualratana, whose collaboration in research on which parts of this study are drawn was indispensable. Chintana Pejaranonda and Phandhipaya Pharmasaroja were helpful in providing us with official statistical data. Deemar Company, Ltd., and the UNFPA, Thailand Office, kindly made available transcripts of focus-group sessions with southern Muslims.

Special thanks are due to Robert Hanenberg, whose careful reading, critical insights, and detailed comments on a chapter-by-chapter basis as the first draft was being written were invaluable. We also benefited substantially from comments generously provided by the following colleagues: Mary Asher, Tony Bennett, Larry Bumpass, John Casterline, Peter Donaldson, Ronald Freedman, Napaporn Havanon, Jay and Fern Ingersoll, Gayl Ness, Chai Podhisita, Ronald Rindfuss, Peter Schneider, Werasit Sittitrai, Mark Van Langingham, and Nancy Williamson.

Finally, the Institute of Population Studies at Chulalongkorn University, the Institute for Population and Social Research at Mahidol University, and the Population Studies Center at the University of Michigan all provided excellent facilities and atmosphere for carrying out the research and writing of this study.

Thailand's Reproductive Revolution

1

Introduction

Fertility Change in the Third World

In virtually all countries that are commonly considered economically more developed, a transition from previous high levels of fertility to modern low levels has taken place in the course of the last century, in some cases beginning even earlier (van de Walle and Knodel, 1980). A new balance of relatively low birth and death rates is close to replacing an earlier balance of high fertility and mortality. This evolution from high to low birth and death rates, known as the Demographic Transition, is also under way throughout the lesser developed countries, referred to collectively as the Third World. In virtually every country, a movement from higher to lower mortality levels has already taken place. In most Third World countries, the decline in the death rate started recently. Moreover, the decline occurred far more rapidly than in the experience of the more developed countries. So far, as in the case of the more developed countries, declines in mortality in the Third World have shown no signs of reversing.

Declines in birthrates in lesser-developed countries have either lagged behind the mortality decline or have yet to begin. In the vast majority of Third World countries, birthrates are still higher, and often substantially so, than they are in the more developed countries. For example, in 1982, the United Nations (1985) estimated (in their medium-variant projections) that during 1980–85, birthrates still averaged 46 per 1,000 population in Africa, 32 in

3

Latin America, and 27 in Asia. This compares to average birthrates of 14 per 1,000 in Europe and 16 in North America.

The result of these high birthrates has been unprecedented rates of population growth in the lesser-developed countries collectively. Given that the large majority of the world's population live in less-developed nations, this has meant unprecedented growth rates in the world as a whole. Thus, the average rate of close to zero growth that has characterized the world population during most of human history, and that had already risen to approximately 0.5 percent during the first half of the present century, soared to almost 2 percent per annum in recent decades. Such a rate, if maintained, implies more than a quadrupling of the world's population within seventy years, less than the average life span expected of someone born in a more developed country today. Concern over the consequences of prolonged continuation of such rapid growth rates has made population a major international issue.

Sometime during the last two decades, the rate of world population growth peaked and began to slow, finally reversing the previous trend of accelerating increase. Although a complex mix of national situations underlie this international trend, the single most important component of this historic turnaround in world population growth rates has been declining fertility in a number of lesser-developed countries. These selected Third World nations have finally entered the stage of falling birthrates, following the spectacular reductions in death rates over the last several decades.

For developing countries as a group, population growth rates rose from 2.0 percent in 1950 to 2.4 percent in 1965, largely because of falling death rates. Since then, death rates have continued to fall but birthrates have declined even more, so that growth has slowed. Much of the fall in the average growth rate is due to the birthrate decline in China, which alone accounts for almost a third of all the people in lesser-developed countries and where the birthrate has fallen by over 50 percent since 1965. Although the Chinese experience is of considerable interest, in many respects the country is unique, particularly with its capacity to implement at the local level a policy to reduce fertility determined at the highest level of government through a well-developed political-administrative apparatus. Birthrates have also fallen in other Third World countries, however, and in some cases, quite rapidly.

An overview of fertility levels and trends in the fifteen largest Third World countries as assessed by the United Nations in 1982 is shown in table 1.1. The measure used, the total fertility rate, indicates the implied number of births a woman would have if she experienced the average rates at which women of different ages are currently bearing children as she passed through the reproductive age span herself. Between the first half of the 1960s and the first half of the 1980s, total fertility declined in all but one of the countries shown.

Table 1.1. Population Size in 1984 and Total Fertility Rates, 1960–65 and 1980–85, as Assessed by the United Nations in 1982, and Contraceptive Prevalence Rates for the Fifteen Largest Less-Developed Countries

	Population (millions) 1984	Total fertility rate			Contraceptive prevalence[a]	
		1960–65	1980–85	Percent change	Year	Percent
China	1,052	5.4	2.3	−57	1982	71
India	747	6.5	4.4	−32	1981/82	26
Indonesia	162	5.4	3.9	−28	1980	27
Brazil	133	6.2	3.8	−39		
Pakistan	99	7.2	5.8	−19	1979/80	3
Bangladesh	98	6.7	6.2	− 7	1979	13
Nigeria	92	6.9	7.1	+ 3	1981/82	6
Mexico	77	6.7	4.6	−31	1979	39
Vietnam	58	5.6	4.3	−23		
Philippines	53	6.6	4.2	−36	1978	36
Thailand	51	6.4[b]	3.6[b]	−44	1981	56[c]
Turkey	49	6.0	4.5	−25	1978	38
Egypt	46	6.6	5.2	−21	1981	34[d]
Iran	44	8.1	5.6	−31	1978	23
South Korea	40	5.4	2.5	−54	1982	58
All less-developed countries[e]						
Including China	3,597	6.0	4.1	−32	1980–81	38[f]
Excluding China	2,546	6.3	4.8	−24	1980–81	24[f]

Source: United Nations (1984, 1985).

[a] Percent currently practicing among currently married women in reproductive ages.
[b] Based on United Nations estimates and thus differs from total fertility rates presented in chapter 4 from primary sources.
[c] Based on women 15–49 and thus differs from rates given in chapter 5; as of 1984, prevalence was 63 percent for women 15–49.
[d] Including breastfeeding.
[e] Based on United Nations (1984), including less-developed countries not shown; total fertility estimated from gross reproduction rates; total excluding China derived by assigning China a weight proportional to its population size.
[f] Based on median assumptions about countries without prevalence data.

The extent of the decline varies substantially, however, with the largest relative reduction indicated for China.

The place of Thailand within this list of countries is of considerable interest to those concerned with changing patterns of childbearing. The fertility decline in Thailand is the third largest decline, behind only South Korea and China. If the dominating case of China is excluded, the average fertility decline for the remaining lesser-developed countries collectively is only slightly over half the magnitude of the fertility decline in Thailand (24 percent compared to 44 percent). Thailand's total fertility rate of 6.4 during the first half of the 1960s was quite typical of large Third World countries; it was even slightly above average. By the first half of the 1980s, total fertility in Thailand had fallen to 3.6 and was the third lowest rate of all fifteen countries shown, exceeding only that of China and South Korea.

The United Nations (1984) has also compiled results of a number of national surveys measuring the extent of contraceptive use and has made alternative estimates in several of the cases where such surveys were unavailable. The results are also included in table 1.1 for the fifteen largest lesser-developed countries for which data are available. Of the thirteen countries with information on contraceptive prevalence, Thailand shows the third highest rate, again behind only China and South Korea, and is well above the average for all lesser-developed nations. Indeed, more recent data (presented in chapter 5) indicate that by 1984, 65 percent of currently married women aged 15–44 were using contraception, thus approaching the level characteristic of more developed countries. The United Nations (1984:28), for example, estimated an average prevalence of 68 percent for the more-developed countries for the 1980–81 period (based on medium-level assumptions about countries for which prevalence data are unavailable). The relatively high level of recent prevalence in Thailand is particularly remarkable given the very low levels that characterized Thailand less than two decades ago.

The Significance of Thailand

Concern over the social, economic, and political consequences of the developing world's rapid population growth that resulted from falling mortality combined with high fertility has led to considerable interest both on the part of scholars and policymakers in the determinants of reproductive behavior, particularly those related to fertility decline. Developing countries that have experienced substantial reductions in fertility during recent decades are of particular interest in this context. Thailand is an especially intriguing case because of the rapidity and pervasiveness that have characterized the fertility decline there and because reproductive change has occurred during a period when the country is still predominantly rural and agrarian.

The significance of Thailand as a case study of reproductive change in the Third World is further enhanced by the fact that at an early stage of the fertility decline, an official policy and program were instituted to encourage and facilitate the practice of contraception with the explicit goal of reducing the population growth rate through lowering fertility. Such large-scale family-planning programs have been the primary mechanism adopted by many other Third World countries to help curb what governments view as excessively rapid growth rates. A recent tally of government positions on population growth and family planning indicates that 76 percent of the population of the Third World live in countries with official policies to reduce the population growth rate and an additional 17 percent live in countries that support family-planning activities for other than demographic purposes (Nortman, 1985). A number of social scientists have long been critical of the ability of organized family-planning efforts to make a significant contribution to fertility decline, given the inability of these efforts to alter the basic social and economic institutions thought to be the ultimate determinants of reproductive motivations (Davis, 1967). The rapid increase in contraceptive use in Thailand since the government began to support family planning poses important questions about the contribution of the program to the fertility decline. The Thai case is thus a critical and potentially important one both for its policy implications for other lesser-developed nations in which far less spectacular increases in prevalence have paralleled implementation of their family-planning programs and for its implications for a general understanding of the determinants of reproductive behavior.

The population dynamics of lesser-developed countries during the last several decades have also led to a reexamination of traditional explanations of the demographic transition. The original formulation of demographic transition theory derived exclusively from the experience of the more developed countries. According to Notestein, one of the theory's formulators, the growth of Europe in the modern era involved initially declining mortality produced by the process of modernization, including rising levels of living and new controls over disease. Fertility responded more slowly to modernization, but ultimately began to decline with the widespread use of contraception stimulated by such factors as growing individualism and rising aspirations developed in the course of urban industrial living. He noted that the more rapid response of mortality than of fertility to the forces of modernization is probably inevitable and thus that a transitional period of rapid growth is to be expected (United Nations, 1973:58–59).

The idea of demographic transition has been widely adopted by professional population scientists to explain the evolution of populations in both historical and contemporary societies. The implication for the Third World at the end of World War II was that modernization would inevitably cause the same early decline in the death rate, whereas birthrates would remain high; consequently a period of rapid growth was in prospect. Later, only further modernization as part of socioeconomic development would bring about a reduction in fertility.

Although Thailand is not among the least developed of the Third World countries, neither does it rank particularly high with regard to many conventional indices of socioeconomic development (see chapter 3). Most striking, perhaps, is that the fertility transition is taking place while the Thai population is still largely rural and agricultural. There seems to be a general receptivity among broad segments of the population, including those with little or modest education and living in rural areas, to the changes in reproductive patterns that are now taking place.[1] An examination of the Thai demographic transition, and particularly the fertility decline, is important not only in terms of the heightened policy concerns about rapid population growth that have developed over the last few decades but also in terms of understanding the determinants of fertility transition, one of the central problems of modern population science.

The transformation in reproductive attitudes and behavior that has been taking place in Thailand over the last several decades is so far-sweeping and profound that it can aptly be called a reproductive revolution. Our goal in this book is to present a comprehensive study of this revolution, documenting the nature and extent of the changes that have taken place and explaining them in demographic, socioeconomic, and cultural terms, including an assessment of the role of organized family-planning programs. To do so, we follow an approach, described in chapter 2, that draws on both quantitative and qualitative source material and attempts to integrate them to produce a coherent picture of Thailand's fertility transition. Indeed, we view this attempt to combine qualitative and quantitative types of evidence as a major contribution of our study. We intend this book to be of interest to a broad range of readers, including those with an academic interest in population and the process of social change in the Third World in general, those with a special interest in Thai society, and those with a policy- and action-oriented interest in population and development.

1. This study of reproductive change in Thailand excludes consideration of the nonassimilated tribal populations located mainly in mountainous regions, especially in the north and northwest. These groups, known as "hill tribes," constitute only a small minority, although their exact numbers are difficult to determine and depend on the specific definition used. Most surveys in Thailand exclude hill tribes from their sample frames. They are also largely excluded from the national census. Although intensive demographic studies of these groups are only recently in progress, it is safe to conclude that their demographic behavior is quite distinct from the rest of the Thai population. Their fertility still appears to be quite high and it is unlikely that they have experienced much decline in fertility during the period covered in this study. Given their marginality to the rest of Thailand's population, we have defined their demographic dynamics as outside the scope of the present study.

Conceptual Framework

Several decades ago, Davis and Blake (1956) made a major contribution to the conceptualization of fertility determinants by specifying a set of biological and behavioral variables that directly affect reproductive behavior. They distinguished these variables from all others—be they socioeconomic, cultural, political, psychological, or environmental—whose influence on fertility can only operate through them. These direct determinants, originally referred to as intermediate variables by Davis and Blake, are now more commonly called proximate determinants and have subsequently been respecified by Bongaarts (1978) in a manner that more easily lends itself to a quantitative assessment of their contribution to differences or changes in fertility levels (see Bongaarts and Potter, 1984). Our thinking about reproductive change in Thailand, and the presentation of our findings, is guided by this now- familiar distinction between proximate and other fertility determinants. More generally, consistent with our desire to present a comprehensive analysis of Thailand's fertility decline, we operate within a relatively broad and eclectic conceptual framework that starts with the proximate determinants and then moves to the far broader array of influences that indirectly affect fertility through their impact on the proximate determinants.

Figure 1.1 lists the seven proximate determinants identified by Bongaarts with brief descriptions of each. The distinguishing feature of the proximate determinants is that a change in any one of them necessarily results in a change in fertility (assuming the other proximate determinants remain constant). The same is not necessarily the case with other fertility determinants. Thus, for example, a change in the extent of induced abortion, one of the proximate determinants, would necessarily change fertility, whereas changes in nonproximate determinants, such as education, household structure, or religion, may or may not have an impact. Provided adequate information is available, changes in fertility over time can always be traced to variations in one or more proximate determinants. Likewise, the influence of any nonproximate determinant on fertility change can always be accounted for in terms of its influence on the proximate determinants. In a sense, an accounting of fertility change in terms of proximate determinants provides a description of the "mechanics" of reproductive change and as such can serve as an important step in the search for a broader explanation in terms of nonproximate determinants.

The broader framework within which we view changes in the proximate determinants as leading to fertility decline is summarized in figure 1.2. Since many of the proximate determinants are influenced by volitional actions and choice, attitudes directly concerning fertility as well as attitudes about the proximate determinants themselves are an important feature of any explanation of reproductive change. In the cases of explaining the timing and pace of

1. Marriage and Marital Disruption

The proportions of women in reproductive ages who are exposed to coitus
as determined by the age of entry into marriage (or more strictly,
sexual unions) and their durations.

2. Onset of Permanent Sterility

The proportions of couples physiologically incapable of reproduction as
determined by the age at which men and women become sterile. (This
reflects both primary sterility, the inability to bear any children
from the beginning of sexual activity, and secondary sterility,
the eventual loss of reproductive capabilities.)

3. Duration of Postpartum Infecundability

The duration of the anovulatory interval following a birth during
which a woman is not susceptible to conception (dependent primarily
on breastfeeding patterns).

4. Fecundability

The monthly probability of conceiving among menstruating women not
practicing contraception (dependent primarily on coital frequency).

5. Spontaneous Intrauterine Mortality

Nondeliberate miscarriage and abortion.

6. Contraception

The prevalence and effectiveness of contraceptive practices.

7. Induced Abortion

Deliberate interventions to terminate pregnancies.

Figure 1.1. The Proximate Determinants of Fertility. (Adapted from Bongaarts [1982b].)

fertility decline, we believe a particularly crucial aspect of reproductive attitudes is the possible existence and extent of a latent demand for lower fertility
prior to the onset of an actual reduction in fertility levels. Changes in reproductive attitudes as well as in a variety of aspects of the proximate determinants themselves are seen as influenced by a variety of the conditions that
constitute social and economic life in Thailand in recent decades. Particularly
important are those socioeconomic conditions that influence perceptions of
the social, economic, and psychological costs and benefits of children. Given
the importance of organized family-planning efforts as the major policy intervention intended to influence fertility in Thailand, and their operation during
much of the period of fertility decline, we explicitly specify such efforts as a
separate aspect of the broader conditions that potentially contributed to Thailand's fertility decline. Finally, we view all fertility determinants as operating
within a cultural context specific to Thailand and hence the relationship between reproductive behavior and its various determinants as conditioned by it.

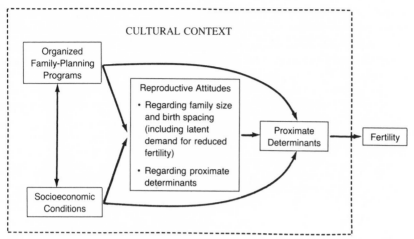

Figure 1.2. A View of the Determinants of Fertility

The organization of this book conforms generally to this view of the determinants of fertility decline. After discussing sources and methods in chapter 2 and providing socioeconomic and related background information for Thailand in chapter 3, we review recent trends in fertility and family-size preferences in chapter 4. The quantitative evidence concerning the proximate determinants of reproductive change is examined in chapter 5 which includes an assessment of the relative contribution of several key proximate determinants to the recent levels and changes in Thai fertility. The results clearly show that increased contraceptive use is the main proximate determinant accounting for Thailand's fertility decline. Chapter 6 also focuses on the proximate determinants but is based on qualitative evidence and includes a discussion of evidence pointing to a substantial latent demand for lower fertility even before fertility went down. The relations between societal change and reduced family size are the topic of chapter 7 with particular attention given to the meaning of the socioeconomic changes described in chapter 3 for reproductive decisions of Thai couples. Chapter 8 focuses on aspects of the Thai culture that are particularly relevant to understanding reproductive behavior and attitudes. Chapter 9 explores the channels through which the means of fertility reduction spread through Thai society, focusing primarily on the role of organized efforts to promote family planning but with some consideration also given to more informal channels of diffusion. The final chapter summarizes our basic arguments regarding the causes and conditions behind Thailand's rapid fertility decline. These involve a series of interrelated and fundamental changes in socioeconomic conditions, a favorable cultural setting for reproductive change, a substantial latent demand for fertility control prior to the actual decline, and a national family planning program that increased awareness and accessibility to acceptable and effective means of contraception. We conclude by assessing the extent to which the Thai experience has wider applicability for other developing countries and for understanding the process of fertility transition in general.

2

Sources and Methods: Integrating Quantitative and Qualitative Approaches

Of all areas of social-scientific inquiry, none have closer association with quantitative data than demographic research. Censuses, vital statistics, and sample surveys, the basic sources of demographic data, provide results that are inherently numerical. As the search for explanation and understanding of demographic phenomena proceeds, however, an increasing number of scholars outside the field of demography as well as demographers themselves are beginning to question the adequacy of an exclusively quantitative approach based on the conventional data sources and research tools of the discipline.

More qualitatively oriented social scientists, particularly anthropologists, have generally treated demographic behavior as only a peripheral interest at best. Moreover, the limited amount of qualitative research on reproductive behavior in developing countries done by anthropologists in the past has often been undertaken without a well-grounded knowledge of quantitative demography. As a result, anthropologists have often been unfamiliar with some of the central issues of concern within the field and with the accumulated knowledge about them, especially as they have emerged from the quantitative results from existing survey research and other standard demographic sources. Consequently, they have often lacked appreciation of the larger statistical profile and demographic trends that could give greater significance to their own localized studies. In short, demographically informed qualitative research on population issues has been relatively sparse in the past.

The situation is beginning to change. Organized efforts to broaden the nature of demographic research are being made by John Caldwell of the Australian National University, his associates, and other sympathetic scholars through their advocacy of what is becoming known as the "microapproach" to demographic investigation. This quasi-anthropological approach combines ethnographic field research with surveys and even censuses of villages or small areas in an attempt to arrive at a holistic understanding of demographic behavior and change within a broad historical and sociological perspective (Caldwell, Reddy, and Caldwell, 1984a,b; Caldwell, 1985a,b).

In part as a result of the recent work by Caldwell and others, considerably more reflection is being given to the strengths and weaknesses of both quantitative and qualitative approaches for the study of demographic behavior. It is our conviction that most is to be gained by a combination of approaches. Thus, the present study follows a mixed-method paradigm, integrating both quantitative and qualitative research to produce a more comprehensive study of Thailand's reproductive revolution than could be done by relying on either type of research alone. To achieve this goal, we draw on a variety of sources, the two most important of which are (1) a series of national sample demographic and social surveys that provide extensive quantitative information and (2) a series of directed focus-group discussions that provide extensive qualitative information on reproductive change and the context in which it has occurred. In addition, other sources including anthropological monographs, local and specialized surveys, and official statistics are utilized to fill out the picture of reproductive change and its socioeconomic and cultural context. A brief review of these sources is the main topic of the present chapter.

Sources of Quantitative Data

Thailand is unusually favored in comparison to most developing countries with respect to the availability of quantitative data for the study of fertility levels, trends, and determinants. These data are generally of good quality, come from a variety of sources, and cover most of the period during which the fertility decline has taken place. Population censuses have been held since 1911 with decennial censuses taking place in 1960, 1970, and 1980. A registration system for births and deaths has been in existence since early in the century, although the data yielded by this system are incomplete. Most important for the quantitative study of determinants of fertility, however, has been a series of sample surveys, conducted during the last decade and a half, that were designed specifically to study fertility and closely related behavior. Although we draw on quantitative information from all relevant sources, much of our analysis is based on data from these sample surveys.

A list of the most important surveys, the abbreviations used to refer to them, the dates of the fieldwork, and a brief comment on the sample coverage are provided in table 2.1. Additional information about the surveys is provided in appendix A. All of these surveys are essentially national in scope and either concentrated on or had substantial components dealing with reproductive behavior and attitudes. Although the samples of the major surveys on which we draw vary to some extent, we believe the results are sufficiently comparable to enable us both to trace the trends in various determinants of fertility over time and to compare quantitative interrelationships at different stages of the fertility decline.[1] Other surveys directed at specific regions or sub-groups of the population, or surveys dealing with nondemographic topics are occasionally drawn upon as well.

All data from the surveys included in table 2.1 refer to individuals or their households. This monograph also draws occasionally on two sets of village-level data, i.e., information collected about the characteristics of villages. In one case, the village level data were collected in 1984 in the course of conducting CPS3 and thus refer to the sample of 208 villages selected for that survey. The other village- level data were collected in 1983 as part of a separate village-level survey whose aim was to gather retrospective information about the sixty-four villages that were included in either LS1, LS2, or NS. We will refer to the first source as the CPS3 Village-Level Survey. Since the Institute of Population Studies (IPS) of Chulalongkorn University conducted the other village level survey as well as LS1, LS2, and NS, we will refer to this source as the IPS Village-Level Survey. In both cases, the data, which refer to rural areas, are more or less nationally representative of rural villages in Thailand.[2] In the case of the IPS Village Survey, an innovative method of group interviews with several village leaders was utilized to collect the information (Chayovan and Knodel, 1985).

In addition to surveys, censuses, and vital registration data, occasional use is made of statistical material both from governmental and nongovernmental

1. Several conventions were followed in preparing the tables included in this study. When referring to the dates of surveys, hyphenated years are reserved for those strictly representing coverage of a span of years, such as SPC2 for 1974–76. Years separated by a slash indicate combined results from two component cross-sectional surveys taking place in successive years namely, LS1 (1969/70) and LS2 (1972/73). Where tables were derived from original tabulations not published elsewhere, the source is simply indicated as the survey itself. Only when tables or parts of tables were derived from previous publications or manuscripts in process are references made to a bibliographical source.

2. This is somewhat less so for the IPS Village Survey, since the sampling frame for LS1, LS2, and NS excluded some of the more remote areas of the country as well as the four predominantly Muslim southernmost provinces.

Table 2.1. Selected Surveys Providing Quantitative Information on Fertility and Fertility Determinants

Abbreviation	Full name	Date of major fieldwork	Sample coverage
LS1	Longitudinal Study of Social, Economic, and Demographic Change—Round 1	Rural—April/May 1969 Urban—April/May 1970	National except for exclusion of sensitive areas and predominantly Muslim provinces in south
LS2	Longitudinal Study of Social, Economic, and Demographic Change—Round 2	Rural—April/May 1972 Urban—April/May 1973	National except for exclusion of sensitive areas and predominantly Muslim provinces in south
SOFT	Survey of Fertility in Thailand (part of WFS)	April/May 1975	National
CPS1	Contraceptive Prevalence Survey—Round 1	December 1978/ January 1979	National except for exclusion of provincial urban places
NS	National Survey of Family-Planning Practices, Fertility, and Morality	April/May 1979	National except for exclusion of sensitive areas and predominantly Muslim provinces in south
CPS2	Contraceptive Prevalence Survey—Round 2	April/June 1981	National
CPS3	Contraceptive Prevalence Survey—Round 3	April/June 1984	National including a special supplemental sample of southern Muslims

16

agencies, especially when dealing with the socioeconomic setting and the performance of the National Family Planning Program. Materials generated by the Ministry of Public Health, the National Statistical Bureau, and the World Bank were particularly useful for these purposes.

Sources of Qualitative Data

The main source of qualitative data on which we draw is a series of focus group sessions conducted specifically with the intent of gaining insights into the nature and determinants of Thailand's reproductive revolution. Although the focus-group technique has been widely used in private industry, especially for marketing research, its use as a tool for basic social-science research has been quite limited.[3] We believe our own use of the technique as part of our research into the Thai fertility transition is quite unusual. Given the newness of focus-group research to the field of population studies, a brief discussion of the approach is in order.[4]

A focus group consists of a small number of participants (usually five to ten) from a target population who, typically under the guidance of a moderator, discuss topics of importance to the particular research study. Although the moderator covers topics according to predetermined guidelines, the discussion is essentially open-ended with leeway to follow up unanticipated lines of discussion germane to the theme of the session. Participants for particular sessions are usually chosen according to criteria that ensure that they are relatively homogeneous with respect to characteristics that might otherwise impede the free flow of discussion. Generally this means that participants of any one session are of similar social status and do not hold sharply conflicting views about sensitive or deeply felt aspects of the topic under investigation. Criteria for inclusion would often include basic background characteristics such as sex, age, education, or income level, as well as characteristics more directly relevant to the study theme. For example, if the main area of concern is with adolescent sexual behavior, groups would be homogeneous according to whether the participants were sexually active or not. The specific criteria on which a group is formed will depend on the nature of the research project. Separate sessions with groups selected on the basis of different sets of criteria permit the in-depth exploration of views of persons with quite different char-

3. The focus-group approach has recently been used as an applied research strategy for aiding in the design and improvement of family- planning programs (see the special issue of *Studies in Family Planning*, December 1981). Wells (1974) provides a useful discussion of the approach as used in marketing research generally.

4. For a fuller discussion of the use of the focus-group approach as means of demographic inquiry, see Knodel and Pramualratana, 1984. Morgan and Spanish (1984) provide a useful discussion of the potential value of focus groups for social science research in general.

acteristics while still preserving the homogeneity of each particular group. Within each session, the full discussion is typically tape-recorded and later transcribed. These transcripts serve as the basic data for analysis.

The informal and supportive group situation and the open-ended nature of the questions are intended to encourage participants to elaborate on behavior and opinions to an extent that might be difficult in individual interviews or in groups containing persons of opposing views and diverse statuses. When focus groups work properly, participants react to comments made by each other. Remarks by one participant may lead another to pursue a line of thinking that would not have emerged in an individual interview. Interactions among participants stimulate memories and expressions of opinion and thus lead to a fuller discussion of the topic at hand. This group dynamic distinguishes focus-group sessions from individual in-depth interviews typical of ethnographic research and from group interviews in which participants are expected to provide concrete factual answers to questions posed rather than to discuss issues in an informal manner. Caldwell (1985a) has recently noted the value of interaction when interviews are conducted within a group setting, although in his own research such group discussions were conducted in a less systematic way than in the case of focus-group sessions.

Our use of focus-group material is based on a central tenet shared by practitioners of micro-approach, namely that, "most actors involved in major social changes know that something is happening, have some idea of the direction and shape of the changes, and have speculated—at least to themselves—about what is happening and why" (Caldwell, Reddy, and Caldwell, 1984a). Given the qualitative nature of the data and the analysis, a considerable amount of subjective judgment on the part of the researcher is involved in interpreting what was said or even in determining what views appear to be more pervasive among the many opinions expressed. Not all statements can be taken at face value. Interpretation based on the context in which they are made and in light of information available to the researchers from other sources is required. Relationships between variables of interest to the researcher are not always spelled out by the participants, even with probing, and may have to be inferred. Part of the problem arises from the difference in the level of abstraction and explanation sought by social scientists and that which seems of direct relevance to participants. Nevertheless, in our own case, with proper scrutiny and interpretation, the information, perceptions, opinions, and attitudes expressed by the participants regarding the rapid decline in fertility yield valuable and otherwise unavailable insights into the nature and causes of Thailand's reproductive revolution.

Probably the most important advantage of focus groups is their group-dynamic aspect, whereby participants stimulate each other with respect to the thoughts expressed. There are a number of other advantages as well over standard survey interviews. When questions are misunderstood by participants, it usually becomes quickly evident to the moderator and can be easily corrected. Since comments are typically made within the context of a broader discussion, they are less likely to be misinterpreted by the analyst. A group situation can facilitate open discussion of some types of sensitive topics if other participants are perceived as sharing the same perspective. Moreover, whereas social status differences between an interviewer and a respondent may inhibit or distort responses in a typical individual interview situation, it is less likely to have an impact in a focus-group session where the individual participant has greater anonymity vis-à-vis the moderator.

The focus-group approach, although it sacrifices some rigor, encourages fluidity in the process of hypothesis development and hypothesis testing. Hypotheses and concepts often emerge during the data-collection process rather than being determined beforehand. There is flexibility to introduce new topics into the discussion guidelines and to discard less useful ones as the project proceeds. Moreover, the focus-group approach permits closer involvement of principal investigators at the primary level of data collection. It is usually more practical for the researcher to observe a substantial proportion of focus-group sessions, or even to moderate them himself, given the limited number of sessions, than it would be to attend a large proportion of individual survey interviews. This allows the analyst to be considerably closer to the data and provides a far better vantage point when interpreting results.

The focus-group approach also has limitations and potential problems. The determination of whether hypotheses have been disproved or confirmed is a less precise process than with quantitative research and rests largely on the judgment of the investigators. The qualitative nature of the data, the small size of the total sample, and the intentionally purposive manner in which participants are selected make statistical generalizations based on focus-group results inappropriate. In addition, covert behavior or opinions that may be disapproved by substantial segments of the community may be less likely to be revealed in a group than to an individual interviewer, unless they are perceived to be shared by others in the group. Basic values and concerns are not always readily verbalized, in part because they are taken for granted and considered too obvious to discuss. Mechanisms that operate in subtle or indirect ways may be difficult to detect in direct discussions of the behavior that they influence. Moreover, there is always a risk that one or two participants may dominate the discussion.

The use of focus-group sessions is a less ambitious approach to collecting qualitative data than a full-fledged anthropological study or the microapproach to demographic investigation advocated by Caldwell. These latter approaches permit far greater in-depth analysis of linkages between demographic behavior and socioeconomic and cultural underpinnings in the context of local communities than is possible with a focus-group study. However, because focus groups do not require long-term residence and extensive participant observation in the communities in which they are conducted, a greater number of communities can be included in a given study and thus a broader coverage attained. Moreover, because transcripts are produced in the course of a focus group study, verification of findings and reanalysis can, in principle, be undertaken by others besides the original investigators. Such an endeavor would be far more difficult with the field notes of an anthropologist or practitioner of the microapproach to demographic studies.

The focus-group material comes mainly from research we conducted comparing older- and younger-generation Thais with respect to attitudes and circumstances underlying recent changes in reproductive behavior. Focus groups were chosen to represent modal pre- and post-fertility- decline situations. For this purpose, the older-generation participants selected were generally over age 50 and had at least five children who survived childhood. Younger-generation participants, in contrast, were generally under 30 for women and under 35 for men, wanted no more than three children, and had not yet exceeded that number. Both older and younger participants were to have no more than an elementary education, reflecting the educational status of the majority of the Thai population. Separate sessions were held for older and younger generations of each sex.

Complete sets of four focus-group sessions were held during late 1982 and early 1983 in five villages: one each in the central, northern, and northeastern regions, and one each in both a Buddhist village and a Thai-speaking Muslim village in the south (the region where Muslims are concentrated). In addition, all but an older-generation men's session were held among rural migrants living at construction sites in Bangkok. There were twenty-three sessions in all. Although the total sample is not statistically representative of the Thai population, each major region is included as well as a village of the Muslim minority and a group of rural migrants. The sample had a strong rural emphasis by intent, since our major interest was in the rapid reproductive changes of the rural majority. In four of the villages, resident anthropologists collaborated with us, providing background information and helping in the selection of participants. Fuller details of the design of the focus-group project, as well as a copy of the discussion guidelines used by the moderators, are provided in appendix B.

We also draw on an additional set of focus-group transcripts produced in connection with a study of attitudes toward family planning among Muslims in the south sponsored by the United Nations Fund for Population Activities (UNFPA) and conducted by Deemar, a commercial marketing-research firm in Bangkok. The topics covered are narrower and oriented more toward applied issues concerning increasing acceptance of family planning rather than to the broader theoretical issues involved in understanding fertility transition in Thailand, as is the case with our own focus-group project. Nevertheless, the Deemar transcripts are of value because they provide rare qualitative data related to the reproductive behavior of Thai Muslims, a group of particular interest because they have not been fully participating in the reproductive change that has recently characterized virtually every other easily identifiable group in Thai society (see chapters 4 and 5).

In our own focus-group project, we included only one Muslim village, which is probably atypical of most Muslim villages in several respects. Given that the villagers speak the southern Thai dialect and that the village is located in a mixed Muslim-Buddhist area near a main highway, the residents are probably more integrated into Thai society and more modern in their attitudes toward family size and contraception than is true of most Thai Muslims. The Deemar study involved eight focus-group sessions with both Thai- and Malay-speaking Muslims and thus expands considerably the amount of qualitative data available for Thai Muslims.

Unless it is specifically stated otherwise, focus-group material summarized and cited in the following chapters is drawn from our own focus-group project. Whenever material from the Deemar Muslim study is used, it is identified as such. To illustrate the focus group findings, direct quotations from the focus group sessions are occasionally used. We have attempted to select quotations that are both typical and clear. Implied words are included in brackets when necessary to improve intelligibility. Following each quote, we identify the session from which it comes.

In addition to focus-group research, we draw on existing ethnographic and anthropological studies to provide qualitative material for our study. Although most such studies do not deal directly with reproductive behavior, they nevertheless provide important information on the cultural and social context, particularly in rural areas, of Thailand's fertility transition. Moreover, at least three recent anthropological village studies have been directed specially at an analysis of demographic behavior including fertility decline and thus are particularly valuable for our own purposes (Lauro, 1979; Mougne, 1982; Podhisita, 1985a).

Integrating Quantitative and Qualitative Research

Because the use of qualitative data for the study of demographic behavior is relatively novel, this chapter has described more extensively the qualitative than quantitative source material for the present study. Particular attention has been given to the focus-group approach since it is the primary source of qualitative data used. This is not intended to imply, however, that qualitative data are necessarily more important. Both types of data are useful, can complement each other, and, when integrated into a single analysis, can provide a more complete picture than if each were analyzed separately. Although qualitative research gives investigators considerable leeway for exercising intuition, such intuition is better grounded when placed in a perspective of a solid knowledge of available quantitative data. As one commentator on focus groups has pointed out, the greatest threat to qualitative research findings is probably not so much their lack of generalizability as their potential lack of validity, a liability that can be best assessed by comparing results obtained by alternative methods (Calder, 1977). Even when different approaches yield conflicting results, this is important information to have, ideally leading to a reevaluation of each approach and perhaps to a reformulation of the issues under investigation.

We view social science research in general and demographic inquiry in particular as an ongoing process aiming at a fuller understanding of the phenomena under investigation rather than as final and definitive analyses. Demographic inquiry is thus best undertaken as a total package, combining not only results from different methods but also familiarity with theoretical arguments and knowledge of previous research efforts. The incorporation of qualitative techniques into what has been largely a quantitative field will bring us further along toward this goal. We hope that the promise of such an approach is at least partially illustrated in the content of the chapters that follow.

3

The Country Setting: Thailand in Transition

Thailand is a tropical country in the Indo-Chinese peninsula of southeast Asia bordered by Kampuchea and Laos on the east and northeast, by Burma on the west and northwest, and by Malaysia on the south. Thailand includes tropical rain forests, agriculturally rich plains, and forest-clad hills and mountains. The patterns of rivers and mountains divide Thailand into four natural regions: the mountainous north; the northeast, consisting primarily of the Korat plateau; the central region, consisting primarily of the Chao Phraya Basin; and the south, consisting of the long peninsular extension of Thailand south from the Chao Phraya Basin to the Malaysian frontier (see map—figure 3.1).

Unlike many other developing countries and all its southeast Asian neighbors, Thailand has never been colonized by a foreign power. There have been periodic invasions by Burmese and Khmers in the more distant past and a brief occupation by the Japanese during World War II, but by and large the country has been an independent nation throughout its history. The current royal dynasty has been in power since 1782. Although absolute monarchy was replaced by constitutional monarchy as a result of a bloodless revolution in 1932, the royal family serves as an important unifying symbol for the vast majority of Thais. Despite a series of coups and constitutions since the overthrow of the absolute monarchy, the basic political situation in Thailand has remained relatively stable throughout this period with the military, in one form or another, exercising considerable influence in the government most of

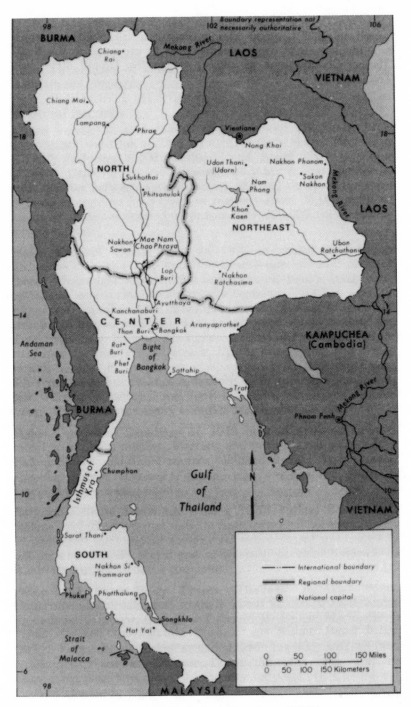

Figure 3.1. Map of Thailand. (From Bunge [1981].)

the time. Although insurgency problems have not been negligible, especially during the late 1960s and much of the 1970s, they never escalated to the level of conflict that eventually resulted in the establishment of Communist regimes in south Vietnam, Laos, and Cambodia (Szaz, 1983).

Administratively, the country is currently divided into seventy- three provinces (*changwat*), one of which is the Bangkok metropolis. Each province is further subdivided into districts (*amphur*), townships (*tambol*), and villages (*muban*). Some areas are also designated as municipalities, including all provincial capitals. Economically and politically the country is dominated by Bangkok, the only major urban area. Although it is located geographically within the central region, for most purposes the Bangkok metropolis is usefully considered a distinct region on its own because its population differs considerably in many characteristics from the remainder of the central region.

In socioeconomic terms, Thailand's features are typical of the developing world. Like many other Third World nations, Thailand has been experiencing rapid and fundamental social and economic change as it undergoes the process of modernization and development and becomes increasingly enmeshed in the world economic system. In this chapter we provide a variety of statistical indices intended to portray Thailand's present stage of development and to document some of the basic social and economic changes that have been taking place during the period when reproductive behavior has changed so radically. These indicators, however, capture only imperfectly the nature and speed of the changes that have engulfed the Thai population and that underlie the ongoing revolution in reproductive behavior. Many of the indices, by their very nature, change only slowly and thus do not reflect rapid shifts in attitudes and outlooks that have taken place. Moreover, it is people's perceptions of change, rather than the objective conditions themselves, that influence their actions. These perceptions include not only their assessment of how the present situation differs from the past, but also their anticipation of what the future holds.

We have attempted to tap these perceptions of present conditions, past changes, and future prospects through the focus-group sessions. Discussion of these qualitative results, however, is deferred to later chapters in which they are related specifically to reproductive change. In addition, most discussions of Thailand's cultural context, other than a brief examination of religious composition and household structure, are also deferred to later chapters where they are related to the qualitative data collected through the focus-group sessions. The present chapter thus is largely restricted to providing information about Thailand's level and direction of development as measured by more conventional statistical indices. Such information, despite its limitations, is still valuable for understanding the context of changing reproductive patterns. Particular emphasis is placed on changes taking place over the last decade or two, since this corresponds to the timing of rapid changes in reproductive behavior among Thai couples. Comparisons of the results of the last two or three censuses are particularly useful in this respect.

Thailand in Comparative Perspective

As a starting point, it is useful to examine Thailand's socioeconomic situation within the broader context of Third World countries in general. Data published by the World Bank (1985) provide a useful basis for such a comparison. Results are summarized in table 3.1 utilizing the World Bank's classification of developing countries into low- and middle-income groupings based on a ranking of gross national product (GNP) per capita. The low-income countries all had a per capita GNP of no more than 400 U.S. dollars in 1983. Because averages (weighted by population) for this group are dominated by China and India, the two largest countries, indices are shown separately for these two countries and the combined group of all other low-income countries. Moreover, because the middle-income group includes a large number of countries and covers such a wide range of average income levels, results are shown separately for the lower and upper divisions of this broad category. Not included are results for a small number of high-income oil-exporting countries of the Middle East, whose status as Third World countries is questionable, as well as countries with industrially advanced economies.

In terms of GNP per capita, Thailand is squarely middle-range among those developing countries classified as being lower-middle-income, which ranged in 1983 from 440 U.S. dollars for Senegal to 1,430 for Colombia. This is the case even though Thailand's rate of economic growth since 1960 has been well above the average of less-developed countries generally. Nevertheless, Thailand's population remains predominantly rural and agrarian. In comparison with other developing countries, including even those in the low-income category, the urban proportion is unusually low and the percentage of the labor force engaged in agriculture is unusually high.

In a number of other respects, such as energy consumption, primary and secondary school enrollment, availability of physicians, and daily calorie supply, Thailand is fairly typical of the lower-middle-income group of Third World nations, although generally a little lower than average. In terms of infant mortality and life expectancy, Thailand's situation appears more favorable, resembling more closely the average for the upper-middle-income group. In brief, based on standard socioeconomic indications, Thailand can be considered to be at a level of development well within the range encompassing most of the Third World, better off in some respects than the poorest countries but by no means unusually advanced compared to the middle range countries of the developing world.

Table 3.1. Comparative Indicators of Social and Economic Development, Thailand and Other Low- and Middle-Income Countries

	Thailand	Low income		Middle income	
		China and India	Other countries	Lower middle	Upper middle
GNP per capita (U.S.$), 1983	820	280	200	750	2,050
Percent annual growth in GNP per capita, 1965–83	4.3	3.2	0.7	2.9	3.8
Percent of labor force engaged in agriculture, 1981	76	73	72	54	30
Percent of population living in urban areas, 1983	18	22	21	36	64
Energy consumption per capita (1,000s of kilograms of oil equivalent), 1983	269	341	80	382	1,225
Primary school enrollment (as percent of age group), 1982	96	98	70	103	102
Secondary school enrollment (as percent of age group), 1982	29	33	19	35	51
Population per physician, 1980	7,100	1,858	17,990	7,555	2,018
Daily calorie supply per capita, 1982	2,296	2,503	2,118	2,495	2,880
Infant mortality rate (per 1,000 live births), 1983	50	61	115	87	59
Life expectancy at birth, 1983	63	62	51	57	65

Source: World Bank (1985).

Note: All figures are based on World Bank estimates and thus may differ from results presented in subsequent tables or chapters based directly on primary sources.

Population Growth and Land Availability

According to recent population projections by Thailand's National Economic and Social Development Board (NESDB), Thailand's population exceeded the 50 million mark sometime during 1984. This represents more than a sixfold increase since 1911, when the population, according to the first census (as shown in table 3.2), was only 8 million. As in many developing countries, population growth, particularly since World War II, has been relatively rapid. Although the intercensal rates of growth can be considered as only approximate due to uncertainties about the completeness of the census enumerations, it seems likely that the rate of growth peaked at over 3 percent per year during the 1950s and the early 1960s. By the first half of the 1980s, according to the recent NESDB estimates, the population growth rate had declined to below 2 percent.

Table 3.2. Enumerated Population for Census Years 1911–70, Adjusted Population for Census
Years 1960–80, and Average Annual Intercensal Growth Rates

Census date	Enumerated population (in 1000s)	Intercensal annual growth rate (percent)	Adjusted population (in 1000s)	Adjusted annual growth rate (percent)
4-1-1911	8,266.5	—	—	—
4-1-1919	9,207.4	1.3	—	—
7-15-1929	11,506.2	2.2	—	—
5-23-1937	14,464.1	2.9	—	—
5-23-1947	17,442.7	1.9	—	—
4-25-1960	26,257.9	3.2	27,357.0	—
4-1-1970	34,397.4	2.7	36,825.0	3.0
4-1-1980	44,824.5	2.6	46,269.5	2.3

Sources: 1911–70 census enumerated totals and intercensal growth rates are from Arnold,
Retherford, and Wanglee (1977); 1980 enumerated total from 1980 census volume; adjusted
populations for 1960 and 1970 from U.S. Bureau of the Census (1983); adjusted population for
1980 from Pejaranonda, Arnold, and Hauser (1983).

Clearly rates of growth of 3 or even 2 percent cannot persist indefinitely in
any country, since the force of exponential growth inevitably leads to absurdly
large population sizes over the long run. The force of the relatively rapid
growth over recent decades and the sixfold increase since the first census in
1911 has already made itself felt by creating pressure on agricultural land.
Indeed, whereas the amount of land under cultivation has been increasing, it
has not kept pace with population growth. As is shown in table 3.3, between
1963 and 1983 the total area of agricultural holdings increased by 43 percent;
during the same period, the population increased by over 60 percent. Moreover, much of the new land is probably of a more marginal quality than that
already under cultivation. However, since the proportion of households engaged in agriculture has decreased, the size of the holding has changed little,
averaging about 3.5 hectares both in 1963 and 1983.[1] The rate of expansion of
the area of agricultural holdings has also slowed recently. On average between
1963 and 1978, the area increased annually by 0.25 million hectares compared to 0.19 million hectares between 1978 and 1983. There is general
agreement that by 1980 most of the usable new agricultural land in Thailand
had been occupied except in parts of the south (Whitaker, 1981:127).

1. There has been some suggestion that the rural landless have been increasing (Turton,
1978:112, 1982:28). Census results, however, indicate little change between 1970 and 1980 in
the percentage of males working as paid employees in agriculture, the category that would presumably represent landless agricultural laborers. The excess rural population is presumably
entering the nonagricultural sector.

Table 3.3. Growth in the Area of Agricultural Holdings and Average Size of Holding, 1963–83

	National	Central	North	Northeast	South
Percent growth in area of agricultural holdings					
1963–78	34.1	13.5	58.8	53.3	−2.7
1978–83	6.4	− 0.4	8.4	10.6	1.0
1963–83	42.8	13.0	72.2	69.7	−1.8
Average size of holding (hectares)					
1963	3.5	4.3	2.6	3.5	3.7
1978	3.7	4.5	3.2	3.9	3.1
1983	3.6	4.3	3.1	3.8	2.9

Source: Thailand National Statistical Office.

Although the average size of holding differs only moderately by region, there is considerable variation within regions and localities. Agriculture is dominated by small holders, most of whom have either outright title to the land or effective possession of it. Tenancy is significant only in the central plains (Whitaker, 1981). According to a study conducted in 1973/74, the proportion of farm operators who were full owners of their holding was 77 percent for the country as a whole. Regionally, the proportion who were owners was 89 percent in the northeast, 83 percent in the south, 69 percent in the north and 7 percent in the central region. Many of the remainder were part owner and part tenant, with only a small proportion full tenants (World Bank, 1980). In general, productivity has increased somewhat over the last few decades, but is low by regional standards. For example, the average yield per hectare in rice, the most important crop, rose from slightly under 1.25 metric tons during the 1950s to almost 1.75 metric tons during the 1970s. Productivity seems to have leveled, however, with yields during the late 1970s and early 1980s not much different from those a decade earlier. During the last two decades, substantial crop diversification has taken place and production of many secondary crops has increased substantially. This represents a considerable change from the previous almost total dominance of rice (Whitaker, 1981).

Rural-Urban Distribution

Social, economic, and often cultural forces typically differ sufficiently between rural and urban settings to result in observably different ways of life. The distribution of population with respect to rural and urban areas is thus an important dimension of a country's socioeconomic condition.

There is no question that Thailand has been and continues to be a predominantly rural society and is relatively so even within the context of the developing world in general. It is also clear that there are pronounced differences in social and economic conditions between the rural and urban populations. Nevertheless, the situation is less straightforward than might at first appear. Two issues are involved. The first concerns the technical definition of urban and rural; the second concerns the changing implications of any rural-urban categorization during a time of substantial socioeconomic change.

There is no official definition of rural and urban in Thailand. The usual practice is to define the officially designated municipal areas, including the entire Bangkok metropolis, as urban, and the remainder of the country as rural.[2] This definition is increasingly being criticized as unrealistically narrow and most observers agree that it results in an underestimation of the "true" urban population. One partial remedy is to include officially designated sanitary districts, or at least the larger ones, as urban. Sanitary districts are localities that achieve a minimum population size and density and develop some urban characteristics. In the present study, however, analyses in subsequent chapters utilize the usual, more limited definition of urban based only on municipal areas because such a definition has been incorporated in most of the data sources used.[3]

The percentage of Thailand's population living in urban areas, defined both in terms that include and that exclude the larger sanitary districts, is shown in table 3.4 based on the last three censuses. According to the 1980 census, exactly 17 percent of Thailand's total population lived in municipal areas including the Bangkok metropolis. This figure is the one typically used to designate

2. Prior to its formation in 1972, the Bangkok metropolis consisted of two separate provinces, each of which contained certain areas classified as rural. For this reason, the definition of "urban" employed in a number of sample surveys utilized in the present study corresponds to the population living inside municipalities or the formerly urban sections of the Bangkok metropolis; the remaining population is defined as rural. In other surveys, the entire population of the Bangkok metropolis is treated as urban.

3. The basic problem with a definition based only on municipal areas (including Bangkok) is that it is becoming increasingly out of date. There has been almost no change in the number of officially designated municipalities over the last several decades even though the nature of many places in the nonmunicipal category has changed considerably, including places both on the fringe of municipal areas and elsewhere. Instead, localities that achieve a minimum population size and density and develop some urban characteristics are frequently designated as "sanitary districts." As such, they remain in the rural category when rural is defined exclusively in terms of municipalities. (In 1980, 17.0 percent of Thailand's total population lived in municipal areas, including the Bangkok metropolis, 6.6 percent in large sanitary districts, and 2.7 percent in small sanitary districts.) In addition, there has been insufficient redefinition of the boundaries of existing municipal areas to allow for their de facto expansion (ESCAP, 1982; Robinson and Wongbuddha, 1980).

An argument has been made that even inclusion of large sanitary districts in the definition of "urban" is inadequate to capture the "real" urban population because it does not adequately take into account recent spatial expansion of larger provincial municipal centers. However, no estimate

Table 3.4. Indices of Urbanization, Based on Censuses, 1960–80

| | Percent urban of total population | | Percent of total population | | Bangkok as percent of municipal population |
	Excluding sanitary districts	Including large sanitary districts	In Bangkok[a]	In provincial municipalities	
1960	12.5	16.2	6.5	6.0	51.9
1970	13.2	20.8	7.3	6.0	54.8
1980	17.0	23.6	10.5	6.5	61.5

Sources: 1980 census and Economic and Social Commission for Asia and the Pacific (1982).

[a] The municipal-area portions of Bangkok and Thonburi provinces in 1960 and 1970; the Bangkok metropolis in 1980.

the urban percentage of the population. However, if the definition of urban were expanded to include the larger sanitary districts, the urban percentage would increase to 24 percent. Thus, although the proportion of the Thai population living in urban areas has increased with each successive census, it was still less than one fourth of the total in 1980, even when the expanded definition is used. Although the usual definition of urban as the equivalent of municipal areas is likely to understate the extent of urbanization in Thailand, any reasonable adjustments are unlikely to alter the impression that Thailand not only is predominantly rural but is unusually so in comparison to most Third World countries.

The evidence on urbanization presented in table 3.4 also makes clear the increasing and overwhelming dominance of Bangkok in the overall urban population. More than half of the total urban population, defined in terms of municipal areas, lived in Bangkok in 1960; by 1980, more than six out of ten urban residents resided in the capital city. Moreover, most of the increase

---

is available of how different the urban proportion would be if this were taken into account (ESCAP, 1982:30).

One reason a consensus on how to redefine the urban population is lacking is evident from data provided in the 1980 census on the proportion of population designated as living in agricultural households. In contrast to the municipal area population, where only 4 percent live in agricultural households, 35 percent of the population in the large sanitary districts and 38 percent in the smaller sanitary districts are agricultural. This compares to 73 percent living in agricultural households among the population outside both municipalities and sanitary districts. Thus, the population of sanitary districts appears to occupy an intermediate position and as such forms an ambiguous category. Indeed, a case can be made for making a finer distinction between rural and urban than is implied in a simple dichotomy (Goldstein and Goldstein, 1978; Sermsri, 1980).

in the urban percentage is attributable to the growth of Bangkok; the share of the total population living in provincial urban places has increased little over the last two decades.[4]

Bangkok has often been noted as an extreme case of a primate city (ESCAP, 1982). According to the 1980 census, for example, the largest provincial city at that time, Chiang Mai, had only about 100,000 inhabitants, compared to the 4–5 million inhabitants of Bangkok. Even more recent figures, based on registration data, taking into account new, expanded boundaries of both Chiang Mai and Korat (Nakorn Ratchasima), the largest city in the northeast, indicate that Korat is now the largest provincial city but that the populations of both Korat and Chiang Mai are still less than 200,000 each. This dominance of Bangkok in the urban hierarchy has profound economic, social, and political implications (London, 1980). Moreover, the population differs in many important respects from the provincial urban population (Prachuabmoh et al., 1972). There is thus ample reason for treating Bangkok as a distinct "region" in itself.

The second conceptual problem concerns the changing sociological nature of any set of rural-urban categories when basic socioeconomic change is affecting the entire society. Although rural and urban life-styles may differ considerably from each other, both are changing. In particular, influences that were formerly associated primarily with an urban setting are increasingly permeating the countryside. The result is that, in some respects, the difference between the two settings is becoming less distinct. For example, educational and health-care facilities are improving in the countryside, a wide array of consumer goods are increasingly available in village shops, and villagers have increasing access to urban areas, to mention just a few of the aspects that are blurring the difference. The dynamic nature of both the rural and urban populations should be kept in mind when interpreting rural- urban comparisons in the analysis of changing reproductive behavior (ESCAP, 1984).

Mortality Change and Health Facilities

Mortality has been improving in Thailand for some time. One recent set of estimates indicates a fairly steady decline in the crude death rate in Thailand since 1920, with the exception of the turbulent years during World War II (ESCAP, 1976). Expectation of life at birth probably increased by some two

---

4. Part of the apparent lack of increase in the level of urbanization in the provinces is a result of the restrictive definition of "urban" as discussed above. In addition, part of the increasing proportion living in Bangkok is attributable to the redesignation of the Bangkok metropolis in 1972 by combining the entire former provinces of Bangkok (Phra Nakorn) and Thonburi and eliminating the former nonmunicipal classification of some areas within these provinces.

or three years between the mid-1960s and the mid-1970s, reaching about 58 years for males and 64 years for females by the end of the period. An important component of the improved mortality, since 1960 at least, has been a reduction in infant and child mortality. The probability of a child dying before age 5 was approximately 10 percent in the mid-1970s, which is less than half the risk estimated for the period between 1937 and 1947 (National Research Council, 1980; Rungpitarangsi, 1974). Recent trends in infant mortality are summarized in table 3.5. Direct estimates based on the dual-record system methodology of the two Surveys of Population Change agree reasonably well with indirect estimates based on the proportions deceased among all children reported ever born to a woman as recorded in various sources. Nevertheless, there is the possibility that the indirect estimates, especially the most recent ones, understate somewhat the true level.[5] Both types of estimates indicate moderate declines in infant mortality at the national level between the mid-1960s and mid-1970s; the indirect estimates suggest a continuing decline since then. Even in the mid-1960s, however, the level of infant mortality appears to have been quite moderate by Third World standards, lower than many countries even recently, including Indonesia and all of south Asia with the sole exception of Sri Lanka (World Bank, 1985:218).

The estimates of infant mortality point to a substantial and persistent difference between the rural and urban populations. The chance of a rural infant dying before reaching age 1 remains considerably greater than for an urban infant, although the most recent indirect estimates, based on the 1980 census and the 1984 CPS3, indicate the difference is contracting. Part of the reason for the decline in infant mortality, particularly among the rural population, may well be the substantial expansion of public-health facilities over recent years.

The health-service system in Thailand is a complex mixture of public and private providers. In urban areas, private health services are very important. In addition, the Ministry of Interior administers a variety of public-health facilities in Bangkok and other municipalities. For the large rural population, however, the major source of service is the Ministry of Public Health, operating through an extensive network of outlets including regional health centers, provincial and district hospitals, and local midwifery and health stations. As discussed in detail in chapter 9, the public sector is also the most important source of family-planning services for the Thai population.

---

5. One possible source of understatement, in addition to the underreporting of dead children, is the choice of the North model life tables as the basis for the calculations. This was done to maintain consistency for the whole series of indirect estimates. There is some suggestion, however, that, at least for more recent years, the West model is more appropriate. If the West model were used, for example, the estimated infant-mortality rate based on CPS3 would increase from 41 to 45 per 1,000 live births (Kamnuansilpa and Chamratrithirong, 1985).

Table 3.5. Direct and Indirect Estimates of Infant Mortality, by Place of Residence

Type of estimate and source	Approximate years to which estimate applies	Infant mortality per 1,000 births		
		National	Rural	Urban
Direct estimates				
SPC1	1964–65	84[a]	86	68[a]
SPC2	1974–76	52	59	20
Indirect estimates				
1970 census	1966	70	74	31
Second SPC (Round 1)	1970	61	65	27
1980 census	1976	43	44	31
CPS3	1980	41	42	34

Sources: Thailand National Statistical Office (1978); Knodel and Chamratrithirong (1978); Chamratrithirong and Pejaranonda (1984); Kamnuansilpa and Chamratrithirong (1985).

Note: The indirect estimates of infant mortality were obtained from the North family of model life tables corresponding to indirect estimates of $2q0$, $3q0$, and $5q0$. For a description of the method of calculating the indirect estimates, see Knodel and Chamratrithirong (1978). Direct estimates are based on a dual-record methodology.

[a] Excluding Bangkok-Thonburi.

The substantial expansion of the public-health system during the last two decades is evident in the data provided in table 3.6 on the number of local health stations and provincial and district hospitals under the Ministry of Public Health. It is particularly significant that virtually all the health and midwifery stations are located in rural areas and that the increase in hospitals is almost entirely at the district level, with the number of provincial hospitals increasing only modestly.

At present, the vast majority of rural Thais have at least reasonably easy access to primary health care, as indicated by the finding from CPS3 that 88 percent of married rural women lived in villages within 5 kilometers of a health station or hospital (Kamnuansilpa and Chamratrithirong, 1985). This represents a considerable change from 1971 when, according to the IPS Village Survey, 69 percent of rural villages were within 5 kilometers of a health station (Chayovan, Hermalin, and Knodel, 1984a). The IPS survey provides another indicator of improved access, namely, that between 1971 and 1979 the proportion of villages that were either within 5 kilometers or a half hour's travel time of a health station or hospital increased from 72 to 94 percent, reflecting both the expansion of the number of health service outlets and improved transportation. Although rigorous studies linking the provision of government health services to improvements in health and the decline of mortality are lacking, it seems likely that the major expansion of such service in recent years has been an important contributing factor.

Table 3.6. Number of Health-Service Outlets of the Ministry of Public Health, 1965–84

	Health and midwifery stations[a]	Provincial and district hospitals[b]
1965	2,119	237
1970	3,358	312
1975	4,676	342
1980	5,862	386
1985	7,189	513

Source: Rural Health Division, Ministry of Public Health.

[a] Midwifery stations have a midwife and sometimes an assistant; health stations have, in addition, a junior sanitarian. The Ministry of Public Health is in the process of upgrading all midwifery stations into health stations.

[b] There has been little change in the number of provincial hospitals, which has remained under 100 during the entire period.

Social and Economic Change

As in most other developing countries, Thailand is experiencing rapid and fundamental social change affecting virtually all segments of the population. This change is reflected in part in the trends shown by a variety of social and economic indicators reviewed in the present chapter.

The Labor Force

The predominantly agrarian nature of the Thai population is evident in table 3.7, which shows the distribution of the economically active population according to the industry in which they practiced their principal occupation during the year preceding the census. Although the agricultural sector of the population has been declining, in 1980 agriculture was still the overwhelmingly dominant industry providing employment for over seven out of every ten workers. Between 1960 and 1980, agriculture's share of the labor force declined from 82 to 72 percent. Increases in the shares attributable to the tertiary service sector, manufacturing, and commerce absorbed the shift out of agriculture. As would be expected, the labor-force composition by industry is markedly different for rural and urban areas. Over four-fifths of the rural labor force worked in agriculture. In contrast, in urban areas, services, commerce, and manufacturing predominated.

To some extent, these statistics based on the principal occupation over the last year exaggerate the importance of the agricultural sector, since a substantial proportion of the agricultural population works part time in nonagricultural jobs during the agricultural slack season (Pejaranonda and Arnold,

Table 3.7. Percentage Distribution of the Economically Active Population Aged 11 and Over,
by Industry, 1960–80, and by Residence, 1980

	1960	1970	1980	1980 Rural	1980 Urban
Agriculture (including forestry, hunting, and fishing)[a]	82.4	79.3	72.2	82.8	7.1
Manufacturing	3.4	4.1	5.6	3.6	18.0
Construction (including repair demolition)	0.5	1.1	1.5	1.0	4.7
Commerce[b]	5.7	5.3	7.3	4.1	27.1
Transport, Storage, and Communication	1.2	1.6	1.8	1.0	6.8
Services	4.8	7.1	8.1	4.6	29.3
Others, unknown	2.0	1.5	3.4	2.8	7.0

Sources: 1960 and 1970 censuses as reported by Pejaranonda and Arnold (1983) and 1980 census report.

Note: The economically active population refers to all persons who were employed at the census date or at any time during the preceding twelve months.

[a] Forestry, hunting, and fishing constitute only a very small percentage of this group; in 1980, for example, they represented less than 0.5 percent of the economically active population.
[b] Combined with banking and other related financial institutions in 1980 and presumably for prior years.

1983). There is also some evidence that this tendency has been increasing recently (ESCAP, 1984).[6] Despite this qualification, it is clear that agricultural activities retain a predominant importance in the economic lives of the large majority of the Thai population.

Thailand has relatively high female labor-force participation rates (Debavalya, 1983). Measurement of labor force participation, particularly for women, however, is very sensitive to the definition used. In the case of Thailand, it is important to realize that all unpaid family workers are included in the census definition of the economically active population (i.e., the labor

6. The 1980 census provides information on the occupational distribution of the population based on the occupation practiced in the week prior to the census and on the principal occupation during the past year for those who worked in the past year. Since the 1980 census took place during the slack season in most parts of Thailand, a comparison of these distributions provides some indication of the magnitude of the shift into nonagricultural pursuits during the slack season. Such a comparison makes evident that most farmers during the slack season either continue to engage in agriculture or remain idle waiting for the farm season to begin. Nevertheless, a substantial minority work in crafts, as nonagricultural labors, or work in sales or transportation jobs

force) in contrast to many other countries where stricter definitions are employed. In the 1980 census, two alternative definitions of the economically active population were used: one based on activity during the prior week and the other on activity during the prior year.[7]

As table 3.8 shows, the resultant economic activity rate (i.e., percent active) for men is almost the same for both definitions, but for women is somewhat higher if the one-year rather than the one-week definition is used. Thus, among females aged 11 and over, 69 percent were economically active based on the one-year definition, compared to 62 percent based on the one-week definition. Regardless of the definition used, the proportion of women who are economically active is lower than men. This holds at all ages except under 20, where economic activity is slightly higher for females. Of particular interest is the fact that economic activity rates are quite high for women during the reproductive ages. Even when the one-week definition is used, about three-fourths of women aged 20 through 49 are economically active.

Most economic activity among Thai women involves unpaid family work, particularly as farmers. This accounts for the substantially higher activity rates among rural than among urban women. Nationally, among women who worked in the year prior to the 1980 census, 70 percent were employed as unpaid family workers in their principal occupation and 65 percent worked as unpaid family workers in agriculture. Among economically active women in urban areas, the situation was quite different, as only 22 percent worked as unpaid family workers. Nevertheless, definitional problems aside, most observers agree that labor-force participation is high among women in Thailand compared to most developing countries and that women play important economic roles in Thai society (Sharp, 1970–71). In addition to producing a

---

when there is no farm work (Pejaranonda and Arnold, 1983). The number of employed persons in these categories during the week prior to the census exceeds the number who state this as their principal occupation by almost 1,120,000 or about 7 percent of the total who indicate their principal occupation is in agriculture. This is undoubtedly a minimal estimate, since some persons whose principal occupation was in agriculture might also work during part of the slack season outside of agriculture but were not doing so during the week prior to the census.

7. More precisely, in one case, anyone who had worked during the week prior to the census or who was looking for work or waiting for the farm season to begin is considered economically active; in the other case, anyone who had worked during the year prior to the census is defined as economically active. In the published census reports, economic activity *rates* are reported only in terms of the one-week definition. However, the *number* of economically active persons based on the one-year definition is also given, thus permitting calculation of *rates* based on both definitions. Since the number whose economic-activity status is unknown is only given based on the one-week definition and not for the one-year definition, the one-year rate must include them in the denominator even though they are excluded from the denominator of the rate based on the one-week definition. The result is to bias downward slightly the one-year rates compared to the one-week rates.

Table 3.8. Percent Economically Active among Population Aged 11 and Over, by Age, Sex, and Residence, 1980

| Age at time of census | Active status in year prior to census[a] | | Active status in week prior to census[b] | | | | | |
| | Whole country | | Whole country | | Rural | | Urban | |
	Male	Female	Male	Female	Male	Female	Male	Female
11–19	47	50	49	50	53	54	27	29
20–29	88	80	90	73	92	75	81	63
30–39	97	86	96	75	96	78	95	65
40–49	97	86	95	75	95	78	94	60
50–64	77	56	84	60	85	64	77	41
65 and over			40	20	42	21	31	12
11 and over	75	69	76	62	78	65	68	49

Source: 1980 census.

Note: See text for definition of activity status.

[a] Includes persons with unknown activity status in the denominator.

[b] Excludes persons with unknown activity status in the denominator.

sizable proportion of the family income through their marketing activities, Thai peasant women generally control family finances, as is often the case with their urban counterparts (de Young, 1955:24). In urban areas, it is not uncommon for women to work for wages or as independent vendors both before and after marriage (Prachuabmoh et al., 1972; Thailand National Commission on Women's Affairs, 1980).

Education

Universal compulsory education in Thailand was enacted into law in 1921. Implementation has been a gradual process but by 1980 was virtually complete. Government efforts have focused mainly on primary education, and until recently the highly educated segment of Thai society consisted almost exclusively of a small elite in Bangkok. This has changed to some extent in recent decades, especially since the establishment of Rhamkhamhaeng University in 1971, a large open-admissions institution in Bangkok, and the opening of regional universities. In the last few decades, education has been a vital government activity representing a critical part of the overall effort to accelerate social development (Kaplan, 1981). Nevertheless, advancing through the educational system is still a long and difficult task, especially for rural Thais. After finishing primary education (presently six years) in a village school, a student would typically have to enter a secondary school in a district or provincial center located a considerable distance away. If there are no relatives or other potential hosts in the town where the school is located, the costs of room and board put further education out of reach of most rural Thais. After completing grade 10 or 12, depending on whether vocational or university education was sought, a student often would need to move to Bangkok or at least to a regional center to study further. Centralism and an extremely hierarchical educational system have prevented many poor and rural children from continuing their studies (Sudaprasert, Tunsiri, and Chau, 1980).

Until recently, school attendance was compulsory only through the first four grades, known as "lower primary" education. During the 1970s, as part of a reform of the educational system, primary education was reduced from seven to six grades and the distinction between lower and upper primary levels eliminated. Compulsory attendance has also been extended and now covers the entire six primary years. Implementation of the increase in the number of years of compulsory education has been an ongoing process rather than a sudden universal change, but by the mid-1980s was largely in effect. Since the change is quite recent, it is only starting to have a major impact on the educational distribution of the adult population. In 1980, the majority (59 percent) of Thais aged 15 or over had exactly a fourth-grade education and only 21 percent had attended more than fourth grade. According to the 1960 census, only 4 percent of women in the major reproductive ages 20–44 had more than fourth-grade education. This increased to 8 percent by 1970 and to 17 percent by 1980. Moreover, 70 percent of women aged 20–44 in 1980 had exactly a fourth-grade education.

The substantial improvements over time in the level of educational attainment are reflected in the experience of successive age groups in Thailand. Table 3.9 shows several indicators of educational attainment according to age groups based on the 1980 census. Although literacy is close to universal at present among younger and middle-aged cohorts, a substantial proportion of the older generation, particularly older women, were unable to read or write. The proportion with at least a fourth grade education has improved rapidly over time. For the older generation, as represented by those aged 55 or over, only a little more than one in four had finished at least fourth grade, compared to close to universal attainment of this level by the youngest cohorts. Going beyond a primary education to attend at least some secondary school was a rarity for the older generation. The percentage with at least some secondary education has increased substantially, especially recently, although even for the youngest cohort shown, only a little more than one in four studied beyond primary school.

A comparison of educational attainment among older men and women reveals that, in the past, men received substantially more education than women.

Table 3.9. Indicators of Educational Attainment, by Age in 1980

Age in 1980	Percent literate			Percent with four or more years of education			Percent with at least some secondary education		
	Total	Men	Women	Total	Men	Women	Total	Men	Women
15–19	97	98	97	94	94	93	27	29	25
20–24	97	97	96	95	94	92	24	27	20
25–29	96	97	94	92	94	90	16	20	13
30–34	94	96	93	90	92	87	14	18	11
35–39	92	94	89	85	88	81	12	16	8
40–44	88	92	84	77	82	72	8	11	4
45–49	86	90	81	71	76	65	5	7	3
50–54	80	88	72	64	73	54	5	8	3
55 and over	52	69	36	28	42	16	3	4	1
15 and over	88	92	84	81	85	76	15	19	12

Source: 1980 census.

Note: Persons of unknown educational attainment or classified as "other education" are excluded; persons with a primary education but unknown grade or classified as "vocational primary" are distributed proportionately within the primary range.

Literacy, for example, is almost twice as high for men than for women among the oldest age group and attainment of at least a fourth-grade education is more than two and a half times more likely for men. Information available from the 1970 census indicates an even more striking difference. Among the population aged 60 and over in 1970—that is, among those who would have been at or past school age in 1920—only 11 percent of the women were literate compared to almost 60 percent of the men. One reason for the previously large sex differences in education was that formerly most teachers were Buddhist monks who are forbidden by their vows to have contact with women (Hanks and Hanks, 1963). The sex difference in educational attainment, however, diminished considerably over time, as evidenced by the far less marked differences for the middle-aged cohorts and the only minor differences for the youngest age groups. Improvements in educational attainment, while benefiting both sexes, occurred disproportionately among women and thus have helped to close the gender gap in education over recent decades.

In sum, examination of indicators of educational attainment in Thailand leads to several observations. First, although literacy is very high, the current level of educational attainment for the majority of adult Thais is modest, usually not exceeding fourth grade. Thus, for many Thais, literacy is at a very rudimentary level. Second, there has been a steady improvement in the educational levels of successive cohorts, leading to substantial intergenerational dif-

Table 3.10. Percent Attending School, by Age, 1970 and 1980; by Sex and by Residence, 1980

	Total population		By sex, 1980		By residence, 1980	
Age	1970	1980	Males	Females	Rural	Urban
10	85	91	91	91	91	93
11	66	88	89	87	87	93
12	46	78	80	76	76	90
13	32	58	62	54	54	81
14	25	42	46	38	36	73
15	18	33	36	30	27	66
16	15	30	33	28	24	60
17	12	27	29	25	21	55
18	10	24	26	22	18	50
19	7	19	21	18	13	42
20–24	3	8	9	7	5	20

Source: 1970 and 1980 censuses.

ferences. Third, a formerly pronounced difference in the educational level between men and women is beginning to disappear.

Some idea of the rapidity with which educational change has been occurring recently is provided by data on school attendance in the last two censuses. Since the census takes place in April, during the school vacation period, the census question on attendance refers to the previous January. As is evident in table 3.10, school attendance has increased at all ages from 10 to 24 during the decade of the 1970s. Clearly, teenagers as well as younger school-aged children were considerably more likely to be attending school in 1980 than was the case just ten years earlier. The unusually large percentage point increases at ages 12 and 13 reflect the extension of compulsory primary education from four to six years. The percentage of older teens attending school, while still a modest minority in 1980, more than doubled during the decade.

At all ages shown except age 10, males were more likely to attend school than females in 1980. However, the sex differential is not large even at the older ages, when students would be finishing secondary education or attending some form of higher education. In contrast, rural-urban differences in 1980 are very pronounced except at the youngest ages. This is in part an artifact of the geographical location of secondary schools, which are disproportionately urban, and the overwhelmingly urban location of institutions of higher education (Sudaprasert, Tunsiri, and Chau, 1980). Thus many students from rural areas must migrate or commute to towns to study beyond the primary levels. However, since the census takes place during school vacation time, many students from rural areas who are studying in towns are at home at the time of the census and are counted as rural residents. This should minimize the distortion in the results created by the urban location of higher-level schools. Thus the large rural-urban difference in school attendance at older ages is probably for the most part genuine.

Electrification, Consumer Durables, and Mass Media

Among the changes that probably have the most far-reaching impact on the daily lives and aspirations of the people of Thailand and other Third World populations are the interrelated processes of electrification, expanding availability of consumer goods, and increasing exposure to mass media, particularly radio and more recently television. Access to electricity spurs consumption of a variety of consumer goods, especially electrical appliances including television sets. Television viewing further stimulates consumer aspirations and demand for goods through exposure to commercials and portrayals of modern, urban life-styles, including those of the very rich.

In Thailand, these processes are occurring at a remarkably rapid rate. Data from the more than 200 villages in the CPS3 sample indicate that the percentage of villages with access to electricity increased from only 6 percent in 1965 to 36 percent by 1980. The increase in rural electrification efforts has been even more rapid since 1980, with the result that fully 70 percent of the sample villages reported access to electricity by 1984, the year of the survey. Information on the proportion of private households with electricity (as measured by electric lighting) is available from the 1970 and 1980 censuses. As the results summarized in table 3.11 indicate, there has been a dramatic increase in the spread of electricity during the decade of the 1970s, particularly in rural areas, where the proportion of households with electric lighting increased from less than one in ten in 1970 to almost one in three in 1980.[8]

Information on household possession of selected consumer durables, including radio and television sets, is also provided by the 1970 and 1980 censuses and is summarized in table 3.11. The data point to substantial increases in the ownership of durable appliances over the 1970s. For every item shown, a higher percentage of households owned one in 1980 than in 1970. Although ownership of every item except the bicycle was considerably higher for urban households than rural ones, increases over the decade in ownership of many of

---

8. The increasing use of electricity can be viewed as part of a more general "energy transition" associated with modernization and consisting of a shift from use of renewable to nonrenewable energy sources. Thus, electrical and fossil-fuel energy is increasingly being substituted for wood, animal, and human energy. A general discussion of the nature of the energy transition as it is taking place in Thailand and its impact on rural Thais is provided in Ingersoll and Ingersoll (1984, 1985).

Table 3.11. Percent of Private Households with Electric Lighting and Selected Durable
Appliances, by Place of Residence, 1970 and 1980

	National		Urban		Rural	
	1970	1980[a]	1970	1980[a]	1970	1980[a]
Electric lighting	19	43	86	94	9	32
Radio	66	87	80	89	64	86
Television	7	21	39	68	2	11
Telephone	n.a.	4	n.a.	17	n.a.	1
Sewing machine	14	n.a.	41	n.a.	10	n.a.
Refrigerator	4	16	21	53	1	9
Electric fan	9	29	49	81	3	18
Air conditioner	n.a.	2	n.a.	7	n.a.	1
Bicycle	31	45	29	31	31	48
Motorcycle	7	19	15	22	6	18
Automobile	3	7	13	17	2	4

Source: 1970 and 1980 censuses.

[a] The published figures in the 1980 census report on the percent of households with specific types of durable appliances are based on an incorrect base number of households. Figures shown here have been recalculated using the correct base number of households and thus differ from the published figures.

n.a. = not available.

the items was more pronounced among the rural population than among the urban. The increasing importance of the motorcycle in expanding the mobility of the rural population is reflected in the tripling of the percentage of rural households that possessed one, from 6 to 18 percent. Given that purchases of major consumer durables in Thailand are frequently made through installment payments, the trend toward increasing ownership of goods is probably also associated with increased indebtedness (Ingersoll and Ingersoll, 1985).

Data on household possession of consumer durables are also available from several of the national sample surveys. A comparison of LS1, LS2, and NS results agrees well with the general trend toward a marked increase in ownership of a variety of goods during recent years, including a number of items not covered by the census. For example, between 1969 and 1979, the number of rural households owning a clock or a watch increased from 36 to 46 percent, those owning an electric iron increased from 4 to 14 percent, and those owning a sewing machine from 10 to 18 percent. Among urban households, ownership of a clock or watch was already close to universal (84 percent) in 1970. Between 1973 and 1979, the proportion of urban households with stereos increased from 13 to 22 percent and the proportion with an electric hair dryer from 8 to 26 percent.

Additional data on the percentage of households with radio and television are available from the periodic Radio and Television Survey conducted by the National Statistical Office. As table 3.12 indicates, there has been a substantial increase in both radio and television ownership since the late 1960s.[9] In rural areas, the spread of the radio is far more extensive, both because radios are far cheaper than television sets and because their use is virtually independent of access to electricity. Moreover, television reception was not possible in many rural areas until recently.

Data from LS1 for 1969 indicate that by that year 67 percent of rural men listened to the radio "often, daily, or almost daily" and data from LS2 indicate that in 1972, 68 percent of rural women reported they did so. In contrast, television viewing outside of urban areas is quite recent. According to NS results, in 1979 only 11 percent of rural women, compared to 64 percent of urban women, reported viewing television "often, daily, or almost daily." With the rapid spread of television in rural areas after 1979, television viewing in rural areas has undoubtedly increased substantially since then, but equivalent data are not available from subsequent surveys.

The pervasiveness of the radio, even in the late 1960s, is impressive and important for understanding recent social change, particularly in rural areas, given the radio's potential as a medium for the diffusion of information, ideas, and values. Although reliable statistics on the extent of radio ownership are not available for earlier years, there are several indications that exposure to radio in the countryside at that time must have been quite limited. Interviews in the mid-1950s with Bangkok pedicab drivers from the northeast revealed that none of them had a radio in his village home and about half of them said they came from villages in which no one owned a radio (Textor, 1961). Even for the village of Bang Chan, now within the boundaries of the Bangkok metropolis but formerly outside the city limits, data for the mid-1950s indicated that only 14 percent of households owned radios (Goldsen and Rales, 1957). The advent of inexpensive transistor radios made possible the rapid spread of the radio throughout rural areas, expanding the awareness of rural dwellers about the outside world and increasing their exposure to the whole array of messages conveyed through advertisements, popular music, news broadcasts, and so on.

Although television was quite common in urban areas even at the end of the 1960s, only recently has it made substantial inroads into rural areas. By 1983

9. The apparent decrease between 1980 and 1983 in the percentage of households with radios may be an artifact of terminology. In recent years, simple radios are being replaced by compact stereo cassette tape player and recorder combinations with built-in radios. Many people think of these not as radios but as stereos or tape players and may not refer to them if asked about radios as such when surveyed.

Table 3.12. Percent of Households with Radio and Television Sets, 1968–83

	Households with radio			Households with TV		
	National	Rural	Urban	National	Rural	Urban
1968/69	44.5	40.9	75.5	4.2	0.8	33.0
1974	70.9	69.8	79.0	10.2	4.7	48.7
1980	79.4	79.2	80.8	20.7	11.5	63.8
1983	75.3	74.5	78.7	33.1	24.1	73.1

Source: Thailand National Statistical Office, Reports of the Radio and Television Survey.

almost a quarter of rural households had a set, representing more than a doubling of television ownership between 1980 and 1983 alone. The recent, rapid increase in television in the countryside is undoubtedly the result of increased access to electricity and the broadening of geographical areas able to receive television transmission.

The increase in exposure to television in rural areas is considerably greater than the statistics on household possession of television sets would indicate, since it is common for neighbors and acquaintances without television to view programs at the home or shop of those who do have sets. A more relevant indicator, then, is the proportion of villages with sets. Data collected from a recent village-level survey of 64 villages throughout the country found that although only a few villages had any television around 1970, by 1983 there was at least one set in all but three of the villages. Even in villages without access to public sources of electricity, car batteries or private generators provide power for the television sets. Of course, public access to electricity in a village results in far more households obtaining television sets, but even just one household or shop with a set frequently permits large numbers of villagers at least some exposure.

Transportation

There can be little doubt that in Thailand, as is generally true throughout the developing world, contact between the rural and urban population is increasing. Rural villagers are less and less isolated from urban styles of life. This is a result not only of the increasing penetration of the mass media but also of a major change in the increased mobility of the rural population, made possible by dramatic improvements in the transportation system. The basis of this transformation is an expanded road system extending to many once-remote villages and the proliferation of bus services ranging from relatively primitive mini-buses and converted trucks along the feeder roads to air-conditioned tour-style buses along the major highways connecting Bangkok and the provincial capitals in every region of the country.[10] In addition, the motorcycle is rapidly becoming a common means of private transportation. Moreover, increased travel in Thailand is facilitated by the relatively favorable geography of the country, which permits an extensive and interlinked road system to be built, unlike the situation in nations of many islands, such as Indonesia or the Philippines, or countries of difficult mountainous terrain, such as Nepal or Laos. The result is that far more villagers are traveling than ever before and they are doing so more frequently to further destinations, especially to Bangkok.

Extensive development of the road network greatly accelerated after World War II. From the mid-1950s on, considerable road construction took place, in part spurred by foreign aid, especially from the United States (Whitaker, 1981). Although a major impetus for building or improving roads was to enhance the government's ability to respond to insurgency or other potential military problems, the long-run effect was to increase the integration of once remote villages into the national economy and society (Wyatt, 1984:297). By 1965, there were about 9,500 kilometers of state highways. This increased to just over 15,000 kilometers by 1984. Even more dramatic, however, was the expansion of primary and secondary roads forming the provincial road system. Such roads increased between 1965 and 1984 by about sevenfold, from less than 3,000 to close to 20,000 kilometers. Along with the expansion of the road system, the number of registered buses increased, from fewer than 20,000 in 1970 to more than 32,000 in 1979, the last year for which comparable data for buses are available. Vehicle-registration data also provide an idea of the rapid spread of motorcycles. Between 1965 and 1980, registered motorcycles outside of Bangkok increased from fewer than 80 thousand to almost 750 thousand, and by 1983 exceeded 1 million.

Cultural Factors: Religion and Household Structure

Although an extended discussion of Thailand's cultural setting is deferred to chapter 7 and in general is not easily portrayed in statistical indices, statistical information on religious composition and household structure is available from the 1980 census.

Religious and Ethnic Composition

A common religion is one of the most important factors contributing to the relative cultural homogeneity of the Thai population. As indicated by table 3.13, almost the entire population (95.5 percent in 1980) professes Buddhism as its religion. Most non-Buddhists adhere to Islam, which is practiced by

---

10. For a vivid description of the nature and impact of the transportation revolution in Thailand from the perspective of villagers, see Ingersoll and Ingersoll (1984, 1985).

Table 3.13. Percentage Distribution of the Population by Religion

	National	Bangkok	Central	North	Northeast	South
Buddhist	95.5	95.1	98.0	98.4	99.5	75.4
Muslim	3.8	4.1	1.4	0.1	0.0	24.6
Christian	0.5	0.8	0.5	0.9	0.4	0.1
Other	0.1	0.1	0.0	0.6	0.0	0.0
Total[a]	100	100	100	100	100	100

Source: 1980 census.

[a] Sum of categories may not add to exactly 100 because of rounding.

about 4 percent of the population. The large majority of Thai Muslims, about 80 percent, live in the south, where they constitute the majority of the population in the four southernmost provinces and make up one fourth of the total population of the south, despite their small percentage nationally. About half of the Muslims living outside the south reside in Bangkok and most of the rest are in the central region. Muslims are a negligible proportion of the populations of the north and northeast. In no region do Christians or members of other religions constitute as much as 1 percent of the population.

In a number of important respects, Thai Muslims are culturally distinct from the Buddhist majority and thus are of interest as a source of comparison in a study of reproductive change. Thai Muslims, however, are themselves not culturally homogeneous. The Muslim communities in Bangkok and the central region go back for many generations and thus have had the opportunity to develop their own historical legacy quite different from that of the southern Muslims. Perhaps the most important division among Thai Muslims is with respect to language. In three of the four predominantly Muslim provinces in the south—Pattani, Yala, and Narathiwat—the mother tongue of the vast majority of Muslims is a Malay dialect. In contrast, most Muslims in Satun, the fourth predominantly Muslim province, as well as elsewhere in the south are native speakers of the southern Thai dialect. Bangkok and central-region Muslims speak central Thai. Since most Thai Muslims are ethnic Malays, they constitute both a religious and ethnic minority.

The Chinese probably constitute an even larger ethnic group. It is difficult, however, to estimate their numbers with any precision, since they are not distinct in terms of religion and there is no question in the census that would permit their identification. A question on citizenship indicated that the number who identified themselves as citizens of China diminished from 37 percent in 1937 to less than 1 percent in 1970, the last census in which the question was included. Indeed, because considerable assimilation, including intermarriage, has taken place, there is no agreed-upon definition of Chinese ethnicity in Thailand. Various estimates suggest they constitute from 7 to 12 percent of the total population (Kaplan, 1981). They are disproportionately concentrated in the urban areas and are predominantly involved in commercial activities. For example, in the first round of the Longitudinal Survey (LS1) in 1969 and 1970, 3 percent of rural households, compared to 25 percent of urban households, were found to have at least one indication of Chinese ethnicity, such as having a Chinese altar or displaying paper strips with Chinese characters (Prachuabmoh et al., 1972:43–46). Other numerically smaller minorities include Indians and Pakistanis, who are engaged largely in trade, Cambodians concentrated largely along the border areas near Kampuchea, Vietnamese living largely in the northeast, and a variety of hill tribes located mainly in the mountainous regions, especially in the northwest.

Household Structure

In much of Thailand, and particularly in the northeast and north, the norm is that a newly married couple resides initially with the bride's parents for a period of a year or two or until the first child is born or until another, typically younger, daughter marries (Foster, 1975; Kaplan, 1981:82–83; Smith, 1979). The last daughter to marry resides permanently with the parents, taking care of them in their old age, and as a reward inherits the house and compound; any farmland is divided equally among the siblings. The extent to which this ideal is followed varies considerably and the practice is apparently in a state of transition (Podhisita, 1985a; Mizuno, 1978a). However, temporary residence with the bride's parents or, to a lesser extent, with the groom's parents, continues to be fairly common following marriage (Lauro, 1979:79–80; Foster, 1977:121–22; Mougne, 1982; Hanks and Hanks, 1963:435). Coresidence, except for the child remaining permanently with the parents, typically lasts for only a short period, after which neolocal residence is established, though often in close proximity to the parental home of the bride or groom. (Henderson et al., 1971; Limanonda, 1979; Smith, 1979).

The 1980 census provides information, summarized in table 3.14, on household structure as defined by family type. In addition to non-family households (one person or unrelated individuals) and nuclear family households, stem (vertical extension), joint (horizontal extension), and stem-joint (both vertical and horizontal extension) households were distinguished. The nuclear family predominates, and if nonfamily households are ignored, virtually all other households consist of a stem family, consistent with the norm previously discussed. Given the nature of coresidence norms in Thailand, the composition of any particular household will vary over time, depending on the life-cycle stage of the family (Foster, 1975). Cross-sectional data on household structure, such as provided by the census, necessarily masks this dynamic process and must be interpreted in terms of the developmental cycle. This is clearly

Table 3.14. Percentage Distribution of Households Defined by Family Type, by Age of
Household Head, 1980

Household type	Age of household head				
	Under 30	30–44	45–59	60+	Total
Including nonfamily households					
Nonfamily	8	2	3	8	4
Nuclear	82	83	64	40	71
Stem	9	13	32	51	24
Joint or joint-stem	1	1	1	2	1
Total[a]	100	100	100	100	100
Excluding nonfamily households					
Nuclear	89	85	66	43	74
Stem	10	14	33	55	25
Joint or joint-stem	2	1	1	2	1
Total[a]	100	100	100	100	100

Source: 1980 census.

Note: Nonfamily households refer to one-person households and households of unrelated individuals; family households refer to households with at least two related individuals. In the case
of stem families, extension is vertical; for joint families, the extension is horizontal.

[a] Sum of categories may not add to exactly 100 because of rounding.

evident from the variation in the relative frequency of nuclear and stem families with the age of the household head. Stem families are very rare for households headed by younger persons but constitute the majority of those headed
by someone 60 years old or over, corresponding to differences in the life cycle
stage of the family.

Regional and Rural-Urban Variation

In many important respects, the Thai population is relatively homogeneous.
The vast majority adhere to Buddhism, are ethnic Thais, and speak some form
of the Thai language. Moreover, the official central Thai language is understood virtually everywhere. There is generally a sense of national identity
reinforced by a widespread allegiance to the monarchy, which serves as an
effective symbol of national unity. Nevertheless, to varying extents, cultural
and socioeconomic differences characterize the four major regions. The most
obvious cultural difference is in the dialects spoken. In the north, the Thai
Yuan dialect is common; in the northeast, Thai Lao is prevalent; in the south,
the southern Thai dialect and Malay (among Muslims) are common.

As is evident in table 3.15, Bangkok is in a class by itself on virtually all socioeconomic measures. Of the four major regions excluding Bangkok, the central region generally ranks the highest in socioeconomic terms. It is also the cultural center of the nation, closest in physical and psychic distance to the Bangkok metropolis. The central plain is the heartland of rice cash crop in a country where rice is the mainstay of the economy. Substantial parts of the Chao Phraya Basin have benefited recently from a major irrigation project that has opened up wide expanses of land to the possibility of rice double-cropping.

The poorest region is the northeast, which contains about one third of the total Thai population. It is the driest region and suffers from periodic droughts combined with a lack of a well developed irrigation system. Although lower primary education is close to universal in all regions, discrepancies still exist with respect to the percentage of children who continue their education beyond this level. Past discrepancies are evident in the regional differences in the percentage of young adults (aged 25–29) who continued beyond primary education; the northeast ranks lowest in this respect.

The north is the second poorest region. Because of its mountainous terrain, rice farming in many areas is concentrated in densely settled narrow valleys and involves particularly intensive agricultural practices. Communally run small-scale water control systems are common and perhaps are part of the reason why social commitment to the structural organization of the valley community is generally judged to be greater in the north than elsewhere.

The smallest region in terms of both land area and population is the south, which tends to rank higher on most socioeconomic indexes than either the north or the northeast. It is the region of heaviest rainfall and is least dependent on rice as either a subsistence or export crop. Tin mining, rubber planting, and coastal fishing are important contributors to the local economy.

Despite the reservations previously discussed about the adequacy of defining rural and urban in terms of municipal and nonmunicipal areas, table 3.16 makes clear that such a definition captures very pronounced socioeconomic differences. Moreover, provincial urban places generally differ significantly in most measures from Bangkok. As would be expected, the proportion engaged in agriculture is very high in the rural areas and very low in urban places. Although literacy is very high regardless of residence, educational attainment is far greater among the urban population, as indicated by the much higher percentage of young urban adults with at least some secondary education. School attendance is also higher in urban areas among children and teenagers. Radio is as widespread in the countryside as in the towns but television is far more common in the towns. Health conditions, as indicated by the infant mortality rate, and sanitary conditions, as indicated by the prevalence of sanitary-type toilets, are also far better among the urban population.

Table 3.15. Selected Socioeconomic Indicators by Region

	Source	Whole country	Bangkok	Central	North	Northeast	South
Percent of national population, 1980	A	100	10	22	20	35	13
Percent urban, 1980	A	17	100	10	7	4	12
Percent with principal occupation in agriculture among economically active aged 11+, 1980	A	72	5	62	80	89	75
GDP per capita, 1982 (in U.S.$: 23 Bht = $1)	B	770	2,207	1,185	497	278	625
Percent annual growth (in constant prices) in GDP 1975–82	B	6.7	10.5	6.1	4.7	3.5	5.1
Percent of population above official poverty line, 1975–76	C	75	91	87	73	64	75
Percent literate among population aged 10+, 1980	A	90	93	91	84	93	85
Percent with at least some secondary education among population aged 25–29, 1980	A	16	46	16	11	8	16
Percent attending school among population aged 6–19, 1980	A	56	71	68	50	52	60
Percent of households with electric lighting, 1980	A	44	98	55	38	26	31
Percent of households with radio, 1980	A	87	92	92	86	83	85
Percent of households with TV, 1980	A	21	77	29	12	7	13
Infant mortality per 1,000 live births, 1974–76	D	52	25	49	74	52	51

Sources:
  A. 1980 census.
  B. Thailand National Statistical Office, Statistical Yearbook, various editions.
  C. World Bank (1980).
  D. Thailand National Statistical Office (1978).

Table 3.16. Selected Socioeconomic Indicators by Rural-Urban Residence

		Urban		
	Rural	Total	Bangkok	Provincial urban
Percent with principal occupation in agriculture among economically active population aged 11+, 1980[a]	83	7	5	10
Percent literate among population aged 10+, 1980[a]	88	92	93	92
Percent with at least some secondary education among population aged 25–29, 1980	9	44	46	41
Percent attending school among population aged 6–19, 1980	53	71	71	71
Percent of households with electric lighting, 1980	32	96	98	93
Percent of households with radio, 1980	86	89	92	84
Percent of households with TV, 1980	11	68	77	53
Percent of households with sanitary types of toilets, 1980[a]	39	95	97	92
Infant mortality per 1,000 live births, 1974–76	59	20	25	n.a.

Sources: 1980 census except for infant mortality, which is from Thailand National Statistical Office (1978).

Note: Unless otherwise stated, the unknown category has been excluded from the denominator.

[a] Including unknown in denominator.

n.a. = not available.

Concluding Comments

Although the basic changes transforming Thai society over recent decades have been discussed one by one, in categories convenient for the presentation of statistical indices, none of these trends is taking place in isolation from the others. Instead, changes in virtually all aspects of social and economic life are occurring in concert and typically reinforce each other. Thus, it is more realistic to view the ongoing transformation of Thai society in terms of an evolving socioeconomic environment rather than in terms of specific changes in the components of this broader setting. Moreover, the transformation of this socioeconomic environment is occurring along both temporal and spatial axes (Ingersoll and Ingersoll, 1984). In a particular village, town, or city, changes proceed more or less in a parallel manner over time, but at any particular time the stage of development characterizing communities conforms to a rural-urban, regional, and general spatial pattern in which Bangkok forms the center, major regional towns and provincial capitals serve as subcenters, and the level of development diminishes the further away from the center and subcenters a community is located. National averages mask this spatial dimension although to some extent it is captured through the rural-urban and regional comparisons.

One result of the social changes that have been taking place over recent decades is the emergence of a new Thai middle class that is predominantly urban and nonagricultural and for which modern education at the secondary level and above, rather than income per se, is the crucial determining factor. Access to this status has been greatly facilitated by the expansion of secondary schools and particularly technical and commercial colleges and nonelitist universities. Critical to their life-style is access to the mass media, particularly television, and sufficient income to assure the higher education of their children and the achievement of some sense of upward social and economic mobility. Although numerically still a modest proportion of the total population, their rapid growth is illustrated by the doubling of the number of Thais with any college or university education during the 1960s and the quintupling of this number during the 1970s. Moreover, a similar trend is evident for those with a secondary (tenth grade) education (Wyatt, 1984:294–97). It is probably this emerging new middle class, rather than traditional Thai elites or the truly rich, that serves as the model for many in the rural population or among the urban poor who aspire for better lives for their children and indeed is the likely group for those who are successful to eventually join.

Our qualitative research into social change in Thailand based on the focus-group discussion yielded a clear impression of the great extent to which many of the socioeconomic changes taking place are interrelated. This is also evident from virtually any anthropological village study in Thailand. Caldwell and colleagues, on the basis of an intensive study of an area in south India, have likewise stressed the extent of the interdependence among the many types of changes that are currently transforming local societies (Caldwell, Reddy, and Caldwell, 1984b). Thus, in order to understand more fully the nature of the socioeconomic transition taking place in Thailand and its relation to reproductive change, it is important to keep in the mind the interacting nature of these changes as well as their temporal and spatial dimensions.

4

Recent Trends in Fertility, Family Size, and Demand for Children

A major reduction in fertility has taken place in Thailand during the last two and a half decades. Although deficiencies in vital registration, the lack of fertility surveys prior to the mid-1960s, and the imprecision of fertility estimates make determination of the exact timing and extent of the decline difficult, there is extensive evidence both to document the broad outline of the fertility decline and to make clear that the decline was among the most rapid ever experienced by any Third World country.

Most evidence suggests that there was little or no fertility decline at the national level prior to the 1960s. According to an extensive study of recent fertility trends by the National Research Council (1980), the total fertility rate was in the range of 6.3 to 6.6 births per woman in the early 1960s and began to decline fairly sharply in the mid-1960s, reaching a level of 5.4 to 5.8 in 1970 and 4.5 to 4.9 by 1975. Several sources of estimates indicate an acceleration of fertility decline in the early 1970s, although the evidence on this is not conclusive. Urban fertility was probably already declining by 1960 and continued to decline thereafter, whereas rural fertility probably remained relatively constant until the second half of the 1960s and then began a rapid decline. More recent evidence attests to a continuation of the fertility decline since 1975, with some data indicating that the total fertility rate had fallen below 3 by 1985.

National, Rural-Urban, and Regional Fertility Trends

For the last three mid-decade periods, the National Statistical Office attempted to estimate fertility and mortality levels as well as the completeness of vital registration through a dual-record system approach. These efforts, called the Surveys of Population Change, provide estimates of the total fertility rate. Total fertility has also been estimated from the 1970 and 1980 censuses based on the number of children in the household. These estimates are typically referred to as "own-children" estimates, since they are based only on the number of natural-born children born to women members of each household enumerated in the census (see Cho, 1973). Total fertility rates have been derived additionally from information on full or partial pregnancy histories as retrospectively reported by ever-married women in a number of sample surveys. The 1984 Contraceptive Prevalence Survey (CPS3) provides a recent estimate of this type and has the advantage over earlier surveys of being specially designed to provide estimates at the regional level. National, rural-urban, and regional estimates of total fertility are presented in table 4.1 from each of these sources.[1]

A comparison of the first two Surveys of Population Change indicates a national decline of 22 percent in total fertility between the mid-1960s and the mid-1970s but with the decline concentrated mainly in the north and the central region. Preliminary estimates from the first year of the 1984–86 Survey of Population Change suggest that the total fertility rate has fallen below 3 at the national level, which would represent a decline in total fertility of over 50 percent since the mid-1960s.[2] Estimates based on the number of children in the household from the 1970 census covering the prior decade indicate a substantial decline in urban fertility between the first and second half of the 1960s, but only a very modest decline in rural areas and hence for the country

1. There are a number of technical reasons why estimates derived by different techniques and based on different sources may not agree completely. For example, the own-children estimates depend on the accuracy of the age distribution of the children and on the mortality assumptions employed. Dual-record systems, like the Survey of Population Change, are dependent on the accuracy of the matching procedure and the assumption of independence between births not reported in the survey and those not registered. Cross-national surveys, such as CPS3, often derive fertility estimates from retrospective reports of respondents on the dates of their one or two most recent births and thus are particularly dependent on the accuracy of this information.

2. A full report of the 1984–86 Survey of Population Change is to be issued only after the two years of fieldwork are completed. However, preliminary results indicating a crude birthrate of 25–26 per 1,000 population, based on the first year of fieldwork, have been released in an official communiqué to the National Economic and Social Development Board. Given the current age structure of the Thai population, a birthrate of this magnitude implies a total fertility rate in the range of 2.8–2.9.

Table 4.1. Total Fertility Rates by Residence and by Region

Source and year	Residence			Region				
	National	Rural	Urban	Bangkok	Central	North	Northeast	South
Survey of Population Change								
1964–65	6.30[a]	6.49	—	—	5.90	6.47	6.61	6.02
1974–76	4.90	4.98	4.49	3.46	4.11	3.74	6.25	6.12
% Change	–22	–23	—	—	–30	–42	–5	+2
Census (derived from number of children in household—"own-children" estimates)								
From the 1970 census								
1960–64	6.48	6.70	5.17	6.06		6.36	6.97	6.52
1965–69	6.19	6.55	4.15	5.32		5.71	7.20	6.48
% Change	–4	–2	–20	–12		–10	+3	–1
From the 1980 census								
1965–69	6.59	6.91	5.03	4.52	6.08	6.26	7.63	6.70
1970–74	5.41	5.84	3.53	3.15	4.75	4.74	6.78	5.45
1975–79	3.88	4.21	2.57	2.40	3.43	3.23	4.88	4.59
% Change	–41	–39	–49	–47	–44	–48	–36	–31
Contraceptive Prevalence Survey 3								
1982–84[b]	3.36	3.54	2.76	2.75	2.83	2.91	3.82	4.76

Sources: Thailand National Statistical Office (1978); Retherford et al. (1979); Arnold, Pejaranonda, and Choe (1985); and Kamnuansilpa and Chamratrithirong (1985).

[a] Excluding Bangkok-Thonburi.
[b] Based on births two years prior to the survey.

56

as a whole. Again the decline is concentrated in the north and central region. Similar estimates from the 1980 census provide total fertility rates for the 1965–80 period. They indicate a 41 percent decline nationally between the last half of the 1960s and the last half of the 1970s, with a considerably greater share of the decline occurring during the 1970s than between the last half of the 1960s and the first half of the 1970s. Substantial declines are apparent for both rural and urban areas as well as for all regions, with the north and the central region again showing the most pronounced fertility reduction.

Comparison of the own-children estimates of total fertility rates for 1965–69 based on the 1970 and the 1980 censuses indicate that those based on the 1980 census are uniformly higher. Although the reasons for this discrepancy are undetermined, its existence serves as a reminder that all fertility estimates for Thailand must be considered as only approximations and that each set of estimates is dependent on the quality of data used and the assumptions involved in applying the particular technique. In addition, there is a discrepancy between the own-children estimates for the 1970s and the Survey of Population Change estimates for 1974–76 with respect to the extent of a rural-urban difference in total fertility. The former shows a much larger rural-urban gap than the latter. There are technical reasons, however, to suggest that the own-children estimates probably exaggerate the rural-urban contrasts.[3]

Recent estimates of total fertility are available from CPS3. As with the results emerging from the latest Survey of Population Change, they suggest a continuation of the fertility decline into the 1980s. Consistent with results from the other sources, CPS3 indicates a persistence of considerable regional variation in fertility and its trend. The north and the central region, including Bangkok, are characterized by relatively low and similar fertility levels but total fertility is greater by about one child in the northeast and by almost two children in the south. At the same time the CPS3 results indicate that moderate rural-urban differences in total fertility still persist. Additional statistics on fertility trends are presented in appendix C. They show clearly that the decline evident in total fertility rates, which refer to all women, is more or less paral-

---

3. Because of the way they are calculated, it is likely that the own-children estimates overstate the rural-urban fertility difference. In order to allow for the fact that some young children are in the care of someone other than their own parents, initially derived fertility rates based on "natural" children in the household are inflated for absent children by an adjustment factor based on the national average. In the case of Thailand, however, we suspect that urban mothers are far more likely to send one or more children to the countryside to be taken care of by the grandparents or other relatives than rural mothers are to send young children for long-term care to the urban areas. Although we are unaware of data to document the extent of this difference, we believe it could be substantial. If so, the effect would be to underadjust the urban fertility estimates and overadjust the rural estimates. The resulting distortion leads to a greater understatement of urban rates rather than an overstatement of rural rates because the composition of the national population is heavily rural.

leled by a reduction in measures of marital reproduction. Despite various minor inconsistencies, the bulk of the evidence points to a major and rapid decline in Thai fertility since the early or mid-1960s and that the decline appears to be continuing during the 1980s.

Completed and Expected Family Size

The high fertility of Thailand's recent past is still evident in the cumulative fertility of women currently at the end of their reproductive ages. According to CPS3, the most recent survey, ever-married rural women aged 45–49 reported an average of five and one-half children ever born. This is already lower than the almost seven births per woman reported in the earliest surveys (Kamnuansilpa and Chamratrithirong, 1985; Institute of Population Studies, 1981). Of course, some of these births are lost through mortality early in life. According to the earlier surveys, the number of living children reported by women in their forties averaged about one less than the number of children ever born. This difference, however, is beginning to decrease as a result of the recent declines in both fertility and infant and child mortality.

As indicated in table 4.2, over 70 percent of all ever-married women aged 45–49 in 1970 experienced at least five live births with over 50 percent having borne five to nine children. Overall, these women average over six and a half births each. Data from the 1980 census show a considerable change in both the distribution and the mean and median number of children ever born compared to the 1970 census. Although about half of the ever-married women aged 45–49 in 1980 still experienced between five and nine births over their reproductive life, the proportion with ten or more children ever born has decreased substantially. As a result, the proportions who had at least five births declined to just over 60 percent. At the same time, the proportions with two to four children ever born increased noticeably. This shift in the distribution resulted in a decline in the mean number of children ever born by about one birth compared to the 1970 census results and is consistent with the evidence of fertility decline in the intervening period.

Results from the 1980 census also provide information on the distribution of the number of living children among women at the end of their reproductive span. The mean number of living children is over half a child less than the mean number of children ever born. Nevertheless, over half of Thai women aged 45–49 reported having five or more living children and only 30 percent reported three or fewer.

During a period of fertility decline, the completed family size of women at the end of their reproductive ages no longer accurately predicts the completed fertility that younger women will eventually achieve by the time they themselves reach the end of their childbearing years. Based on the 1984 CPS3, the

Table 4.2. Percentage Distribution of Ever-Married Women of Selected Ages, by Children Ever Born, Living Children, and Expected Number of Children

	Number of children ever born to ever-married women aged 45–49		Number of living children born to ever-married women aged 45–49	Expected number of children born to ever-married women aged under 30
	1970 (census)	1980 (census)	1980 (census)	1984 (CPS3)
0	1.7	2.9	3.2	0.2
1	5.5	4.8	5.8	6.7
2	6.1	7.3	8.8	46.2
3	7.0	10.3	12.5	31.1
4	8.6	13.3	15.4	12.2
5–9	51.5	52.4	50.6	3.6
10+	19.7	9.0	3.7	0.0
Total[a]	100	100	100	100
Mean	6.55	5.52	4.86	2.60
Median	6.04	4.81	4.27	1.93

Note: The expected number of children is calculated by adding the number of living children and the number of additional children desired.

[a] Sum of categories may not add to exactly 100 because of rounding.

future completed family size of currently married women still in the midst of their childbearing span has been estimated by adding the number of additional children a woman wanted to the number of living children she already had. This measure is labeled the "expected number of children."[4]

The distribution of younger ever-married women (those aged under 30) in 1984 by their expected number of children provides a sharp contrast to the distribution of women by completed family size who were at the end of their childbearing years in 1980. More than half of the younger women expect no more than two children and only 4 percent expect five or more. The mean number of children expected is only 2.6, which is only slightly more than half as many as the mean number of living children for women aged 45–49 in 1980. It is possible that the actual fertility of these women will exceed their expected family size due to unwanted births, although the increasingly wide-spread use of contraception makes limiting family size to the desired number

4. In a strict sense, this measure is based on future fertility *desires* rather than expectations. Moreover, it is based on living children rather than all live births, assuming that respondents are expressing their future fertility desires in terms of living children rather than simply live births.

increasingly feasible. Moreover, some women may change their mind regarding the number of additional children they wish to have, but this could operate in either direction. Even allowing for some unwanted births, the actual completed family size of these women seems virtually certain to be far lower than their predecessors a decade or two ago.

Desired Family Size

Attempts to measure family-size preferences have been incorporated into many surveys in developing countries. Although a variety of more sophisticated approaches have been developed, undoubtedly the most common source of such information is a relatively simple question asking for the number of children the respondent would have if he or she could have just the number wanted. In cases where the respondents are married, the question often is phrased in terms of how many children the respondent would like to have if he or she were starting marriage over again.

Trends in family-size preferences based on such questions are indicated in table 4.3, which shows the mean preferred number of children across several successive surveys for currently married women aged 15–44. In addition, separate results are shown for women married less than five years. The responses of such women are less likely to be affected by ex post facto rationalization since they are still at an early stage of family building and are unlikely to have already exceeded their desired family size. Moreover, their responses should reflect the most recent trends in family-size preferences and thus be more indicative of fertility developments in the near future.

The mean preferred number of children declined substantially during the period of fertility decline both for women aged 15–44 and for recently married women. In each survey, the mean preferred number of children is lower for recently married women, but the declines are quite parallel, so the difference of just over half a child indicated at the time of LS1 is still evident more than a decade later. Rural women consistently expressed higher preferred numbers of children than their urban counterparts throughout the period. By the time of the 1984 CPS3, however, the rural-urban difference had almost disappeared among recently married women. Since 1979, both rural and urban women who were married less than five years indicated they wanted fewer than three children on the average. The fact that total fertility rates are still well above the preferred family size of recently married women suggests that Thailand's fertility transition is not yet at its end.

One noteworthy feature of the trends is that the mean preferred number of children stated by rural women remained constant at 3.9 between 1969 and 1972 and declined only slightly by 1975, despite a major increase in the use of contraception (see chapter 5) and a decline in marital fertility dur-

Table 4.3. Preferred Number of Children among All Currently Married Women Aged 15–44 and among Those Married Less than Five Years

	1969/70 (LS1)	1972/73 (LS2)	1975 (SOFT)	1979 (NS)	1984 (CPS3)
National					
All married women	3.8	3.8	3.6	3.3	3.0
Married less than five years	3.2	3.2	3.0	2.8	2.4[a]
Rural					
All married women	3.9	3.9	3.7	3.3	3.0
Married less than five years	3.3	3.3	3.0	2.8	2.4[a]
Urban					
All married women	3.6	3.4	3.3	3.0	2.7
Married less than five years	3.0	2.9	2.8	2.6	2.3[a]

Note: Results for all married women 15–44 are standardized by age. The national age distribution of currently married women as reported in the 1970 Census serves as the basis for the age standardization.

[a] Refers to recently married women 15–49.

ing the same period (see appendix C). Interestingly, earlier data from the Potharam district in central Thailand indicate that desired family size in the mid-1960s was almost identical, suggesting that preferred family sizes may have been relatively constant for some time prior to the decline in fertility (Hawley and Prachuabmoh, 1971a:77). In Taiwan and Korea, initial increases in contraceptive practice and decreases in fertility also took place in the absence of any noticeable concomitant change in desired family size (Freedman et al., 1974; Ross and Koh, 1977). In all three countries, fertility preferences were below the completed family size of women at the end of their childbearing years. This situation, which suggests potential demand for effective family limitation, may have arisen as a result of improved child survival during the preceding decades, leading to an increase in the number of surviving children above that which traditionally had been accepted as appropriate. Under such a situation, a demand for family limitation may develop prior to attitudinal changes in the preferred number of children.

An important feature of Thailand's reproductive revolution is the pervasiveness of the small-family norm across a broad spectrum of Thai society. The fact that at present there is virtually no difference in the mean preferred number of children between recently married rural and urban women indicates that a desire for small families has permeated at least one very fundamental societal division. Results for 1984 based on CPS3 and presented in table 4.4 indicate the extent to which family-size preferences differ according to educational background, both a basic determinant and a reflection of a women's

Table 4.4. Preferred Number of Children among All Currently Married Women Aged 15–49
and among Those Married Less than Five Years, by Residence and Education, 1984

Years of education	All currently married women aged 15–49 (age-standardized)[a]			Currently married women married less than five years		
	National	Rural	Urban	National	Rural	Urban
Less than four	3.4	3.4	3.0	2.5	2.5	2.4
Four	3.1	3.1	2.9	2.4	2.5	2.3
Five or more	2.7	2.7	2.5	2.3	2.4	2.3
Total sample	3.0	3.1	2.8	2.4	2.4	2.3

Sources: Kamnuansilpa and Chamratrithirong (1985) and original tabulations from CPS3.

[a] The national age distribution of currently married women as reported in the 1970 census serves as the basis for the age standardization.

socioeconomic position. The mean preferred number of children is shown for all currently married women standardized for age as well as separately for recently married women. Age standardization is useful in the case of all married women, since recent trends toward increasing education result in considerably different age distributions within each educational category.

For all women together, a moderate inverse association between level of education and preferred number of children is evident—both within the rural and the urban areas. However, results for recently married women suggest that this relationship is largely a legacy of the past, given that educational differentials in the number of children desired for the new generation starting their families are virtually absent. Regardless of education or residence, recently married women express a preference for a modest-size family averaging no more than two and a half children. Indeed, the least-educated recently married rural women indicate a family-size preference of only slightly larger than the best-educated urban women.

The distribution of the preferred number of children, based on CPS3, is shown in table 4.5 for recently married rural and urban women. The responses indicate a remarkable consensus for a two-to-three-child family at present among women embarking on their reproductive careers. Nationally, 57 percent stated a preference for a two-child family and over 80 percent stated a preference for either two or three children. Although a clear modal preference for two children is evident, it is also clear that there is virtually no one who wants only one child. Over time, support for a two-child family has increased considerably but there has been almost no change in the apparent aversion to having fewer than two children. For example, the proportion of

Table 4.5. Percentage Distribution of Currently Married Women
Married Less than Five Years According to the
Preferred Number of Children, by Residence, 1984

Preferred number	National	Rural	Urban
0–1	7.5	6.8	10.1
2	56.8	55.5	61.3
3	25.6	26.6	21.9
4+	10.1	11.0	6.6
Total[a]	100	100	100

Source: Kamnuansilpa and Chamratrithirong (1985).

[a]Sum of categories may not add to exactly 100 because of rounding.

recently married women stating a preference for two children rose from 27 percent at the time of LS1 in 1969/70 to 56 percent by 1984. At the same time only 9 percent indicated a preference for fewer than two children in 1969/70 and only 8 percent in 1984. Thus, although the two-child family represents the target for an increasing number of women in Thailand, it also appears to set a lower limit on the extent to which fertility will decline in the foreseeable future.

There is a small difference in the distribution of ideal family sizes among recently married rural and urban women, with the latter more likely than the former to express a preference for two children. Nevertheless, the majority of rural women also preferred two as the ideal number.

The meaningfulness of responses to questions on desired family size, particularly in developing countries, has often been questioned. Especially in settings where the practice of birth control is rare or absent, family size may not be thought of as a matter of conscious choice but rather as the inevitable consequence of sexual activity, God's will, or events outside of one's control. In contrast, the role of individual decision making, and hence family-size preferences, becomes more salient as control over one's "demographic fate" increases (Back, 1967).

There is some survey evidence indicating that concern about limiting family size was not well entrenched in the thinking of much of the population at the onset of the fertility transition but that it gained salience during the early stages. Several regional surveys as well as the rural round of LS1 in 1969 indicated that at the end of the 1960s only a minority of married women said that they had discussed either the number of children they wanted or the possibility of fertility control with their husbands or with others such as relatives or friends and neighbors. Several surveys during the 1970s suggest discussions of such matters increased measurably (Knodel et al., 1982).

Results of focus-group discussions also suggest that, for the pretransition generations, family size was generally not thought of as a matter of choice, but rather considered the product of a natural process over which the couple had minimal control. This is clearly reflected in the many comments by participants that there were no effective means of birth control in the past and thus that children continued to come until the end of the couple's natural reproductive span. Some older-generation participants indicated they consciously wanted many children and others seemed at least accepting of large families even if they did not actively seek them. Neither group, however, seemed to have had specific family-size goals but rather accepted whatever number came along. There was also a substantial number of older-generation participants who indicated they thought about limiting family size but felt helpless to control childbearing.

"We didn't think about how many [children] we should have. [My husband] felt sorry for me when I had lots of children but no one knew what to do." (older Buddhist woman, south)

"I didn't intend [to have any particular number of children]. I never decided at all." "It wasn't like nowadays when they have pills to limit the number of children to what you want and then stop." (two older men, north)

"We never thought about [how many children to have] so [my husband and I] never disagreed [about family size]." (older woman, central region)

Focus-group participants of both generations agreed that the situation nowadays is very different. Today virtually everyone considers the number of children to be a matter of deliberate choice. Most young husbands and wives already start out their married life with a fairly clear idea that they want only two or three children. Thus, in the course of the fertility transition, family size has emerged as a matter of choice. Among younger-generation participants, the idea of letting the number of children nowadays be the result of a process of uncontrolled fertility is as remote as the idea of effectively limiting family size to a specific target number was just a few generations ago.

Gender Preferences

Parental attitudes and aspirations concerning the sex of their children can be an important influence on reproductive behavior since couples may continue childbearing beyond their overall desired family size if they have not achieved some favored number of one particular sex or some preferred distribution of sons and daughters. Such gender preferences may be simple or complex and can originate from a variety of sources including economic considerations, religious beliefs and observances, cultural practices regarding marriage and coresidence, inheritance systems, and concerns about lineage. The extent to which gender preferences will actually affect fertility will depend on the extent to which fertility is under deliberate control. Under conditions of natural fertility such preferences are unlikely to have a behavioral impact, whereas under conditions of widespread use of birth control their impact could be quite pronounced. Recent studies reviewing evidence from a wide variety of countries indicate that the extent of gender preference and their impact on reproductive behavior varies considerably on a cross-national basis (Williamson, 1976; Cleland, Verral, and Vaessen, 1983).

In Thailand, children of both sexes are valued, although for different reasons. Only a son can become a Buddhist monk, an act thought to bring considerable merit to parents and a reason frequently cited as underlying the importance of having a son. On the other hand, in much of rural Thailand, couples typically reside with the wife's parents immediately following marriage, thus adding the labor of the son-in-law to that of the household. Although such coresidence is often temporary, it is common for the youngest daughter and her husband to live in her parental household permanently, to take care of her parents in their old age, and eventually to inherit the house (Smith et al., 1968: 120; de Young, 1955: 23; Foster, 1975, 1978). Thus, there is reason to expect that many couples will feel it is important to have at least one child of each sex. In his study of a central Thai village, Riley (1972) points out that many women, when asked about their ideal family size, said they wanted two children and then volunteered the information "one boy and one girl." This was also a common occurrence in the focus-group sessions when younger-generation participants discussed the number of children they wanted. In addition, different reasons were frequently cited for wanting a daughter and for wanting a son.

Although most anthropologists agree that both sons and daughters are viewed positively, they differ in the extent to which they believe sons are preferred over daughters. Some report at least a moderate son preference (e.g., Kingshill, 1960: 187; Podhisita, 1985a); others stress the lack of son preference (Hanks and Hanks, 1963; Blanchard, 1958: 435); and some suggest a preference for daughters (Potter, 1976: 127; Kemp, 1970: 83). Attitudinal data from surveys generally show some preference for sons over daughters, with the preference stronger among men than among women. At the same time, however, very few respondents indicate they wish to have only sons. There clearly is a desire to have at least one child of each sex, and for couples who wish only two children, the increasingly common choice among Thai couples, almost all say they want one son and one daughter (Knodel et al., 1982).

Recent quantitative evidence on the potential impact of gender preferences

Table 4.6. Percent of Currently Married Women Aged 15–44 Who Want No More Children,
and Percent Sterilized, by Residence and Number and Gender Composition of
Living Children, 1984

Number of living children and gender composition	Want no more children[a]			Sterilized[b]		
	Total	Rural	Urban	Total	Rural	Urban
One child						
One daughter	23	22	30	2	2	2
One son	23	21	31	1	1	1
Two children						
Two daughters	56	56	60	20	20	20
One son, one daughter	75	76	74	34	33	38
Two sons	57	55	66	32	32	32
Three children						
Three daughters	70	67	87	42	42	42
One son, two daughters	84	83	89	48	43	71
Two sons, one daughter	86	87	86	53	49	68
Three sons	72	67	98	43	40	60

Source: CPS3.

[a] For pregnant women, desire for additional children refers to children after the expected birth.
[b] Includes both ligation and vasectomy.

on reproductive behavior is presented in table 4.6 based on the 1984 CPS3.[5] The results show the percentage of couples not wanting additional children, as well as the percentage in which either the husband or wife is sterilized, according to the composition of the family with respect to sons and daughters at the time of the survey. Since many couples are now practicing contraception for spacing (see chapter 5), the percent using permanent methods of contraception can serve as a better indicator of a true commitment to stop childbearing than overall contraceptive use. Given the emerging consensus for small families, results are limited to couples with one, two, and three living children.

The findings generally confirm that a preference for at least one child of each sex is strong. Among women with two living children, three-fourths of those with one child of each sex indicate they want no more children, compared to 56 percent of those with two daughters and 57 percent of those with two sons. A similar pattern holds for women with three living children. Those

5. For a concise and clear summary of some of the limitations of the type of tabulations used in the present analysis for detecting gender preferences and their fertility impact, see Cleland, Verral, and Vaessen (1983).

with at least one child of each sex are more likely to indicate they wish no more children than those with children of all one sex. Couples with three children are also more likely to be practicing a permanent method of contraception if they have a child of each sex than if all are the same sex.

The behavioral data on sterilization also suggest that some son preference exists. Among urban couples with three children, sterilization is distinctly less common for those with all daughters than for those with at least one son. In addition, both rural and urban couples with two children are less likely to be sterilized if they have no son than if they have one or two sons. This suggests some son preference. That there is not a pronounced preference for sons over daughters, however, is suggested from the finding that women with all daughters are about as likely not to want more children as those with all sons, regardless of whether they have one, two, or three living children already. Moreover, once three children are reached, a substantial proportion practice permanent contraceptive methods regardless of the sex of the children.

In terms of expressed desires to stop childbearing, only a modest proportion of women with one child say they wish no more children, whereas the large majority of women with three children say they want no more, again regardless of composition with respect to sons and daughters. Nevertheless, the findings do suggest that some women may continue childbearing beyond their preferred number of children if they do not have at least one child of each sex. Moreover, the desire to have both a son and a daughter may underlie the apparent aversion to one-child families evident from the data on the preferred number of children and thus set a lower limit, at least for the foreseeable future, on Thailand's fertility decline.

Religious Differentials

Given the small proportion of the total Thai population represented by Muslims, the demographic impact of Muslim fertility on national parameters is minimal. Nevertheless, religious differentials in fertility and related behavior are of interest because cultural differences between Buddhists and Muslims are relatively sharp within the otherwise relatively homogeneous Thai society. Information on reproductive differentials has generally been limited because the low proportion of Muslims in the population typically resulted in only small numbers being included in any national sample survey. The 1984 CPS3, however, incorporated a special supplemental sample of respondents in predominantly Muslim villages in two of the four southern provinces, where Muslims are the majority, thus enabling more extensive comparisons between Buddhists and Muslims to be made than is possible with previous surveys.

Thailand's fertility decline, including the adoption of a small family norm, has cut across important socioeconomic boundaries, as indicated by the very modest rural-urban and educational differentials that exist at present. Regional differences are evident, however, and the south in particular stands out as currently being characterized by higher levels of fertility and a lesser extent of fertility decline during the recent past than the other regions. The south is also unusual in having a high proportion of Muslims in the population, most of whom are concentrated in the four southernmost provinces. It is thus of interest to determine the extent to which the lesser participation of the south in Thailand's reproductive revolution is related to the substantial Muslim population there.

Earlier research based on the 1960 census and the 1970 Rural Employment Survey in southern Thailand, and thus not reflective of recent fertility change, has pointed to *lower* cumulative fertility among Muslims than Buddhists by the latter part of the reproductive span (Goldstein, 1970; Jones and Soonthornthum, 1971). Given that Muslims marry at a considerably earlier age than Buddhists, this lower cumulative fertility prior to the recent decline is particularly interesting. The authors of these earlier studies speculated that more frequent divorce and remarriage, greater use of traditional birth-control methods, and poor health may have accounted for the lower Muslim fertility rates, although they lacked data to document these explanations.[6]

More recent evidence suggests that religious differentials in fertility in Thailand are changing as the Buddhist majority experiences rapid fertility decline while reduction of fertility among the Muslim minority lags behind (Knodel et al., 1982; Kamnuansilpa, Chamratrithirong, and Knodel, 1983). As a result, current fertility is now higher among Muslims than Buddhists. Differentials in cumulative fertility are more complex and in a state of transition, reflecting the different recent histories of fertility trends. The 1984 CPS3 provides the most up-to-date information on fertility and family-size preferences for the two religious groups. Table 4.7 summarizes these results. Since Muslims are concentrated primarily in the south and to a lesser extent in Bangkok and the central region, comparisons within these areas are shown separately.

Nationally, recent marital fertility as well as the percentage of women reporting themselves as pregnant are clearly higher for Muslims than for Buddhists. Cumulative fertility as measured by children ever born is shown for selected marriage durations rather than by age to minimize the influence of the earlier age of marriage that characterizes Muslims. Unlike earlier studies, even among women at the end of their reproductive careers (represented by those married at least twenty years), Muslims are characterized by higher cumulative fertility than are Buddhists. Among women married ten to fourteen

6. For an extensive review of previous research on the fertility of Thai Muslims, see Rachapaetayakom (1983).

Table 4.7. Fertility and Family-Size Preference Measures, by Religion, 1984

	National		South		Central region, including Bangkok	
	Buddhists	Muslims	Buddhists	Muslims	Buddhists	Muslims
General marital-fertility rate for two years prior to survey	161	277	195	288	155	220
Percent pregnant among currently married women, 15–44	8.1	12.7	9.3	13.4	7.9	8.6
Children ever born to ever-married women married for						
10–14 years	2.8	3.8	3.1	3.8	2.7	3.4
20+ years	5.2	6.1	5.8	6.0	5.2	6.6
Expected number of children to women married 10–14 years	3.0	4.3	3.4	4.5	2.8	3.6
Preferred number of children among currently married women						
All aged 15–49	2.9	3.9	3.3	3.9	2.7	3.4
Married less than five years	2.3	3.1	2.5	3.2	2.2	2.5

Sources: Kamnuansilpa and Chamratrithirong (1985) and original tabulations from CPS3.

Note: The expected number of children is calculated by adding the number of living children and the number of additional children desired.

years, not only are the number of children ever born higher for Muslims but so is the final expected family size. Muslim family-size preferences are consistent with their higher current cumulative and expected fertility. Both among all currently married women and among recently married women, Muslims express a preference for a larger number of children than Buddhists, although the desired number is smaller than the actual number of living children Muslim women in the past had by the end of their childbearing years.

Higher fertility and family-size preferences characterize Muslims compared to Buddhists both in the south and in the central region including Bangkok, although cumulative fertility among women married twenty years or more differs only modestly between southern Buddhists and Muslims. It is interesting, however, that consistently for both Muslims and Buddhists a pronounced regional difference is evident with women of either religion in the south characterized by higher fertility and family-size preferences than their counterparts at the national level or in the central region including Bangkok. Thus, although the lagging reproductive change in the south can be in part attributed to the higher proportion of Muslims there, other regional influences are also operating.

Popular Perceptions of Fertility Decline

Focus-group results make clear that both older- and younger-generation participants are well aware of the changes in reproductive behavior and attitudes that have been taking place in Thailand and identify these changes as a widespread phenomenon. Older-generation participants were almost uniformly convinced that the present younger generation will have far fewer children than they themselves had, often mentioning two or three as the choice of young couples. Likewise, the younger-generation participants felt that couples nowadays desire smaller families than were typical of their parents' generation and frequently mentioned two or three children as their new family-size goal.

"Every day now they have fewer children." (older man, northeast).

"Almost everyone wants few children, at most no more than three. When I say this, I mean those my age . . ." (younger man, central region)

A small family size is not only widely acknowledged but appears to be approved among both younger and older generations because it is seen as being more adaptive to present-day conditions. When disapproval was expressed by older participants, it primarily reflected the judgment that younger couples were not exercising enough foresight about help and support from children later in life. Among those indicating disapproval, many saw advantages as well to the small family when asked directly about this. Indeed, in most groups there was some recognition of both advantages and disadvantages of smaller family size, although most agreed that under present circumstances the advantages were predominant.

"It is not at all good to have many children today because it is very difficult now to make a living, to raise a family. People with fewer children are okay. If people have many children it will be difficult." (older Muslim man, south)

"[Having fewer children nowadays] is good because making a living is different than before." (older Buddhist man, south)

"Few is good. The expense is lower. Money is hard to find now." (older woman, northeast)

It is particularly noteworthy that the older generation had generally favorable attitudes toward the change in family size even though they themselves had many children. Their favorable disposition to this change in large part stems from their perception that changes in the socioeconomic environment virtually make small families imperative today. In addition, it is consistent with the view expressed by a number of older-generation participants, discussed more fully in chapter 6, that they themselves would have had fewer children if effective means of fertility control had been available earlier. Thus, a deeply rooted large-family ideal seems to have been absent among rural

Thais for at least a generation before the onset of the fertility transition and hence does not seem to have been an important impediment to rapid fertility decline. The small-family norm has become imbedded in people's thinking and behavior and is now recognized as a new generation's way of life.

Summary

Although it is difficult to identify precisely the year in which Thailand's reproductive revolution began, there is clear evidence of a major fall in fertility between the end of the 1960s and the present. As measured by the total fertility rate, reproductive rates at the national level have probably declined by over 50 percent within less than a two-decade period, thus representing one of the most rapid fertility transitions on record. The magnitude of this ongoing change is well illustrated by the contrast between the average of six to seven live births that represent the actual completed fertility of women who finished their childbearing just a generation ago and the small-family size of two to three children preferred and expected by recently married Thai couples in the early 1980s. Qualitative data from focus group sessions make clear that both older- and younger-generation couples are aware of the major changes that have taken place in reproductive behavior and attitudes and that both generations see small families as appropriate for present-day circumstances.

One impressive feature of the recent reproductive change in Thailand is the extent to which it permeates almost all segments of Thai society. The small-family norm is now espoused by young couples regardless of educational level or whether they live in a rural or urban area. Regional differences are evident in the timing and extent of fertility decline and in the current level of fertility and preferred family size. Yet it is also true that by the turn of the present decade, reproductive change was underway in each of the major regions. In terms of readily identifiable groups, Muslims stand out most conspicuously in terms of experiencing less of a fertility decline and professing larger family-size preferences, particularly among the concentration of Muslims living in the south. However, given that Muslims constitute only a small minority of the Thai population, their impact on national demographic trends and levels is relatively insignificant.

Although most younger reproductive-aged Thais want to limit their families to a small number of children, they also wish to have at least one child of each sex. There is some evidence of son preference, but it is only moderate. More important for most couples is to have both a son and a daughter and this may explain the general aversion to the one- child family in terms of expressed family-size preferences. At the same time, there is little evidence that many young couples would be willing to continue childbearing past three children for the sake of achieving a more desirable sex distribution.

5

The Proximate Determinants of Reproductive Change: A Quantitative Assessment

As described in chapter 1, reproductive change can be accounted for in terms of seven proximate determinants that directly affect fertility (see figure 1.1). Empirically, Bongaarts (1982a) has found that four proximate determinants—the proportions married among women, contraceptive use and effectiveness, prevalence of induced abortion, and duration of postpartum infecundability—account for nearly all the variations in fertility levels among populations. The other proximate determinants—fecundability (frequency of intercourse), spontaneous intrauterine mortality, and prevalence of permanent sterility—are far less important. The present chapter focuses on quantitative evidence concerning the proximate determinants, especially the four that Bongaarts found to be of greatest importance.

The seven proximate fertility determinants can be grouped into three broad categories: factors relating to exposure to intercourse (marriage), those related to "natural" marital fertility, i.e., fertility in the absence of birth control (postpartum infecundity, fecundability, intrauterine mortality, and sterility), and those related to deliberate marital fertility control (contraception and induced abortion). We divide our discussion of the role of proximate determinants in Thailand's fertility decline along these lines.

Marriage and Marital Disruption

In most societies, including Thailand, exposure to sexual intercourse, at least among women, largely occurs within marriage. For Thailand, there is little reliable quantitative data on the extent of premarital and extramarital sex, premarital pregnancies, or illegitimacy (see Knodel et al., 1982; Porapakkham, Vorapongsathorn, and Pramanpol, 1986). Birth registration, for example, does not include information on legitimacy status and thus data on births outside marriage are unavailable from the vital-statistics system. Probably the extent of nonmarital sexual relations and their implication for fertility has been changing over time. It is likely that there has been some increase in premarital sexual activity during recent decades. Nevertheless, despite the lack of solid quantitative data, it is reasonable to assume that trends in nonmarital fertility have had only a negligible impact on the recent fertility decline.

In contrast to the situation regarding nonmarital unions, there is considerable quantitative evidence on nuptiality in Thailand. Although marriage registration data are seriously flawed because of underregistration, tabulations of the population by age, sex, and marital status, particularly in the censuses, provide useful information for examining marriage patterns. The proportions single at different ages are shown in table 5.1 based on the 1960, 1970, and 1980 censuses. Because age was determined by a direct question on age in the 1960 census rather than calculated from date of birth as it was in the 1970 and 1980 censuses, some minor adjustment is required to make the 1960 results comparable to those from the later censuses. The results show a continuous moderate increase in the proportion single at most ages for both women and men during the two-decade period covered, reflecting a trend toward postponing marriage. Data from the 1947 census indicate that this trend was already underway before 1960 (Knodel et al., 1982).

A convenient summary measure of the changes in nuptiality is provided by the singulate mean age of marriage, an estimate of the age at first marriage derived from the proportions single by age. According to this estimate, the age at marriage rose by just over one year for women and by just under half a year for men between 1960 and 1980.[1] A rise in the age of marriage appears to

---

1. Calculations of the singulate mean age at first marriage, when based on a single cross-section from a census or survey, incorporate an assumption of unchanging marriage patterns over the recent past. Since the evidence seems to point to increases over the last two decades in the age at marriage and in proportions single, particularly at younger ages, this assumption is not met and the estimates of the singulate mean age at marriage tend to be biased upward. An alternative method of calculating the singulate mean age at marriage that avoids the assumption of unchanging nuptiality can be used, provided data are available for two points in time (United Nations, 1983). The resulting calculation reflects the age at marriage implied by the nuptiality experience

Table 5.1. Proportions Single and Singulate Mean Age at Marriage (SMAM), by Sex, Age
Group, and Residence, Based on Censuses, 1960–80

	National			1980	
Sex and age	1960[a]	1970	1980	Rural	Urban
Women					
15–19	.830	.810	.833	.817	.899
20–24	.352	.379	.435	.379	.628
25–29	.126	.156	.209	.162	.370
30–34	.062	.081	.118	.090	.226
35–39	.040	.053	.073	.058	.140
40–44	.030	.039	.053	.043	.099
45–49	.026	.030	.041	.034	.077
SMAM	21.6	22.0	22.7	22.0	25.4
Men					
15–19	.959	.963	.958	.955	.972
20–24	.663	.651	.664	.626	.801
25–29	.242	.249	.270	.285	.456
30–34	.088	.106	.115	.090	.216
35–39	.050	.058	.061	.050	.111
40–44	.036	.038	.043	.037	.073
45–49	.032	.032	.035	.031	.055
SMAM	24.5	24.7	24.9	25.1	27.3

Sources: National Research Council (1980) and 1980 census.

Note: Persons of unknown marital status have been proportionately distributed except for male
priests, who are treated as single.

[a] Adjusted to account for differences in age reporting between the 1960 and subsequent censuses;
see National Research Council (1980).

be a general phenomenon taking place in many developing countries (Smith,
1980; Coale, 1983). It is interesting to note, however, that even in 1960, female age at marriage in Thailand was above 21, a relatively late age in comparison with many other developing countries. At present, Thailand is less
distinctive in terms of late marriage because increases in age at marriage have
been even more rapid elsewhere.

during the period intervening between the two sets of observations and is no longer biased by
changes that may have occurred prior to the first observation. Such calculations based on the
censuses yield a singulate mean age at marriage for women of 21.7 for the 1960–70 intercensal
period and 22.2 for the 1970–80 intercensal period. As expected, these estimates of the singulate
mean age at marriage are slightly lower than would be obtained if we simply averaged the estimates derived from each census separately.

Analyses of nuptiality information collected in connection with sample surveys provide some evidence supporting a trend toward a rising age at marriage. In particular, results from both CPS2 and CPS3 indicate that the average age at first marriage among women marrying before age 30 rose steadily, if modestly, during the twenty-year period prior to each survey.[2] In the case of CPS2, the increase was from 19.7 to 20.4 from 1961–65 to 1976–81 (Knodel et al., 1984); for CPS3 the rise was from 19.3 in 1964–68 to 20.1 in 1979–84. Thus, although the two surveys do not agree in terms of the average age at any given point in time, they agree quite well in terms of the direction and magnitude of the change.

In Thailand, the difference in the age at first marriage between men and women is not large. Judging from the singulate mean age at marriage, men are about two to three years older than women when they marry for the first time, with this difference declining somewhat over time. This is low compared to most other developing countries, where the age gap between spouses can be as large as eight years (Durch, 1980; Smith, 1980).

The census data indicate that marriage is close to universal in Thailand, with over 95 percent of both men and women having married at least once by the time they reach age 50. It should be noted, however, that the rise in the proportions single at younger ages over the last two decades may signal somewhat higher proportions remaining permanently single in the future.

Table 5.1 also indicates that the proportions single in 1980 were lower in rural areas at all ages than in urban areas for both men and women. The singulate mean age of marriage is over two years older for urban residents than for rural residents of each sex. The largest absolute rural-urban differences are in the age groups in the twenties and thus for ages at which fertility is potentially highest. Some difference still persists even at the end of the reproductive ages, although the percentage remaining single is low enough to suggest nearly universal marriage even in urban areas. The lower proportions single among rural women in reproductive ages contribute to the higher total fertility rates in rural areas compared to urban areas, as discussed in chapter 4.

A special analysis of the 1980 census also provides information on differentials in nuptiality within the population (Pejaranonda and Chamratrithirong, 1985). It generally shows that couples with more modern characteristics, such as as higher educational attainment or higher-level urban occupations, marry later than average. For example, the singulate mean age at marriage increases with educational attainment. It is slightly under 21 for women with no education, slightly under 22 for women with primary education, and somewhat above 25 for women with secondary or university education. Similar educa-

2. Limitation of results to women marrying before age 30 is necessary in order to avoid biases that would result from the increasing truncation effects on estimates for successive years prior to the survey, given the exclusion of women above age 49 in the survey coverage.

tional differentials in age at marriage were evident in the 1970 census as well (Chamratrithirong, 1980). There is also more than a two-year difference in age at marriage between Buddhist and Muslim women according to the 1980 census, with the former marrying later (22.8 versus 20.5).

Anthropologists have noted that divorce and remarriage are common in Thailand (Henderson, 1971:70). Divorces are often not officially registered. Instead, marital dissolution is typically the product of an informal process whereby one of the partners simply moves out. Quantitative information on marital dissolution from surveys may be impaired to some extent because it is sometimes a sensitive area of inquiry. Nevertheless, in many surveys, a substantial proportion of ever-married women report being married more than once when questioned about their marital histories. Estimates based on SOFT suggest that almost one out of five Thai women can expect their marriage to end within the first fifteen years and close to one out of four within the first twenty years. During the early years of marriage, divorce and separation are far more important sources of marital disruption than widowhood, and even by the end of twenty years they jointly account for over 60 percent of total dissolution (Smith, 1981).

Although marital disruption is frequent in Thailand, so is remarriage, particularly for younger women. Again estimates based on SOFT indicate that almost two-thirds of women in the reproductive ages remarry within five years of marital disruption. Among women in the younger reproductive ages, remarriage is particularly rapid and extensive (Smith, 1981).

The distribution of women by marital status at different ages within the reproductive age span at any given time is the net result of past trends in marriage, marital dissolution, and remarriage. Given the strong association between age and fecundity within the childbearing span, the implications of different marital-structure distributions for fertility depend not only on the overall proportion in a given marital status, but also on the age profile of women in different marital-status categories. On average, reproductive potential, known in demographic terminology as fecundity, increases for some years following puberty, reaches its maximum for women in their twenties, and declines thereafter, with the decline particularly rapid after the late thirties. Coale (1969) has proposed an index of the proportion currently married among women in the reproductive ages. This index incorporates a set of weights thought to represent the age profile of fertility in the absence of deliberate control. This idea has been extended to indices of other marital statuses (Hull and Saladi, 1977; Smith, 1978). The main advantages of these indices are that they reflect not only the marriage pattern of women, but also the potential effect of their marital status on fertility, taking into account that reproductive potential varies with age. Thus, for example, the same proportion

Table 5.2. Marital Status Indices for Women, 1970 and 1980

	1970	1980
Index of proportion currently married (I_m)	.646	.604
Index of proportion single (I_s)	.302	.350
Index of proportion divorced or separated (I_d)	.031	.026
Index of proportion widowed (I_w)	.021	.020

sums to 1.0

Source: Results calculated from 1970 and 1980 census reports.

of women divorced or separated toward the end of the reproductive span carries less weight than at earlier ages, when reproductive potential is presumed to be higher.[3]

Table 5.2 shows a complete set of these marital status indices for Thai women based on the 1970 and 1980 censuses. Since the sum of the indices is 1, it is possible to determine the extent of reproductive potential that is realized through marriage or lost through women being in various unmarried statuses (under the assumption that illegitimacy is negligible). Thus, the results suggest that approximately 65 percent ($I_m = 0.646$) of the reproductive potential of Thai women in 1970 and about 60 percent in 1980 was realized through the existing marriage pattern. Of the potential unrealized, most was unrealized because of delayed or forgone entry into first marriage as indicated by the far greater values of I_s than I_d or I_w. Indeed, in both 1970 and 1980 only about

3. Age-specific marital fertility of Hutterite women married 1921–30 serves as the standard age profile of fertility in the absence of deliberate birth control. Hutterites are an Anabaptist religious sect in North America that has a strict prohibition on the use of birth-control methods. The fertility rates of the 1921–30 marriage cohort represent the highest reliably recorded marital fertility known at the time of construction of the original I_m index. More precisely,

$$I_m = \frac{\Sigma m_i F_i}{\Sigma W_i F_i} \qquad I_s = \frac{\Sigma s_i F_i}{\Sigma W_i F_i}$$

$$I_d = \frac{\Sigma d_i F_i}{\Sigma W_i F_i} \qquad I_w = \frac{\Sigma w_i F_i}{\Sigma W_i F_i}$$

where m_i, s_i, d_i, and w_i refer to the number of married, single, divorced, and widowed women respectively in age interval i, W_i equals the total women in age interval i, and F_i is the Hutterite fertility rate in age interval i. The indices are calculated on the basis of summation from age intervals 15–19 through age intervals 45–49.

5 percent (the summary I_d and I_w) was unrealized because of marital dissolution. Thus, the increasing proportions of single women are having a depressing effect on overall fertility but changes in marital dissolution are having little effect, at least over recent years.

In addition to the permanent dissolution of a marriage, temporary separation can reduce exposure to intercourse and thereby influence fertility levels. Davis and Blake (1956) cite the separation of couples due to migration as an example of such a situation. Although available evidence does not permit a definitive judgment on the extent of temporary separation of spouses, there are several indications that temporary separations are fairly frequent (Knodel et al., 1982; Goldstein, Goldstein, and Piampiti, 1973). Of particular interest is the recent overseas migration of Thai workers, especially to the Middle East, since such migration often results in absences of a year or more (Arnold and Shah, 1984). Statistics from the Department of Labor indicate increasing migration of Thai workers overseas with the numbers rising from about 1,000 in 1975 to over 20,000 in both 1980 and 1981 and then to over 100,000 in 1982, followed by a decrease to 67,000 in 1983 (Pitayanon, 1983; Thailand, Department of Labor, 1984). Depending on the coverage of these statistics, the duration of stay of migrants and their distribution with respect to their sex, age, and marital status, the impact of overseas migration of workers on fertility could be significant.

Officially published census reports do not distinguish currently married persons with spouses present from those with spouses absent. However, some information is available from special tabulations from the 1960 census and more recently from the Contraceptive Prevalence Surveys. Analysis of the 1 percent sample of the 1960 census indicated that 3.3 percent of currently married women reported their husbands absent (Knodel et al., 1982). Results from CPS2 in 1981 suggest that the figure was only slightly higher (3.6 percent) two decades later. In contrast, CPS3 indicates a substantially higher figure of 6.4 percent for 1984. This may reflect the sharp increase in migrant workers overseas indicated in the statistics from the Department of Labor. The amount of separation is particularly high for the northeast, where almost 9 percent of currently married women under 50 reported their husbands absent. This conforms with the common impression that the overseas migrant workers come disproportionately from that region. If all these figures are accurate, and temporary separation of spouses remained at a relatively low and similar level between 1960 and the start of the 1980s, it would appear that this factor has played little role during the bulk of the observed fertility decline. Very recent increases in the amount of relatively long-term but still temporary migration overseas, or possibly increased temporary rural-urban migration by one spouse, may currently be exerting some influence.

Natural Marital Fertility Factors

Even in the absence of deliberate attempts at birth control, marital fertility can vary substantially. The most important proximate determinant of variation in "natural" marital-fertility levels is the duration of postpartum infecundability, which is closely related to infant-feeding practices in the population. Before examining the evidence relating to this factor, we review information related to two of the other three marital-fertility factors: primary sterility, which is an important component of permanent sterility, and coital frequency, which is an important determinant of fecundability. Reliable information on the fourth factor, spontaneous interuterine mortality, is lacking for Thailand.

Primary Sterility

In any population, at least a small proportion of couples is unable to bear any children from the start of cohabitation because of physiological impairment of either or both of the spouses. The extent of this situation, referred to as primary sterility, can be approximated by the proportion of ever-married women who remain childless to the end of the reproductive span, provided voluntary childlessness is negligible. Census results on the extent of childlessness suggest that primary sterility in Thailand is quite low and has been for some time. For example, only about 3 percent of ever-married women aged 45–49 and fewer than 4 percent of women in their fifties never had a child, according to the 1960 and 1980 censuses.[4] A recent comparative analysis of childlessness based on the World Fertility Survey results (including SOFT), confirms that childlessness is low in Thailand and compares favorably with levels in other developing countries. For example, among currently married women aged 40–44, who were married at least five years, only 2 percent never experienced a live birth (Vaessen, 1984). Given the low level of primary sterility in Thailand and the apparent lack of change in the level over recent decades, it is unlikely to have influenced the ongoing fertility decline.

Coital Frequency

Reliable statistical information on coital frequency is rarely available for most societies. For Thailand, several studies, most of which are based on specialized samples, included questions on frequency of intercourse (Knodel et al., 1982). A rural survey based on a more or less representative sample indicated a mean frequency among married couples of about twice a week with the rate

---

4. A variety of biases could affect these results, as has been discussed in Knodel et al., 1982; see also Vaessen, 1984. Nevertheless, it is unlikely that childlessness is substantially greater than the few percent indicated by these figures.

Table 5.3. Indices of Breastfeeding from Selected Surveys, 1969–84

	Rural	Urban
Mean duration of breastfeeding (in months) of all children born within three years of survey[a]		
1969/70[b] (LS1)	22.4	12.9
1972 (LS2)	22.0	9.9
1975 (SOFT)	20.9	9.7
1979 (NS)	17.5	8.4
Median duration of breastfeeding (in months) of last-born child within two years prior to the survey[c]		
1981 (CPS2)	18.3	4.0
1984 (CPS3)	18.3	4.3
Percent of women still breastfeeding their last-born child born within two years of the survey[d]		
1975 (SOFT)	77	37
1979 (NS)	67	36
1981 (CPS2)	66	34
1984 (CPS3)	68	33

Sources: Knodel and Debavalya (1980); Knodel, Kamnuansilpa, and Chamratrithirong (1985).

[a] Estimated from the proportions still breastfeeding among nonpregnant mothers with a child under three years of age.
[b] Rural round in 1969; urban round in 1970.
[c] Estimated by the life-table technique based on the most recent birth to women within two years of the survey.
[d] Based on the most recent birth to women within two years prior to the survey; standardized for months since last birth.

inversely related to age (Deemar Company, Ltd., 1975, vol. 2: table 15). Although direct evidence is lacking, there is little reason to believe coital frequency is a factor that plays an important role in distinguishing fertility in Thailand from most other countries or that changes in coital frequency have contributed to fertility decline.

Postpartum Infecundability and Infant-Feeding Practices

In contrast to primary sterility and coital frequency, variation in postpartum infecundability associated with different infant-feeding practices is an important determinant of fertility differences in populations characterized by natural marital fertility. The contraceptive effect of breastfeeding is well documented (McCann et al., 1981). Prolonged lactation protects against pregnancy by delaying the postpartum return of ovulation and thus extends the period following a birth during which a woman is not susceptible to conception. Changes in breastfeeding practices can therefore have a significant effect on fertility trends.

Information on the prevalence and trends in breastfeeding is available from a number of the national sample surveys, although comparisons across surveys are complicated by differences in the nature of the data collected and hence in the type of measure that can be constructed. Results based on three different measures are summarized in table 5.3. Estimates of the mean duration of breastfeeding indicate that a moderate but persistent decline occurred between 1969 and 1979 in both rural and urban areas. More recent data from CPS2 and CPS3 suggest that the decline may have ceased at least for the time being, perhaps in reaction to recent efforts to promote breastfeeding (Knodel, Kamnuansilpa, and Chamratrithirong, 1985). This is reflected in the lack of decline in the median duration of breastfeeding between 1981 and 1984 among women with a birth in the two years prior to the survey, as well as in the leveling off after 1979 in the decline in the percentage of recent mothers who were breastfeeding their infants.

The survey results also make clear that rural Thai women breastfeed for much longer durations than their urban counterparts. This differential has been apparent since the earlier survey and is very pronounced at present, with rural women characterized by a median duration of a year and a half compared to a median of under five months for urban women.

Additional information on infant-feeding practices as well as data on postpartum amenorrhea are presented in table 5.4 based on the 1984 CPS3. Clearly, the initiation of breastfeeding is close to universal in rural Thailand, as indicated by the low percentage of mothers who said they never breastfed their infants at all. Even in urban areas, only a small minority indicate they did not breastfeed at all. According to CPS3, nationally only 7 percent of mothers whose most recent birth occurred within four years prior to the survey did not initiate breastfeeding and the average duration of breastfeeding was close to a year and a half.

CPS3 also indicated questions on the return of menses following birth and thus provides the first national data to permit a direct estimation of the duration of postpartum amenorrhea. Since the period of postpartum amenorrhea very closely approximates the period of nonsusceptibility, it is of direct interest for fertility analyses.[5] Nationally, the median is under six months and the

---

5. Although the periods of postpartum amenorrhea and infecundability are not strictly identical, they tend to be quite similar. Since ovulation generally precedes menstruation by two weeks, the period of infecundability would end two weeks prior to the resumption of menstruation or prior to when menstruation would have resumed (in cases where the woman's first menstrual cycle following childbirth is ovulatory or where the woman conceives prior to first menstruation). For

Table 5.4. Indices of Breastfeeding and Postpartum Amenorrhea among Women with a Birth within Four Years Prior to Interview, 1984

Index	National	Rural	Urban
Percent never breastfeeding	6.9	5.0	15.5
Median duration of breastfeeding of last-born child (in months)			
Overall breastfeeding[a,b]	17.5	18.5	4.5
Full breastfeeding[a]	0.9	1.0	0.2
Duration of postpartum amenorrhea (in months)			
Median	5.7	6.5	2.9
Mean	7.2	7.8	4.7

Sources: Knodel, Kamnuansilpa, and Chamratrithirong (1985) and original calculations from CPS3.

Note: The median durations of breastfeeding, full breastfeeding, and postpartum amenorrhea are all derived by life-table techniques. The mean duration of postpartum amenorrhea is based on the prevalence technique (see Ferry and Smith, 1983).

[a] Includes women who never breastfed as duration 0.

[b] Results on the median duration in this table differ slightly from those in table 5.3 because they are based on women with a birth within four years prior to interview rather than only two years.

mean duration slightly over seven months. Given the relatively long average duration of breastfeeding in Thailand, the duration of postpartum amenorrhea is relatively short in comparison with other countries (see, e.g., Bongaarts, 1983; Page, Lesthaeghe, and Shah, 1982).[6]

One plausible explanation for breastfeeding in Thailand not extending postpartum amenorrhea for longer periods may be the very early age at which infants are given supplemental food. The impact of breastfeeding on delaying the return of ovulation is considerably less among women who provide supplements than among those who do not (Van Ginneken, 1974; Lee et al., 1984; Knodel, Kamnuansilpa, and Chamratrithirong, 1985). As CPS3 results indicate, the duration of breastfeeding in the absence of any other foods in Thailand is very short. In rural areas, exclusive breastfeeding ceases at about a

---

some women, however, the first one or two menstrual cycles are anovulatory and the period of infecundability exceeds the period of amenorrhea (McCann et al., 1981; Anderson, 1983:28). To some extent, these two groups of women balance each other out and thus the average durations of postpartum amenorrhea and infecundability should be quite similar at the aggregate level.

6. For example, based on a formula devised by Bongaarts (1983) from cross-national data, a *mean* duration of breastfeeding of 16–18 months typically corresponded to a *mean* duration of postpartum amenorrhea of between 10 and 12 months.

Table 5.5. Contraceptive Knowledge among Currently Married Women Aged 15–44, by Residence, 1969–84

Year and survey	Percent able to mention at least one method without prompting			Mean number of methods mentioned		
	National	Rural	Urban	National	Rural	Urban
1969/70[a] (LS1)	53	48	74	1.2	1.1	1.8
1975 (SOFT)	87	86	92	2.4	2.3	2.9
1978/79 (CPS1)	98[b]	97	98[b]	3.3[b]	3.3	3.5[b]
1984 (CPS3)	99	99	99	4.3	4.3	4.3

Sources: Knodel et al. (1982); Kamnuansilpa and Chamratrithirong (1985).

[a] Rural round in 1969; urban round in 1970.
[b] Excluding provincial urban places.

month, whereas in urban areas it lasts for only a week. Thus, nationally, the year and a half median duration of overall breastfeeding contrasts sharply with the median of under one month for full breastfeeding.

Deliberate Marital Fertility Control

As evident in chapter 4, the recent fertility decline in Thailand has been largely a matter of a reduction in marital fertility. Underlying this change has been a massive increase in the awareness of contraceptive methods and in the extent to which Thai couples deliberately limit their reproduction through birth control. Quantitative data documenting changes in contraceptive knowledge and prevalence are available from a number of surveys.[7]

Knowledge of Contraception

Results summarized in table 5.5 clearly indicate that since 1969 there has been a marked increase in awareness of contraceptives among both rural and urban women. At the time of the first round of the Longitudinal Study, about three out of four married urban women were able to mention a method of contraception without being prompted, but less than half of rural women could. Less than ten years later, almost all women could mention at least one method

---

7. Contraceptive prevalence as discussed in the present study includes use of all methods of contraception including "male" methods such as condoms or vasectomy. For the sake of convenience, however, prevalence is expressed as the percentage of *women* who are currently using or whose husbands are currently using some method, since the information on contraceptive use is typically elicited from female respondents.

and by 1984, 99 percent of both rural and urban women were familiar with contraception.

The average number of methods mentioned by respondents without prompting has also increased substantially, more than doubling for urban women and more than tripling for rural women within a fifteen-year period. The pronounced urban-rural differential in contraceptive knowledge evident in 1969 narrowed considerably by 1975 and had completely disappeared by 1984. The fact that the average Thai woman, especially in rural areas, is now able to mention four different methods when asked about contraception probably reflects (at least in part) the fact that the National Family Planning Program, unlike those in many other countries, has been offering a wide variety of methods on a broad scale over the last decade rather than emphasizing only one or two methods (ESCAP, 1985b; see also chapter 9). According to the 1984 CPS3, the most commonly known method is the contraceptive pill. Nationally, 94 percent of ever-married women in the reproductive ages were able to mention this method without prompting. A substantial majority of women could also name female and male sterilization, the IUD, and injectables without being prompted (Kamnuansilpa and Chamratrithirong, 1985). In short, almost all married Thai women, both rural and urban, are now familiar with the idea of birth control and the large majority are aware of a reasonably wide range of specific modern methods.

Although representative quantitative national-level data are not available prior to 1969, results of a 1964 survey of the Potharam district, a rural area about 80 kilometers from Bangkok, suggest that familiarity with contraception may have been considerably lower then and thus may also have been increasing rapidly during the 1960s. Of the more than 1,000 currently married women aged 20–44 interviewed in the Potharam district in 1964, approximately two thirds had "no knowledge whatsoever of contraceptive methods" (Hawley and Prachuabmoh, 1971b:36). Also of interest is the large-scale national Rural Economic Survey taken in 1930–31. Although it undoubtedly does not conform to modern standards of sampling and survey technique, it nevertheless was the product of a self-conscious effort to collect a variety of representative social and economic data for rural Thailand based on field interviews in forty villages in all regions. This study concludes that "the birth rate does not seem to be under human control. They [the respondents] do not know about birth control nor practice any form to any extent" (Zimmerman, 1931:230).

Information on past awareness of nonmodern methods, particularly withdrawal, which in European populations was a major means of reducing fertility during the demographic transition, is of particular interest. Unfortunately, such data are not available from LS1, the earliest national survey. According to tabulations from CPS1, conducted in 1978, nationally only 3 percent of

Table 5.6. Percent Currently Practicing Contraception among Currently Married Women Aged 15–44, by Residence, 1969–84

Year and survey	National	Rural	Urban
1969/70[a] (LS1)	15	11	33
1972/73[b] (LS2)	26	23	45
1975 (SOFT)	37	35	49
1978/79 (CPS1)	53[c]	51	63[c]
1981 (CPS2)	59	58	65
1984 (CPS3)	65	64	69

Sources: Knodel et al. (1982); Kamnuansilpa and Chamratrithirong (1985).
[a] Rural round in 1969; urban round in 1970.
[b] Rural round in 1972; urban round in 1973.
[c] Excluding provincial urban.

ever-married women in the country as a whole mentioned withdrawal spontaneously when asked what contraceptive methods they knew and another 20 percent indicated recognition of withdrawal when it was specifically mentioned to them (Suvanajata and Kamnuansilpa, 1979:24). Results from NS in 1979 indicated considerably lower figures, especially for rural ever-married women: even with prompting, only 8 percent of rural women indicated any awareness of withdrawal and only 16 percent acknowledged awareness of abstinence as a method of limiting family size or spacing children (Institute of Population Studies, 1981). Presumably, Thai women are not unaware of the connection between coitus and conception. Instead, within Thai cultural context, withdrawal or abstinence are not viewed as acceptable ways of controlling childbearing. Qualitative data presented in the next chapter support the idea that these methods were not part of any longstanding folk tradition in Thailand and were generally not even thought of as means of birth control.[8]

Contraceptive Prevalence

Even more striking than the recent spread of contraceptive knowledge is the increase in contraceptive use illustrated in table 5.6. For the country as a whole, the percentage of married women in the reproductive ages who reported they were currently practicing some method of contraception rose during the decade and a half covered by the surveys from 15 to 65 percent, a level not very

8. More recent data from CPS2 and CPS3 indicate increasing proportions of women acknowledging awareness of withdrawal as a contraceptive method. For example, in CPS3, although only 3 percent mentioned withdrawal spontaneously, an additional 35 percent said they had heard of the method when it was mentioned to them (Kamnuansilpa and Chamratrithirong, 1985:36). This recent spread of knowledge of withdrawal, however, does not contradict the point that it appears not to have been widely known in the past and hence was not a traditional practice.

far below that characterizing many of the developed countries. Moreover, the increase is greater among rural women, of whom only 11 percent were practicing contraception in 1969. As a result, rural-urban differences in contraceptive prevalence have narrowed substantially. Even the low prevalence rate for rural women in 1969 may be the result of a recent prior increase, given that the 1964 survey in the Potharam district found only 4 percent of married women aged 20–44 were currently practicing contraception and only 5 percent had ever practiced contraception (calculated from Hawley and Prachuabmoh, 1971a).

The specific methods of contraception being used by respondents are indicated in table 5.7 (after standardization for age). Both LS1, the first survey, and CPS3, the most recent survey, show female sterilization as the most popular technique. All the surveys in between indicate the contraceptive pill was the most commonly used method. Although CPS3 indicates that female sterilization is the most common method in both rural and urban areas, levels were considerably higher for urban than for rural women, reflecting the greater accessibility in cities and towns to facilities providing sterilization. Even in rural areas, however, over one in five (22.5 percent) currently married women aged 15–44 have been sterilized (Kamnuansilpa and Chamratrithirong, 1985).

The spread of the small-family norm throughout Thai society, with the notable exception of the Muslim minority and to a lesser extent southern Buddhists, was noted in the previous chapter. A roughly parallel situation characterizes the rapid spread of contraceptive use over the last decade and a half. By 1984, contraceptive prevalence was only slightly lower for rural as compared to urban women in contrast to a far more pronounced difference evident a decade or so before. Results in table 5.8 document the rapid increase in the use of contraception among the different educational strata. A direct association between education and percentage using contraception is evident throughout the decade and a half covered, with the exception of the urban figure for 1984. Nevertheless, women in all educational categories experienced increases in contraceptive use of roughly similar magnitudes, again underscoring the broad base of Thailand's reproductive revolution.

Several surveys have attempted to measure differential use of contraception by family income. Although the results of the surveys are not strictly comparable because of differences in the samples and in the way family income was determined, the results are at least suggestive of a considerable contraction of an initially sharp positive association between income and contraceptive use during the 1970s as contraceptive prevalence increased (Knodel et al., 1982). At a minimum, it seems clear that couples in all major income categories have substantially increased their use of deliberate marital fertility control during the course of Thailand's fertility transition.

In contrast to the pervasiveness of increasing contraceptive use across a

Table 5.7. Percent Currently Practicing Specific Methods of Contraception among Currently Married Women Aged 15–44, 1969–84

Year	Survey	Pill	IUD	Sterilization		Injectables	Condom	Others	All methods[a]
				Male	Female				
1969/70	LS1	3.8	2.2	2.1	5.5	0.4	0.0	0.7	14.8
1972/73	LS2	10.6	4.7	2.8	6.8	0.9	0.1	0.5	26.4
1975	SOFT	15.2	6.5	2.2	7.5	2.1	0.5	2.8	36.7
1978/79	CPS1[b]	21.9	4.0	3.5	13.0	4.7	2.2	4.2	53.4
1981	CPS2	20.2	4.2	4.2	18.7	7.1	1.9	2.7	59.0
1984	CPS3	19.8	4.9	4.4	23.5	7.6	1.8	2.6	64.6

Note: Results for LS1 and LS2 are derived by combining separate rural and urban surveys taken one year apart and weighing the results to reflect the different sampling fractions used.

[a]Rounding errors, minor coding discrepancies, and users of unspecified methods account for the small differences between the sum of the percentages practicing individual methods and the percentage for all methods.
[b]Excluding provincial urban.

87

Table 5.8. Percent Currently Practicing Contraception among Currently Married Women Aged
15–44, Standardized for Age, by Educational Attainment and Place of Residence

Residence and years of schooling	1969/70[a] (LS1)	1972 (LS2)	1975 (SOFT)	1979 (NS)	1984 (CPS3)	Increase
Rural						
0–3	7	13	33	48	52	45
4	13	26	36	48	64	51
5+	17	38	45	57	67	50
Urban						
0–3	28	34	44	42	76[b]	50
4	31	42	50	50	68	37
5+	36	54	53	64	67	31

Sources: Knodel et al. (1982); Kamnuansilpa and Chamratrithirong (1985).

Note: The national age distribution of currently married women recorded in the 1970 census
serves as the basis for the age standardization.

[a]Rural round in 1969; urban round in 1970.
[b]Excluding the value for the age group 15–19, which is based on only one woman.

broad socioeconomic spectrum as represented by rural-urban residence, education, and income, a greater difference exists when religion, a basic cultural
dimension, is taken into account. Contraceptive use among Thai Muslims lags
well behind the Buddhist majority. This is clearly evident in results both from
special tabulations from the 1980 census, which included a question on contraceptive use, and more recently from CPS3. Although there is reason to suggest that contraceptive prevalence is generally underestimated by the census,
differentials in use by various subgroups are of interest, particularly religious
differentials, since most surveys include insufficient numbers of respondents
other than Buddhists to make reliable comparisons. According to the 1980
census, among currently married women aged 15–44, prevalence was 48 percent for Buddhists nationally and 16 percent for Muslims. This probably ex-
aggerates the difference somewhat because Muslims are more likely to be
practicing traditional contraceptive methods, especially withdrawal, which
appear to be largely missed by the census. Nevertheless, even taking this into
account, the difference in overall prevalence would be extremely large. That
such differences are not due only to socioeconomic differences is suggested
by the fact that sharp religious differentials characterized each major educational category, although they are less pronounced for women with a secondary or university education. Within the southern region, where most Muslims
reside, contraceptive use also varies with language spoken. Married Muslim
women aged 15–44 whose native tongue is Thai experienced 14 percent

prevalence, compared to 9 percent for those who spoke Malay or a related dialect (Pejaranonda and Chamratrithirong, 1984).

Results from CPS3, conducted in 1984, presented in table 5.9, confirm the sharp religious differential in contraceptive use found by the census: overall prevalence among currently married women aged 15–44 was 34 percent for Muslims and 67 percent for Buddhists. In general, Muslims rely more on withdrawal and other nonmodern methods than do Buddhists, although this appears at least in part to be a regional phenomenon, since southern Buddhists share this pattern. Results from CPS3 also confirm that Malay-speaking southern Muslims were less likely to report using contraception than those who spoke Thai. Among Muslims living in Bangkok and the central region, contraceptive use was lower than for Buddhists living there but nevertheless far higher than for southern Muslims. Southern Buddhists also were characterized by lower contraceptive prevalence than Buddhists elsewhere, although they still had considerably higher prevalence than southern Muslims. Thus in Thailand, both region and religion are associated with the level of contraceptive use at this stage of the fertility transition, suggesting a possibly important role of cultural factors as determinants of reproductive behavior. The significance of the religious differentials for understanding the role the cultural context has played in Thailand's reproductive revolution is discussed in chapter 8.

Induced Abortion

Although the various surveys clearly document both the general increase in contraceptive practice and the methods of contraception used, they are less helpful for determining the amount of induced abortion in Thailand, a potentially important source of fertility control. Because abortion is illegal under most circumstances and, unlike contraception, is believed by most Thais to be contrary to the principles of Buddhism, responses to direct survey questions on the use of abortion are generally assumed to seriously understate its prevalence.

In response to a direct question in each of the three Contraceptive Prevalence Surveys, only 2–3 percent of ever-married women under age 50 acknowledged ever having resorted to abortion as a means of birth control (Kamnuansilpa and Chamratrithirong, 1982, 1985). Several regional surveys have yielded similar figures in response to direct inquiries (Porapakkham and Bennett, 1978:89; Shevasunt and Hogan, 1979:35). It is virtually certain that responses to direct questions in the surveys grossly underestimate the prevalence of induced abortion. It is interesting that Riley (1972:218) indicates that despite the fact that there was an abortionist in the village he studied and that he knew of specific instances of induced abortion, in the course of the systematic interviews he conducted to collect fertility histories, only one woman admitted to having an induced abortion.

Table 5.9. Percent Currently Practicing Specific Contraceptive Methods among Currently Married Women Aged 15–44, by Religion, Region, and Language, 1984

Method	Total population		South only				Bangkok and central region only	
					Muslims by language			
	Buddhists	Muslims	Buddhists	Thai	Malay		Buddhists	Muslims
Pill	20	11	12	17	6		22	23
Condom	2	1	2	1	1		3	2
IUD	4	1	3	0	1		3	4
Female sterilization	24	5	20	6	2		25	15
Male sterilization	5	1	4	2	0		6	3
Injectables	8	6	6	8	4		8	5
Withdrawal	1	6	6	9	5		1	2
Others	2	3	3	1	3		2	2
All methods	67	34	57	44	23		70	56

Source: Kamnuansilpa and Chamratrithirong (1985).

Note: Results from CPS3 in this table are unweighted and thus are not strictly nationally or regionally representative.

90

Results from a number of sources other than direct survey questions suggest that the prevalence of induced abortion may be substantial in Thailand. A 1978 study of abortion practitioners in rural Thailand (Research and Evaluation Unit, National Family Planning Program, 1979) indicates that abortion is widely practiced, using methods ranging from very primitive to modern. Of these methods, massage abortion appears to be the most common. The study estimated that a minimum of about 300,000 illegal abortions occur per year in rural and provincial urban Thailand. This would correspond to approximately one abortion for every four live births or an abortion rate of approximately 37 per 1,000 women, excluding the Bangkok population, which was not covered in the study. A 1980 study in an overwhelmingly rural northeastern province, again based on interviews with indigenous practitioners, indicated a considerably higher incidence of abortion: over eight abortions for every ten live births and an abortion rate of 107 per 1,000 women aged 15–44 (Narkavonnakit and Bennett, 1981). An earlier attempt to estimate the national annual abortion rate, based on countrywide hospital admissions for incomplete abortions, indicated a total of 200,000 to 230,000 cases of induced abortion per year during 1972–73, corresponding roughly to an induced abortion rate of 28 per 1,000 women aged 15–45 (Cook and Leoprapai, 1974, cited in Population Council, 1981).

Although firm estimates of the extent of induced abortion are not available for Thailand, and existing estimates can be called into question on the basis of representativeness and accuracy, it seems fairly clear that the practice of induced abortion is considerable in Thailand and should not be ignored as a factor influencing recent levels of fertility. In this connection, it is worth noting that several studies make it clear that substantial numbers of abortions, perhaps the large majority, are attributable to married women, especially in rural areas, and thus potentially have an important influence on the level of marital fertility (see Population Council, 1981).

Limited evidence suggests that the overall prevalence of abortion has increased during the same period that contraceptive practice has risen sharply. An extensive study based on a large number of hospitals throughout the country indicates a threefold increase between 1966 and 1974 in the number of cases admitted for complications associated with abortion. Although information specifying whether the complications resulted from induced or spontaneous abortion was not available, the author reports that many cases were probably the result of illegally induced abortions (Rauyajin, 1979). Another study based on admissions for induced abortion to a Bangkok hospital indicates a steady 3.6-fold increase between the first three years, 1968–70, and 1977, followed by a slight decline during the next two years (Koetsawang, 1980; Population Council, 1981). These studies clearly suggest a major trend toward increased abortion at the same time contraceptive use is rapidly increasing.

At this stage in Thailand's fertility transition, it may be that both abortion and contraceptive use are part of the same process whereby family limitation is spreading rapidly throughout the population. Given that contraceptive use is becoming very widespread and more efficient, with a high and rising prevalence of sterilization, the number of abortions, at least among married women, may be declining, although there is no solid quantitative evidence to document this. Perhaps the results from the Bangkok hospital study showing a decline since 1977 is signaling such a change.

Deliberate Birth Spacing

There is some evidence from both historical Europe and contemporary experience in the developing world that motivations to limit family size rather than to space births often dominates the initial spread of birth control during early stages of the fertility transition (Knodel, 1979, 1981; Siddiqui, 1979; see, however, Friedlander, Eisenbach, and Goldscheider, 1980). Thus, as birth control spreads throughout the population, we would expect couples who already have all the children they want to adopt birth control more readily than those who want more children. Results presented in table 5.10 clearly show that all the major surveys indicate the percentage of women practicing birth control is substantially higher among those who want no more children than among those who still wish to have additional children. Until quite recently, the increase in contraceptive prevalence has also been more pronounced among the former group, with more than seven out of ten women who want no more children practicing contraception in 1984. Indeed, among the urban population almost 80 percent of women who want no more children indicate they are currently practicing some form of contraception. Nevertheless, the practice of contraception for spacing births is also becoming common, as indicated by contraceptive prevalence among couples in which the wife indicates she still wants more children. By 1984, over half of women who wanted at least one additional child were practicing birth control, presumably for spacing purposes. Thus, although during the first few years of the rapid increase in contraceptive prevalence during Thailand's fertility transition, adoption of contraception for terminating childbearing clearly predominated, more recently use of contraception for birth spacing has also become quite pervasive. Indeed, between 1981 and 1984, the years of the two most recent surveys, prevalence increased more for spacing than for limiting. This probably reflects an inevitable leveling-off of prevalence among couples who want to stop childbearing, given the very high level of contraceptive use that already characterizes this group.

An initial dominance by the motivation to limit family size and the subsequent increasing importance of the spacing motivation over the course of the fertility decline is also evident in data collected from new acceptors in the

Table 5.10. Percent Currently Practicing Contraception among Currently Married Women Aged 15–44, by Desire for Additional Children

Year of survey	Survey	National Want more	National Want no more	Rural Want more	Rural Want no more	Urban Want more	Urban Want no more
1969/1970[a]	LS1	4.5	21.3	1.2	16.7	17.1	46.4
1972/1973[b]	LS2	11.4	35.0	9.7	30.7	19.7	62.6
1975	SOFT	24.6	43.1	22.4	41.0	35.7	59.1
1978/79	CPS1	38.6[c]	61.1[c]	37.5	58.3	43.0[d]	74.5[d]
1981	CPS2	41.2	69.2	40.3	67.5	45.3	77.1
1984	CPS3	51.4	73.4	50.5	72.2	55.1	79.4

Note: In some surveys, for pregnant women desire for additional children refers to children in addition to the one expected.

[a] The rural phase took place in 1969, the urban phase in 1970.
[b] The rural phase took place in 1972, the urban phase in 1973.
[c] Excluding provincial urban.
[d] Bangkok metropolitan area only.

National Family Planning Program. In 1971–72, the first year for which data were available, more than two-thirds of new acceptors indicated they wanted no more children. This share has declined almost steadily, so that by 1983 only slightly fewer than half of new acceptors indicated that they were ready to terminate childbearing altogether. At the same time, the share of new acceptors who still wanted additional children increased almost without interruption, from 14 percent in 1971–72 to 36 percent by 1983. The remainder of acceptors were unsure about their future fertility plans. This proportion has remained fairly steady throughout the period at somewhat less than one-fifth of all acceptors.

Thailand has reached a situation, approximating that of developed countries, in which deliberate fertility control within marriage is exercised widely both for spacing and stopping births. Even during the very short time that the fertility transition has been underway in Thailand, one can see the same evolution in contraceptive practice patterns with respect to spacing and stopping that probably occurred over a much longer period in the past among the developed countries.

An Assessment of Fertility Impacts

As indicated above, Bongaarts (1982a) has demonstrated that four proximate determinants—namely, the proportions married among women, contraceptive use and effectiveness, prevalence of induced abortion, and duration of postpartum infecundability—are of significant importance in the analysis of fertility differences or trends. Variations in the population averages of the other factors usually are not large enough to make a substantial impact on fertility. He has proposed an analytical accounting scheme that permits assessment of the impact of each of these four principal proximate variables on the fertility level at any given point in time and to examine changes in their impact over time (Bongaarts, 1978; Bongaarts and Potter, 1984). The fertility-inhibiting effect of each is assessed by comparing an estimate of the fertility level that would prevail in its presence and then in its absence. The potential fertility level that would prevail in the absence of any inhibiting effect of the four principal proximate determinants (i.e., under conditions in which all women in the reproductive ages were married and there was no breastfeeding, induced abortion, or contraception) is called the total fecundity rate. The level of total fecundity varies from population to population because of differences in the other proximate determinants. On the basis of empirical analysis of a number of populations, Bongaarts has found that the total fecundity rate typically falls within a range of thirteen to seventeen births per women, with an average near fifteen (Bongaarts and Potter, 1983:79).

In the Bongaarts model, the impacts of the four principal proximate fertility determinants are each measured by separate indices that can take values ranging from 0 to 1. When a given proximate determinant has no fertility-inhibiting effect, the corresponding index equals 1; if fertility inhibition is complete, the index equals 0. The four indices are defined as follows:

C_m = index of proportion married (equals 1 in the absence of celibacy and 0 in the absence of marriage);

C_c = index of contraception (equals 1 in the absence of contraception and 0 if all fecund women use 100 percent effective contraception);

C_a = index of induced abortion (equals 1 in the absence of induced abortion and 0 if all pregnancies are aborted); and

C_i = index of postpartum infecundability (equals 1 in the absence of lactation and postpartum abstinence and 0 if the duration of infecundability is infinite).

Since each index equals the proportionate reduction in fertility that it causes, the total fertility rate (TFR) is a product of the four indices times the total fecundity rate (TF):

$$TFR = TF \times C_m \times C_a \times C_c \times C_i$$

The Bongaarts indices can be estimated from a series of reproductive measures. In table 5.11, measures and indices required for the Bongaarts model are presented for four points in time corresponding to the one-year periods on which estimates of total fertility derived from LS1, LS2, SOFT, and NS were

Table 5.11. Estimates of Selected Reproductive Measures and Derived Indices of Four Proximate Determinants According to Bongaarts's Model: Thailand

	Year to which estimates refer			
	1968	1971	1974	1978
Measure				
Total fertility rate (TFR)	6.12	5.30	4.52	3.30
Total marital-fertility rate (TMFR)	9.23	8.07	7.03	5.49
Current contraceptive use (u)	.14	.26	.37	.49
Contraceptive effectiveness (e)	.95	.94	.92	.93
Total induced-abortion rate (TA)	.41	.55	.69	.83
Lactational infecundability (i)	10.7	10.0	9.4	7.7
Model Indices				
Index of proportions married				
$C_m = \text{TMFR/TFR}$	.66	.66	.64	.60
Index of contraception				
$C_c = (1 - 1.08\, ue)$	.85	.74	.64	.51
Index of induced abortion				
$C_a = \text{TFR}/\{\text{TFR} + [.4 \times (1 + u) \times \text{TA}]\}$	.97	.95	.92	.87
Index of lactational infecundability				
$C_i = 20/(18.5 + i)$	.70	.70	.72	.76
Combined Indices				
$C_m \times C_c \times C_a \times C_i$	.38	.32	.27	.20

(handwritten annotations in right margin:)
$0 = $ no one married
$1 = $ everyone married
$1 = $ no use
$0 = $ all use
$1 = $ none
$0 = $ all aborted
$1 = $ no bf
$0 = $ all bf

Note: The actual calculations of the model indices were based on values of u, e, and TA carried to three decimal places; the impact of the combined indices was also calculated from the separate indices carried to three decimal places. Where applicable, data for 1968, 1971, 1974, and 1978 are based on LS1, LS2, SOFT, and NS, respectively. TFR was estimated from the age-specific fertility rates obtained by multiplying the observed age-specific marital-fertility rates by the estimated age-specific proportions married derived by linear interpolation between the 1960, 1970, and 1980 censuses. TMFR is calculated with estimated rates for the 15–19 age group, calculated as .75 times the rate of the 20–24 age group, substituted for the observed rates; u and e are based on age-standardized rates for married women 15–44, as reported in Knodel et al. (1982:110). To calculate e, effectiveness rates of 1 for sterilization, .95 of IUD, .90 for pill and injection, and .70 for all others are assumed, as recommended in Bongaarts and Potter (1983:84). TA for 1978 was based on a rate of 27.75 abortions to married women per 1,000 total women aged 15–44, derived by assuming that the national abortion rate for married women is three-fourths the 37 per 1,000 women rate reported by Research and Evaluation Unit, National Family Planning Program (1979). The rate for 1968 was assessed to be half of this and to increase linearly to 27.75 by 1977. The mean number of months of lactational infecundability was estimated as 7.7 for 1978 from CPS1 (Knodel and Lewis, 1984). Values for earlier years were estimated by inflating the 1978 figure in proportion to the relative difference between the duration of breastfeeding based on the earlier surveys and the duration based on NS.

based. These four surveys were chosen because they were all conducted by or in collaboration with the same organization (the Institute of Population Studies at Chulalongkorn University) and are considered to be relatively comparable. In addition, they cover a decade of major fertility decline. Details on the calculations of the reproductive measures are provided in the notes to the table.[9]

It is worth stressing that several of these measures—in particular those referring to contraceptive effectiveness, induced abortion, and, to a lesser extent, postpartum infecundability—require that a variety of assumptions be made in order to convert the observed data into measures. As long as reasonable, though rough, estimates are possible, however, the model can be useful in providing the orders of magnitude for the extent to which the four principal proximate determinants inhibit fertility, how their contributions change over time, and the contribution each makes to changes in fertility.

The results indicate that, at any given time, the level of marriage alone reduced the total fecundity rate by a third or more. The contribution of changes in proportions married to the decline of fertility during the decade under observation, however, is fairly modest. The intercensal trends toward increasing proportions who are single and corresponding decreasing proportions of women currently married are reflected in the declining C_m index. Thus, the proportions unmarried were inhibiting potential fertility somewhat more by the end of the decade under observation than at the start. As would be expected, the index of contraception declined very substantially, reflecting the increasing importance of contraceptive practice in inhibiting potential fertility. Indeed, the change in this index is by far the greatest of any of those shown. Whereas, in 1968, proportions married had the largest inhibiting effect, as indicated by the fact that C_m has the lowest value of the four indices, by 1974 contraception was of equal importance and by 1978 was of considerably greater importance. The index of induced abortion also declines, suggesting that abortion assumed an increasing importance in inhibiting potential fertility during the decade under observation. However, this is a result of the largely arbitrary assumptions made about changes in induced abortion and thus is not

9. The results presented in table 5.10 differ slightly from previously published results (Knodel et al., 1982). The source of the difference stems from use of final rather than preliminary estimates from the 1980 census of the age-specific proportions married, revised estimates of the mean duration of postpartum amenorrhea, and correction of a calculation error in the estimate of TFR based on NS. The Bongaarts model was also applied to data from the three CPS surveys. The results yielded implied levels of total fecundity for CPS2 and CPS3 well in excess of the normal 13–17 range. Given the variety of assumed values required to calculate the full set of indices, it is difficult to determine precisely the source of the discrepancy. In general, however, the levels of total fertility are relatively high for the levels of contraceptive prevalence, suggesting some possible error in the measurement of either or both.

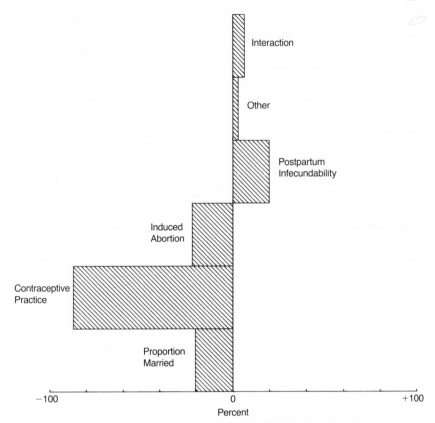

Figure 5.1. Decomposition of the Change in the Total Fertility Rate, Based on Bongaarts's Model, 1968–78

based on solid data. In contrast to the other three indices, the index of lactational infecundability (C_i) increases in value, reflecting the decline in the duration of breastfeeding. Hence, the importance of breastfeeding is decreasing as an inhibitor of potential fertility.

Bongaarts's accounting scheme also permits a decomposition of changes in total fertility into changes in the four principal proximate determinants separately, the remaining three proximate determinants taken collectively, and an interaction factor (Bongaarts and Potter, 1984). The decomposition of changes in total fertility between 1968 and 1978 is shown in figure 5.1. Results are expressed in terms of the percentage of the change in total fertility that is accounted for by each of the four determinants.

According to this analysis, increases in contraceptive prevalence made a far greater contribution to the decline in total fertility than did any other variable.

The contributions to lower total fertility made by the assumed increase in abortion and the decrease in proportions married are substantial but of much smaller magnitudes. The results also indicate, however, that fertility would have increased during the decade by one-fifth because of declining breastfeeding, had the other variables remained constant. When the contributions of contraception and abortion are taken together, it is obvious that Thailand's reproductive revolution is largely the product of increasing deliberate marital-fertility control.

The quantitative data reviewed in this chapter and the preceding one clearly document a rapid and substantial fall in fertility from high levels typical of most developing countries two decades ago and many such countries even today. Fertility preferences have evolved to a point where a two-child family is preferred by the majority of recently married couples and very few wish to have more than three children. Although increases in the age of marriage have contributed modestly to the fertility decline, the use of birth control among married couples, both to space births and to limit family size, has been the dominant proximate determinant involved. These changes have been pervasive, taking in virtually all major segments of the population, with the most clearly identifiable exception being the Islamic minority, especially in the south of Thailand. Given the widespread use of modern contraception, the vast majority of Thai couples are now in a position to act effectively on their low-fertility preferences. In brief, Thailand has already entered the most advanced stages of the fertility transition.

6

The Proximate Determinants of Reproductive Change: A Qualitative Assessment

Quantitative evidence provides important information on the proximate determinants underlying Thailand's fertility decline and clearly points to the primary role of the increased use of contraception. Additional insights can be gained by examining data of a more qualitative nature than are typically obtained through the standard survey questionnaire. Qualitative data also can be used to verify the quantitative evidence provided by surveys.

This chapter reviews qualitative data on the major proximate determinants, much of which was collected through focus-group sessions. The discussion concentrates largely on the knowledge and use of contraception, reflecting the considerable attention devoted to these topics in the guidelines for the focus-group sessions (see appendix B). Some information was also provided on marriage and abortion by the focus groups, as well as on breastfeeding as a potential means of birth spacing. Where possible, findings from anthropological studies are used to supplement the focus-group material. Because marriage generally precedes reproduction, the presentation of qualitative evidence about the proximate determinants starts with a brief discussion of attitudes about the appropriate age to marry.

Age at Marriage

Age at first marriage among the Buddhist majority in Thailand, especially for women, has traditionally been moderately late by Third World standards (see

99

chapter 5). Although the age at marriage has increased somewhat over the last few decades, this trend has contributed only modestly to the reduction of fertility. Nevertheless, it has been an important factor in keeping fertility in the past well below its theoretical maximum level.

In each focus-group session, participants were asked what the appropriate age of marriage was for men and women. Their comments provide some understanding of the normative basis underlying the ages at which men and women enter marital unions. There was reasonable agreement that a woman should marry in her early twenties, with the age of 20 being most commonly mentioned, and that a man should marry in his mid-twenties, with 25 being most commonly mentioned. Participants generally showed more concern about the minimum age at which marriage is appropriate than the maximum age. For women, the reasons mentioned justifying the minimum appropriate age typically concerned her maturity and ability to take responsibility, especially in connection with raising a family and handling the household. Some participants also voiced opinions about an upper limit on the appropriate age for women to marry, implying that if a woman waited too long she would be of little interest to most potential suitors.

The minimum age of marriage for men was linked in the discussion to completion of military service, serving for a temporary period as a Buddhist monk, and being responsible and mature. A Thai ideal is that all Buddhist men should serve at least a short period of time in the monkhood, normally before marriage. This is voluntary, in contrast to universal conscription for military service, which was first introduced in 1902 (Wyatt, 1984:210). It is common for a man to spend some time as a monk, and since normally a man must be at least age 20 before being ordained, the practice of serving as a monk helps set a minimum age for marriage for men.

In Thailand, readiness to marry is defined for both men and women largely in terms of being able to shoulder the responsibilities, both economic and emotional, that go along with living together as a couple and raising a family. The link between age of marriage and completion of military service thus can be seen as part of this more general and very pervasive set of normative expectations about marriage. This norm stipulating responsibility and maturity as prerequisites for marriage probably helps explain the moderately late ages of marriage for both men and women.

"Nobody wants a man who hasn't been in the army already. This is because they have to work in the rice fields. If the man is doing his military service, he cannot help do this work." (older woman, north)

"You should prepare. When you have a wife you should know what should be done. You should know how to provide and support your wife and your children." (younger man, northeast)

"If you are too young, you do not know how to raise children, but if you are older, you do things well and also cook well. If you are too young you cannot do anything." (younger woman, central region)

Although most participants seemed to have some idea of what an appropriate age at marriage should be and were able to provide reasons for their views, there was also a fair amount of flexibility shown. Many participants indicated that individuals had considerable latitude in deciding the timing of marriage for themselves. A frequent comment was: "It depends on the individual." Comments indicating considerable flexibility were found even when the prerequisites of ordination, military service, responsibility, and maturity were being mentioned.

The general flexibility expressed in the focus-group sessions with regard to age at marriage is consistent with the conclusions of much of the anthropological and sociological literature on marriage in Thailand (Limanonda, 1983). It is probably in part a reflection of the fact that in Thailand parents rarely arrange marriages for their children but rather at most play only an advisory role. Men and women typically decide for themselves when they should marry and parents have only limited influence over the choice of the mate and the timing of the marriage (see chapter 8).

The norm stipulating responsibility and maturity as conditions for readiness to marry is probably related to the prevailing patterns of postnuptial residence and household structure. In much of Thailand an ideal exists that a newly married couple will reside initially with the bride's parents for a period of a year or two, except for the last daughter to marry, who resides permanently with the parents, taking care of them in their old age (see chapters 3 and 8). The critical issue is the extent to which support for the newly wed couple, and later their children, falls largely on the couple themselves, rather than being absorbed by a composite household economy, as may be common in countries where age at marriage is quite early (Davis, 1955). The relative economic, social, and emotional independence that is expected of newly formed families and the anticipation that an independent household will be established before too long may well be the crucial factor in accounting for the general avoidance of and lack of support for very early marriage in Thailand. At the same time, complete economic independence is not expected of newly married couples, who generally have some opportunity to accumulate resources during the period of initial coresidence. This may help to explain why the age at marriage for both women and men in Thailand is intermediate between the pattern of early marriage in many Asian populations (at least until recently), where economic dependence on the parental generation is stronger, and the traditional pattern of late marriage in Europe in the past, where more complete independence was expected (Hajnal, 1965).

Perhaps the most interesting aspect of the focus-group discussions about age at marriage from the perspective of analyzing the fertility transition is the fact that participants made little connection between fertility and age at marriage. No link was made between the onset of menarche and the timing of marriage. More important, no one suggested that marriage should be, or was, delayed in order to limit the number of children eventually born. Only in the sense that age at marriage was contingent on readiness to start childbearing in terms of being able to assume the responsibility of child rearing was it apparently linked to fertility in the conscious thoughts of the participants. Thus, it seems unlikely that the older generation viewed delaying marriage as a deliberate way of controlling fertility.

Fertility Regulation before the Fertility Decline

Understanding the extent of knowledge and the nature of attitudes and practices concerning birth control in the past and present is important for understanding the reproductive changes currently underway. In particular, an attempt was made in the focus-group sessions to provide answers to the following questions: to what extent were means of deliberate birth control known and practiced prior to the onset of sustained fertility decline? Were there alternative mechanisms for controlling family size prior to widespread use of birth control? Was there a latent demand for fertility limitation among the pretransition generation? What is the nature and source of increased birth control use among the younger generation?

The General Absence of Birth Control

Many statements made by older- and younger-generation participants in the focus groups indicated that birth control was not practiced in earlier times. These statements usually arose spontaneously in response to a general question on why the number of children differs between the generations.

"Back in our time it was unavoidable to have many [children]. There was no birth control or contraception. You kept on having children until menopause." (older Buddhist woman, south)

"Back then there was nothing one could use for contraception. Children were just born." (older man, northeast)

Thus, the reproductive behavior of the older generation as described by focus-group participants was characterized largely by an absence of deliberate birth control and approximated what demographers term natural fertility (see Bongaarts and Menken, 1983; Knodel, 1983). Moreover, not only was birth control not practiced, but potentially effective means appear to have been either not known or considered inappropriate or unacceptable—indeed virtually unthinkable—within the cultural context. There is no reason to believe this situation was different for still earlier generations. There were some exceptions. Occasional reference was made to massage abortion and, among Muslim participants, to withdrawal, both potentially effective means of birth control, as well as to folk medicine and postpartum rituals intended entirely or in part to prevent or delay pregnancy but unlikely to be consequential. Nevertheless, the overall picture is clear that not only was birth control generally not practiced by the older generation or their predecessors, but there was very little store of traditional knowledge of acceptable and effective birth-control methods. At least one anthropologist doing his work in the 1950s mentions that birth control was not practiced at that time, with the exception of occasional abortions (de Young, 1955).

When discussing where they first learned about birth control, the large majority of older-generation focus-group participants mentioned hospitals or health centers or health personnel, or someone else who heard about it through these sources. Again, this suggests that there was no store of traditional knowledge about birth control upon which couples in the past could draw if they were interested in limiting or delaying births. In itself, this evidence is not decisive, because it is apparent from participants' testimony that some think of the term "birth control" as more narrowly referring to modern contraceptive methods promoted by the family-planning program and health personnel and discussed in the mass media rather than as a generic concept encompassing any means intended to delay childbearing or prevent conception. Nevertheless, the fact that they almost exclusively cited sources directly or indirectly linked with modern efforts to distribute contraception is at least consistent with the contention that the knowledge and practice of birth control was largely absent in the past. Moreover, when asked probing questions specifically about nonmodern methods, most participants generally denied that such methods were widely known or practiced.

Condoms

Although condoms have been available in urban Thailand for quite some time, only one participant in all the focus-group sessions mentioned that they were available at the time the older generation was having its children. Moreover, the other participants in that session then commented that generally only men who patronized prostitutes would have known of condoms. Most likely, awareness of condoms in rural Thailand was not widespread until they were promoted, along with other modern methods, in association with organized family planning activities. Even recently, although awareness of condoms is quite high, very few married couples report using condoms, possibly because of negative connotations derived from their association with prostitution. It is noteworthy that an investigation of the popular images of contraceptive methods among rural Thais in 1975 found a strong perceived association between condoms and their use with prostitutes (Deemar Company, Ltd., 1975).

Herbal Medicine and Postpartum Rituals

Herbal medicine intended either to prevent or to delay the next pregnancy or to abort a present one was the most common means of birth control prior to the relatively recent introduction of modern contraception that the older generation at the focus-group sessions mentioned. Usually participants spontaneously added that such medicines were ineffective.

"There was medicine for driving out [the fetus] but it only worked for some and didn't work for many others." (older woman, north)

"Back then they had herbal medicine to stop childbearing but the more you took, the more children you had." (older woman, Bangkok construction site)

Also acknowledged as ineffective were certain postpartum rituals intended to delay the pregnancy, such as burying the placenta in some special place. The traditional postpartum practice of lying by the fire for a few days to a few weeks, until recently widely practiced in Thailand, was also occasionally mentioned as helping delay the next pregnancy, although it is implausible that it actually had any contraceptive effect. This corresponds with the observations by Mougne (1982), an anthropologist studying a northern Thai village, that women there saw this practice as helping postpone the next pregnancy.

Abstinence

There was near-consensus in denying the use of abstinence as a deliberate means of either spacing births or terminating childbearing. Participants agreed that a brief period of postpartum abstinence should be honored, offering a mixture of reasons. Most frequently mentioned were consideration for the health of the new mother and the belief that resumption of intercourse shortly after childbirth is unsanitary. Only rarely was child spacing cited as a reason. The period of postpartum restraint from sexual relations believed to be appropriate was quite short, commonly one or two months. There is no evidence that this practice differs much between the older and younger generations.

The practices of temporary abstinence (other than for brief postpartum periods) for deliberately spacing births or terminal abstinence for limiting family size seem to be largely foreign concepts to rural Thais. Rarely was abstinence spontaneously mentioned in the focus groups as a way that births could be controlled. When specifically asked if couples ever practiced abstinence, most participants were doubtful that couples would do so for any length of time while still living together. Some women mentioned that husbands would be unwilling to forego sexual relations. The following are some typical reactions to our probing about the practice of abstinence as a method of birth control:

"How can they do that [abstain] if they are married?" (older Buddhist woman, south)

"Even if they were chained down, they would break the chain." (older man, northeast)

"We only did normal things." (older woman, northeast)

Focus-group participants were also questioned to discover whether there was a normative basis for terminal abstinence not directly connected to intentional birth limitation. There was clearly no general feeling that sex relations are inappropriate for older people or that there is any link between reaching some stage of the family life cycle, such as becoming a parent-in-law or a grandparent, and cessation of sexual intercourse, as is apparently the case in some cultures (Nag, 1983). Although many participants acknowledged that the frequency of intercourse dropped off with age and that some elderly couples may stop completely, this was explained in terms of loss of interest, rather than normative proscriptions. Far more common were comments that sex continued until very old ages, at least on an occasional basis, largely due to continued interest of the husband.

"If you stay together as a couple, I can assure you it is difficult to stop." (older Muslim woman, south)

"Women are not interested in it. But men are still interested. It is not certain about men. Until death." (older woman, north)

"People are not the same [with respect to when they stop having sex]. If you stay together you probably keep having sex two or three times a month. But for some, a few months may pass and they won't have sex." (older man, central region)

In the two anthropological studies specifically commenting on deliberate abstinence for birth-control purposes, opposite opinions are expressed. Riley (1972:235) notes in his study of a central Thai village in the early 1970s that despite numerous inquires, he could find no evidence of planned abstinence. In contrast, Potter (1976:53) reports that in his study of a northern Thai village, some landholding families limited family size by deliberate abstinence before modern contraception was available. Although not commenting on deliberate abstinence for birth-control purposes, in a study of a different northern Thai village, Mougne (1982:95) notes the general lack of any normative prohibition of sexual relations during the later stages of the reproductive span. This latter observation accords well with the observation that, in the past, relatively high fertility has persisted at older childbearing ages (Thomlinson, 1971:69–70; Prasithrathsin, 1976:67–68). Several comments were made in the focus-group sessions, however, that indicated bearing children today at an older age is considered embarrassing. Perhaps now with the general acceptance of a small-family norm, it no longer seems appropriate to continue childbearing until the end of the reproductive span. But given the widespread acceptance of birth control, any such norms about appropriate ages for childbearing are not connected to a prohibition or discouragement of sexual relations. Possibly the widespread use of birth control to terminate childbearing early has led people to feel that giving birth at an older age is now inappropriate.

Withdrawal

Previous survey research has indicated that withdrawal is generally not known or practiced in Thailand, except in the south, where it appears to be familiar to substantial proportions of Buddhists and Muslims alike (Kamnuansilpa, Chamratrithirong, and Knodel, 1983; Porapakkham, Pramanpol, and Knodel, 1983; Kamnuansilpa and Chamratrithirong, 1985). In his study of a central Thai village, Riley (1972:235) notes that he found no evidence of special coital practices for the purpose of birth control although he asked about it a number of times. The extent of knowledge and practice of withdrawal as revealed by surveys is apparently sensitive to the wording and structure of the questionnaire. When no specific question about withdrawal is asked, as in the 1980 census, results show its practice as being considerably less than when specific questions are included. This is probably because many respondents consider the concept of contraception to refer only to the modern methods promoted by the National Family Planning Program. In addition, unless the local terminology is used, the respondents may not understand what is meant by the term used to describe withdrawal. In focus-group sessions, there is much less likelihood that participants would not recognize what the moderator is asking about, since there is greater opportunity for the moderator to describe in detail what the method is even if an unfamiliar terminology is used. As soon as one participant is able to recognize what is meant and refers to the local term, if there is one, others in the group are likely to understand.

In the Muslim village, participants of both sexes and generations spontaneously mentioned that withdrawal had long been known and practiced. Withdrawal, referred to by a local expression, was usually discussed in the context of the more general concept of "controlling by yourself" which, for some participants at least, also encompassed douching, the use of herbal medicines, and perhaps abstinence. The concept of "controlling by yourself," however, was not considered to be embraced by the term "family planning," a term that was undoubtedly introduced through organized family-planning program activities and hence associated with and reserved for methods promoted by the program. Withdrawal and the general concept of "controlling by yourself" were also spontaneously mentioned both in Thai- and Malay-speaking focus groups conducted by Deemar with southern Muslims. Thus, among Muslims, potentially effective methods of contraception appear to be traditionally known although, as some participants stated, not to everyone. It seems quite likely that withdrawal has been practiced by Thai Muslims for some time (Suebsonthi, 1980). This may help explain why prior to the recent fertility decline, Muslim women averaged fewer children ever born by the end of childbearing than did Buddhist women, despite an earlier age at first marriage (Goldstein, 1970; Jones and Soonthornthum, 1971).

"When we eat in the kitchen, we spit it out on the porch. It is the same when people wear a hat [condom]. They also would not get children. The only difference is that we take it out and spill it whereas they are controlling it." (older Muslim man, south)

Participant 1—"They had the idea of controlling by themselves; there was no family planning."
Moderator—"What does it mean to control by yourself?"
Participant 2—"When you have sex, you pull it out."
Participant 1—"If the husband does not want the woman to have children because it will be difficult, you will eat in the kitchen and spit it out on the porch. But before one understands [this method] you have many children and you only know about it later or too late and at that time you have half a dozen children already. If I had known about it earlier, I would have wanted only two children." (older Muslim women, south)

"When we [my wife and I] have sex, I let the sperm spill outside every time." (Malay-speaking young Muslim man, Deemar focus group)

In none of the sessions in Buddhist villages was withdrawal spontaneously mentioned, although in the southern Buddhist village a number of participants acknowledged having heard of withdrawal when asked directly. The extent of awareness and practice, however, seems to be substantially less than in the case of the Muslims. Outside the south, only rarely did a participant indicate having heard of withdrawal. Many participants were skeptical anyone would practice such a method and indicated it was a distasteful idea to them.

"I never heard it. Withdrawing when you reach the climax, who is going to do this?" (older man, central region)

"I've never heard of withdrawal before. Back then there weren't even condoms. We just made love naturally." (older woman, northeast)

"We did not think about whether there would be a child or not. When we reached the point of climax we have to continue until the finish. We cannot take it out." (older man, northeast)

One of the few participants outside the south who indicated familiarity with withdrawal, a younger woman in the northeast, volunteered that she and her husband had tried it but only after reading about it in a book, which in itself is suggestive that the method was not part of local traditional practices. This is in sharp contrast to comments of a younger Muslim woman who said she learned about it from her elders.

Abortion

Induced abortion has apparently been known and practiced in rural Thailand for quite some time. Several early anthropological studies commented on this (de Young, 1955; Hanks, 1963). In her study of a northern Thai village,

Mougne (1982:106–7, 214–15) states that although it was known, until recently abortion was only resorted to in truly desperate situations, typically involving nonmarital pregnancies. In the past, an indigenous method involving vigorous massage of the uterus causing the expulsion of the fetus predominated, although herbal medicines of considerably more doubtful efficacy were also taken to induce abortion. More recently, modern techniques are being used as well. Unlike methods of contraception, induced abortion by any technique, although tolerated, is illegal and considered by the vast majority to be contrary to the principles of Buddhism. Although participants in every session knew of abortion, especially the traditional massage technique, they usually stated either that it was uncommon in the past or that it was reserved for pregnancies resulting from extramarital or premarital sex relations. The dangers of abortion, especially by traditional methods, were stressed and cited as the reason abortion was resorted to only in extreme circumstances.

"Most people who get an abortion have the practitioner squeeze it, break the child's neck. They call it 'killing the child in the stomach.' The injection to induce abortion is something new, it's been around only recently." (older man, northeast)

"They used their hands to press it out. It was illegal and dangerous." "Most [who had an abortion] are women who got pregnant but can't find the child's father." (two older men, north)

"In the past, there were no abortions being done. . . . People back then were afraid. It was very dangerous." (older Buddhist woman, south)

Since participants never mentioned any personal experience with abortion, it is difficult to know how much weight to give their general assertion of a very low prevalence of abortion during the period when the older generation was in the active childbearing ages. Many people in the past probably knew of indigenous methods of abortion but apparently did not think of it as a readily acceptable means of fertility control because of the physical danger and social disapproval associated with it. Of those who did resort to abortion, a fair share may have done so in order to avoid the perhaps even greater social disapproval that would have resulted from having a child outside of a marital union. Nevertheless, occasional resort to abortions, if only to a very limited extent, to control marital fertility prior to the fertility decline seems probable.

Western social scientists often recognize that cultural differences affect the receptivity to modern methods of birth control. Rarely, however, do they acknowledge possible cultural differences in receptivity to traditional methods, assuming instead that effective folk methods are both universally known and acceptable and would be used to reduce fertility if motivation were sufficient (Stix and Notestein, 1940; Demeny, 1975). The focus-group results suggest that neither abstinence nor withdrawal was thought of as a means of fertility control in most of Thailand, and when described as such they were generally thought to be objectionable. The fact that withdrawal is acceptable among southern villagers, particularly Muslims, simply underscores the role that cultural differences can play. Although cultural barriers to the use of specific contraceptive methods are not immutable, they may affect acceptability of traditional methods to such an extent that they are in effect unavailable, as appears to be the case in Thailand.

Deliberate Spacing and Breastfeeding

There was near-consensus among all groups that it is better to space children by several years than to have one birth right after the other. Nevertheless, there was little evidence that the older generation took deliberate actions to delay births except for an occasional remark that an abortion might be sought for this purpose or, among the Muslims, that spacing births might be a reason for practicing withdrawal. It is not possible to determine from the focus group discussions the relative importance of spacing children compared to limiting family size as a motivation for adopting birth control or whether views about the importance of each have changed over the course of the fertility decline. It is of interest to note, however, that in an anthropological study of a central Thai village during the mid-1970s, Lauro (1979:243) reports: "Villagers were unanimous in expressing that their objective in practicing family planning was to curtail fertility rather than to space children or defer childbearing to a later time." He indicates that his finding was confirmed through in-depth qualitative investigation. Presumably, spacing has become more important in more recent years, if the survey evidence presented in chapter 4 is accurate, but his observations help confirm that family-size limitation was the predominant motivation during the early stages of fertility transition in Thailand.

In the focus-group sessions, we attempted to find out if participants were aware of the impact prolonged breastfeeding had on delaying conception and if such knowledge partially motivated women in the past to breastfeed their children for extended periods of time. Only among older women in the northeastern village was there a clear consensus that breastfeeding would delay the next birth. They indicated this was knowledge passed from one generation to the next in the past. Elsewhere, however, older women generally denied that breastfeeding delayed pregnancy and often cited as evidence their own experience of becoming pregnant before they had weaned their child. Thus, locally there may have been some intentional prolonging of breastfeeding to space births in the past but it does not appear to have been a general phenomenon.

"In the past, parents would say not to wean the child [soon] because the nipples will get cold and the mother would have a child soon." "The elders told us. We followed their beliefs." (two older women, northeast)

"No, I don't think [how soon you get pregnant depends on breastfeeding]. Some get pregnant even when they feed their children with their own milk." (older woman, north)

Child Transfer

In the absence of or in addition to birth control within marriage, mechanisms that can effectively reduce family size include infanticide, child abandonment, and transferring children to live with people who are willing to care for them. Although such factors cannot be thought of as proximate *fertility* determinants, they can have the effect of limiting family size. Little is known about infanticide, underinvestment in child care (sometimes called infanticide by neglect), or child abandonment in Thailand with reference to either the past or present. The anthropologist de Young (1955:49) believes that outright infanticide is virtually unthinkable by Thai Buddhist standards. The same probability is true for Muslims. Although Mougne (1978:83) does not rule out the possible infrequent practice of infanticide in the northern Thai village she studied, she concludes that it is unlikely to have ever been a major factor in traditional fertility limitation.

In contrast to the nearly unanimous views discounting infanticide, several observers have commented that transferring children through adoption was a way of coping with unwanted fertility in the past. One study of a central Thai village noted that these cases typically involved young mothers who gave up their first births to someone else, mostly kin, to raise (Riley 1972:228–29). However, other studies indicate that child transfer often involves families with large numbers of children who may send one or more to live with relatives, neighbors, or, in the case of boys, to be servants to the monks in the temple and that childless couples frequently adopt children of other couples (Henderson 1971:68–71; Mougne 1982:195). In an article describing his own experience of being sent to live as a monk's apprentice at an early age, Sudham (1980:67) indicates that it was a common practice of peasants with many children, particularly in years of drought, to give a child for adoption to strangers for a sum of money or without receiving any payment.

The focus-group discussions make clear that child transfer was known and occurred throughout Thailand. Participants in almost all sessions cited examples, sometimes from their own family's experience. Most believed child transfer has declined substantially or no longer exists because couples are now able to control the number of births they have. The transfer of children, as described by participants, commonly involved a poor couple with many children giving up one or more children to a couple, often relatives, who were childless or who had few children. The receiving couple was also typically said to be in a better position to provide for the transferred children and, if childless, to be in need of a child to care for them in old age and to inherit their property. Other frequently mentioned circumstances leading to child transfer were nonmarital births and the absence of a spouse due to marital dissolution through death, divorce, or desertion.

"If the husband has a new wife, she may give the child to someone else. Some women get pregnant without [being married to] the [child's] father. Some people have many children and cannot take care of them, so they give them away. They give the children to people who do not have any. [This practice] is well known in our village. During our mothers' time, there were many but now there are only a few. Back then they gave up children for adoption." (younger Muslim woman, south)

"Some people gave away their children permanently because back then parents were very poor and had many children but not enough land. So they gave the children to relatives who had few children to raise." (older man, central region)

Child transfer thus appears to have been an acceptable mechanism for dealing with unwanted children in Thailand before methods of deliberate birth control became widely known and acceptable. Although we cannot judge the frequency of the practice from the focus-group discussions, analyses of life histories of married women from a recent survey in Bangkok and a village in the central region suggest that it occurred on a modest scale involving only a small percentage of children (Knodel et al., 1982:122–23). It is important mainly as a sign of a broader unrealized demand for birth control in the past.

Latent Demand for Birth Control

One important factor underlying the suddenness and rapidity of fertility decline in rural Thailand appears to be the existence of a receptivity or latent demand for effective and acceptable birth control prior to the widespread awareness and availability of modern contraception. The concept of latent demand implies that a receptivity to the use of birth control existed among a substantial segment of the population before acceptable methods were generally known and used and that a reduction in what is sometimes called the "cost" of birth control could, in itself, result in considerably increased use of such methods. In this context, "cost" must be defined very broadly in terms that include not only costs in time and money (obviously negligible in the case of withdrawal and abstinence) but also psychic costs, such as reduced pleasure in sexual relations, normative costs that might be incurred by deviating from established modes of reproductive behavior or by engaging in socially disapproved acts, and, perhaps most basically, the lack of knowledge of an acceptable means of birth control. Determining latent demand is admittedly a difficult task since it is inherently a hypothetical construct. Nevertheless, we believe it is an important concept for understanding the suddenness and rapidity with which fertility in rural Thailand declined.

The frequent references in the older-generation focus-group sessions to attempts to limit or space births through the use of traditional but ineffective means, particularly herbal medicines, is convincing testimony of such a latent demand. As previously noted, participants generally lamented the failure of such means. Presumably, if more effective and culturally acceptable methods had been available, some of the older participants would have practiced them and reduced their fertility.

In a direct attempt to determine if there was a latent demand for birth control in the past, older generation focus groups were asked if they would have had fewer children had modern methods of birth control been available. A similar question was asked of younger-generation groups about their parents. Not all participants were of like minds. Some indicated they had wanted large families; however, the more common opinion, sometimes expressed spontaneously in connection with prior discussion, was that they would have had fewer children had modern birth-control methods been available.

"Back in our time, people also did not want to have many children. They took the traditional medicine to expel the fetus but it didn't work." (older Buddhist woman, south)

"If there had been [birth control] like today, people at that time would have had few children also. I wouldn't have had so many children like this. Probably only four, two daughters and two sons." (older woman, north)

"My mother had a lot of children. I once asked her why. She said she did not know what to do to stop, so she kept on having them until she couldn't have any more." (younger woman, central region)

"I stopped having children before learning about birth control. If I had known about it, I wouldn't have had as many children as I have now." (older woman, Bangkok construction site)

Three, four, and occasionally five children were the numbers older participants most frequently indicated they would have liked to have had. While this is fewer than the number they actually had, it is still more than the number wanted by the present younger generation. The main reason this apparent desire for fewer children did not translate itself into reduced fertility, in the participants' views, was their own lack of awareness of acceptable and effective means of fertility control.

The indication of latent demand in our focus-group sessions with older women in the Muslim village is noteworthy, given that nonmodern methods had apparently been known and practiced for some time. Their discussion made clear that not everyone was aware of the traditional birth-control methods and that others only learned about "controlling by yourself" late in their childbearing years. Such techniques may also not have been wholly effective, thus leading to excess fertility. Since couples seemed to have relied primarily on withdrawal, the exercise of control would depend on the husband, who may not have shared his wife's interest in spacing or limiting births. In the discussions, however, this was never mentioned as a problem.

Answers to hypothetical questions intended to assess latent demand must be interpreted cautiously. The older generation's perception of how they would have reacted earlier is likely to be influenced both by the socioeconomic change that has occurred since then and by their awareness of the younger generation's widespread use of contraception and acceptance of a small-family-size norm. Nevertheless, the combination of their present opinions and the frequent mention of past frustrated attempts to limit childbearing suggests the existence of a substantial latent demand for birth control prior to the start of the sustained fertility decline. Recent anthropological studies have also noted an absence of effective birth control in the past and unsuccessful attempts to control fertility through folk methods (Lauro, 1979; Mougne, 1982; Podhisita, 1985a).

One factor that might have contributed to the existence of latent demand, at least for the generation of couples who completed their reproduction just prior to the onset of sustained fertility decline, could be the reduction in infant and child mortality. With more children surviving, effective family size would have increased above the level prevailing earlier when mortality was higher. As pointed out in chapter 4, this could generate a receptivity to family-limitation practices even in the absence of a change in the preferred number of children.

The focus-group discussions also provide insight into the forces behind the latent demand. Many of the socioeconomic changes that make large families disadvantageous for the younger generation today were already underway when the older generation was having children (see chapter 7). In addition, there are strains inherent in bearing children and raising large families. These include time consumed by child rearing, particularly the mother's time, that could otherwise be spent doing household tasks and contributing economically. Such opportunity costs would be felt by both husband and wife, especially in a society such as rural Thailand where most farming is done by nuclear-family units rather than as a corporate family enterprise. In addition, the pain, suffering, and health hazards associated with childbirth, particularly frequent childbirth, and the general burden of caring for and rearing children, are costs borne predominantly by the mother and of special concern to her.

"When a woman has an infant she can only do work in the kitchen." (older Buddhist man, south)

"It's very good to work together [in the rice fields]. But when we have an infant, we have to work alone while the wife looks after the baby." (older man, north)

"If there had been [birth control] like today, women at that time would have had few children also. Some feared the pain of bearing babies, some of taking care of [many] children." (older woman, north)

An anthropological study of a village near Bangkok based on fieldwork in the early 1950s revealed some of the same concerns and ambivalence toward having large families that were expressed by the older-generation participants (Hanks, 1963). Such costs are not products of social and economic changes but rather aspects of reproductive life that hold for both the older and younger generations. It seems plausible that they played a role in generating demand for birth control in the past.[1] A similar argument has been made with respect to the existence of a latent demand for fertility control in Europe prior to the secular fertility decline (Knodel and van de Walle, 1979). In an analysis of reproductive change in South India, "problems peculiar to women," including their lost work time, have also been cited as forces responsible for receptivity to sterilization and the limitation of family size (Caldwell, Reddy, and Caldwell, 1982a,b). Mention is also made that the legitimacy of women's concerns for influencing reproductive decisions has improved considerably there as a result of a reduction in patriarchal authority. As discussed in chapter 7, patriarchal authority over reproductive decisions appears to be negligible in the case of Thailand.

One feature of the Thai social structure that may also have lessened the desire for large families in the past, thus helping account for latent demand, is the existence of a labor-exchange system in villages. The system consisted of reciprocal-labor groups whose members provided mutual assistance to each other during critical stages of the agricultural cycle when intensive labor was required (such as during transplanting or harvesting). These groups were typically made up of kin and neighbors from several households with agricultural landholdings of similar size. Hence, during these critical periods, families were not forced to rely solely on their own immediate members to meet labor needs, thus reducing the need for many children. In recent decades the ubiquity of such cooperative arrangements has diminished and in some areas these groups have disappeared completely. But during the past, when the older generation was bearing children, they were quite pervasive even if the details of the arrangement differed regionally (Kaplan, 1981:84; Mougne, 1982:319; Lauro, 1979:81–82).

Fertility Regulation among the Younger Generation

In sharp contrast to when their parents' generation was bearing children, the current younger generation of married couples now has virtually universal

---

1. Although these factors are not products of social and economic change, they could be affected by them. For example, the opportunity costs of child raising can vary with changing circumstances: smaller family landholdings could reduce such costs, whereas high levels of education obtained by mothers could increase them. Also, there may have been an increase compared to former times in the extent to which a wife's worries over the risks and burdens of childbearing and child-rearing are considered to be a legitimate concern, not only by herself but also by her husband and the general community, although we have no direct evidence to this effect. With respect to the mortality risks of childbirth, they were even greater in the past than at present.

knowledge of effective means of birth control and shows little hesitation in adopting them in order to limit family size to a few children. This picture, well documented by the survey research reviewed in chapter 5, is confirmed by our focus-group sessions. Also consistent with survey evidence, the focus-group discussions indicated that virtually all contraceptive use today is of modern methods except among Muslims and, perhaps, southern Buddhists. Thus, there has been no general upsurge in the use of withdrawal, temporary abstinence, or any other nonmodern method, with the possible but undocumented exception of massage abortion. Traditional herbal medicine and ritual practices are viewed as inffective means of control by the younger generation (and generally recognized as such now by the older generation as well). In most focus-group sessions, the younger-generation participants clearly rejected the idea of using withdrawal or abstinence as realistic ways to control fertility. Muslims, however, were an exception, as indicated both from our sessions in the Muslim village, and by the Deemar focus-group sessions with southern Muslims.

Differences in the availability and use of modern contraceptive methods were spontaneously mentioned when participants were asked why the younger generation has smaller families than the older generation.

"Nowadays young people can get the number they want." "Now they can control." (two older Buddhist men, south)

"Nowadays there are pills, so we have a smaller number [of children]. Back then there was no pill so they had many children." (younger man, north)

"[Now they have] fewer [children]. In the past they stopped having children naturally. Now it's more advanced. There are many kinds of medicines [to control births]." (older woman, northeast)

Although some participants seem to think of the difference in family size between the older and younger generations only in terms of differences in contraceptive availability, more commonly they cited both differences in the ability to control fertility and differences in socioeconomic conditions (discussed in chapter 7) that would affect the desire for large or small families, sometimes in the same statement. The importance assigned by participants to the introduction of modern contraception for bringing about the reduction in family size accords well with observations by Lauro (1977) based on anthropological research in a central Thai village.

Although negative comments arose concerning specific contraceptive methods, no one in our own focus groups, including the Muslim village, challenged the overall concept of fertility control or the use of modern methods in general. Considerable opposition to modern birth control, however, was evident in the focus groups conducted by Deemar among southern Muslims. Nevertheless, among the large majority of Thais, there is consensus that the widespread use of birth control is now an accepted fact of life in Thailand.

Conclusion

In general, the statistical evidence gathered through surveys on the proximate determinants of Thailand's reproductive revolution and the qualitative data provided by focus-group sessions and observations by anthropologists fit together quite well. This is true both in the sense that the results emerging from the different types of evidence, when they overlap, are quite compatible with each other and in the sense that in other respects they are complementary, providing a fuller picture of reproductive change than any one source alone could do. Documenting and understanding the nature of the proximate determinants is an important and necessary step in explaining Thailand's fertility transition. A fuller understanding, however, clearly requires moving beyond this framework to explain the variety of forces that underlie the changes in the proximate determinants themselves, in particular the forces behind the upsurge in deliberate fertility control among married couples. It is to this task that the remaining chapters are devoted.

7

Societal Change and the Demand for Children

Although Thailand continues to be a predominantly rural and agrarian country, it is also a society undergoing profound socioeconomic change, as has been documented, if only incompletely, by the statistical evidence presented in chapter 3. Some of the changes have been associated with the relatively rapid pace of economic growth over the last several decades which itself has been facilitated by a relatively stable political climate. Other changes are part of a more general process of modernization permeating much of the Third World and at most only loosely related to economic growth. We now turn to a discussion of the meaning of these changes for Thai couples and how they affect reproductive decisions and behavior. We draw heavily on the focus-group discussions for this purpose. Given that the focus groups were conducted primarily among rural villagers and that those conducted in Bangkok were among rural migrants, their findings apply more strictly to the rural majority. Moreover, we have not attempted to differentiate the impact of societal change according to social class. To do so would have taken us beyond the scope of the bulk of the evidence on which our analysis of Thailand's reproductive revolution is based. Although in some contexts, the process of fertility transition differs substantially by class (see, e.g., Schneider and Schneider, 1984), the recent reproductive change in Thailand has been remarkably pervasive, affecting virtually all broad segments of Thai society (see chapters 4 and 5). It seems likely that many of the forces influencing reproductive behavior in atti-

117

tudes in Thailand during the recent past, at least in a general sense are common to most major societal strata.

As was pointed out in chapter 3, the numerous changes taking place tend to interact with and reinforce one another, creating an evolving socioeconomic environment within which Thai couples carry out their social and economic activities. Indeed, such a picture of interwoven social and economic changes intimately affecting both the daily lives of Thai villagers and their plans for themselves and their children emerged from the focus-group discussions. The result of these changes for reproductive behavior is that large families are now increasingly perceived as an economic burden. Extensive market penetration of the countryside, monetization of daily life, and changing consumer aspirations have led to a sense that the general cost of living has increased. Particularly crucial to the increased cost of raising children is the cost of education. Providing children with more schooling is seen as the primary mechanism through which families can cope with limited availability of land and reduced prospects for themselves, and, more important, for their children, for making a satisfactory living through agricultural activities. At the same time, children are generally seen to be less helpful in doing household chores and in contributing to the family's economic activities, in large part as a result of increased school attendance. Many of these changes are reinforced by the mass media, which are increasingly penetrating the countryside. Moreover, reduced infant and child mortality means that couples today would have to cope with larger families than did their parents' generation, if efforts were not made to limit fertility. To think in terms of monetary costs when contemplating raising children is now considered normal, and the view that the more children a couple has, the more costly it will be, has become the accepted way of thinking.

The participants did not explicitly make all these connections themselves. Nevertheless, their comments suggest this basic picture of the social and economic changes underlying the fertility transition in Thailand.

Reduced Child Mortality

Survival rates of infants and children have improved substantially in Thailand over recent decades. Since family size is a matter of surviving children, rather than simply live births, the number of children potentially available to couples as a result of their reproductive efforts has increased as mortality declined. In the terminology of economics, the "supply of children" can be said to have risen (Easterlin and Crimmins, 1985). Thus, if couples had not changed their reproductive behavior, family size would have grown substantially whether or not larger families were consciously desired. This is clearly an important aspect of the context of fertility decline. Nevertheless, marshaling evidence of conclusive links between mortality and fertility reduction has proven to be difficult.

Most focus-group participants were aware that there are far fewer child deaths nowadays than in the past. Others have also found villagers conscious that the infants and young children are more likely to survive now than before (Lauro, 1979:106). Focus-group participants mentioned the greater availability of hospitals, health centers, doctors, and modern medicine as a reason for the improvement. Various examples were offered pointing out that medical and health facilities for prenatal checkups, child delivery, vaccination, and treatments for illnesses exist now, whereas before such facilities were lacking and reliance was primarily on traditional medical practices of questionable efficacy. Younger-generation participants expressed only minimal concern that their children would die of disease or sickness and seemed to worry more about death by accidents such as drowning or vehicle mishaps.

"Nowadays there are few children who die. It is different from the earlier time when there were a lot." (younger Muslim man, south)

"Back then when children had chills, all we could do was to cover them with blankets. Now we can take them to the doctor." (younger woman, north)

"I don't think children will die; I think that they will grow up. I am not afraid of death due to disease but rather due to car accidents. There are many cars." (younger woman, northeast)

A few participants spontaneously mentioned that in the past it was necessary to have more children than today in order to insure against the greater chance of a child dying. When asked directly, however, many others simply denied that this was something they had thought about previously. Some felt couples should consider the possibility of losing a child when making decisions on how many children to have but were uncertain whether couples actually did so in the past.

"Like people said, only a two-ply rope was not enough in the past. They wanted three, four, or five-ply rope. If one or two of the plies were torn, there would still be some left. This is why they wanted more children, because children died a lot." (older man, north)

"You should not think about [having an extra child in case one might die] because it is like condemning your living child." (older Muslim woman, south)

Although the younger generation showed only minimal worry about children dying, some still indicated that it would be a good idea to have an extra child as protection against an unanticipated death of a child. This precaution was not seen primarily as due to a lack of health and medical advances but rather to the fact that death may occur at any time due to an accident regardless of the overall health conditions. However, there were many younger-generation participants who said they had never thought about having extra children for insurance against child loss. Some indicated there was no need to anticipate the death of a child in advance because if a child died, one could have another to replace it.

"I have thought of [having an extra child]. I have two children and I should have one more because I am afraid [one may die]." (younger Buddhist woman, south)

"If anyone has two children and one dies it will be very surprising indeed." (younger woman, north)

It is difficult to draw any firm conclusions from the focus group discussions about the role mortality reduction played in bringing about the sharp decline in fertility in Thailand. It does not seem to be a salient consideration in the participants' own views of the forces leading to the desire to have few children among today's younger couples, although it was mentioned occasionally. This does not necessarily mean that it was insignificant. It is of interest, for example, that in response to an open-ended question about the disadvantage of a small family asked in SOFT in 1975, 11 percent of married men spontaneously said couples with small families would have to worry about child mortality (Arnold and Pejaranonda, 1977).[1]

The fact that personal experience with the loss of children is not a frequent, everyday occurrence, even when child mortality is high, may reduce the saliency of mortality improvement to focus-group participants, particularly when compared with other changes for which the effects are more obvious on a daily basis. Moreover, the selection criteria for older participants may have favored those with a lower than average proportion of children lost through mortality (see appendix C). Undoubtedly the improvement in child survival facilitated the reduction in fertility. It is difficult to imagine that had infant and child mortality remained at the levels of several decades ago that fertility would have fallen to the current levels, since this would have resulted in substantially smaller families, in terms of living children, than is presently the case. In addition, lower mortality at infant and childhood ages is an important part of the overall improvement in mortality that led to the rapid population growth over the last several generations thus contributing to the pressure on land resources. As is discussed below, this is perceived as an important reason for rural couples to limit family size. Nevertheless, direct evidence of improved child survival contributing to the decline of fertility in Thailand is largely lacking.

1. In a survey of two northern provinces, a majority of married men interviewed agreed it was necessary to have an extra child to insure against infant mortality (Shevasunt and Hogan, 1979). The fact that fertility has fallen rapidly to quite low levels in these same provinces and desired family size is very modest, however, casts some doubt on the meaning of these responses.

Some additional insights into mortality-fertility linkages is provided by analysis of survey data. In situations where effective efforts to limit family size are absent, the idea of replacing a child that died with an additional birth or insuring against potential loss of a child by having an extra birth has little practical meaning for behavior, since women continue childbearing through the end of the reproductive age span regardless of experience with child mortality. Only when marital fertility is deliberately controlled through contraception or abortion can volitional responses to experience with child mortality have an impact on fertility (Knodel, 1982). Thus, prior to the widespread use of birth control in Thailand, a couple's experience with child mortality is unlikely to have directly affected their reproductive behavior except through nonvolitional mechanisms, in particular the physiological effect through which the curtailment of breastfeeding leads to a shortening of postpartum amenorrhea when a child dies before being weaned. It is not surprising, therefore, that an elaborate regression analysis based on the 1969 LS1 rural sample found no statistically significant evidence of a replacement effect, given the very low prevalence of contraception in rural areas up to that time (Hashimoto and Hongladarom, 1981). In contrast, results based on the 1970 urban sample, for which contraceptive prevalence was much higher, were significant. At present, contraception is common all over and thus influences of child mortality on couples' reproductive motivations can now be effectively translated into actual behavior among both the rural and urban populations, at least for couples who are not sterilized.

Indirect evidence based on CPS3, and shown in table 7.1, suggests that a couple's experience with child mortality does affect fertility desires, both in the sense that couples may wish to "replace" a child that dies at an early age with another birth and in the sense that some couples who have lost a child through a premature death may wish to "insure" against future loss by having an extra child. The analysis is limited to couples with two or three live births when examining evidence concerning replacement motivations and to couples with two or three living children when examining evidence of insurance motivations. In addition to unadjusted results, results are also shown adjusted statistically for several potentially confounding background characteristics (age, region, and rural-urban residence) known to be associated with fertility desires.

Motivation to replace a child that died with another birth is evident from the finding that women with the same number of live births are more likely to want to have an additional child if a previous child had died than if all previous children were still alive. The difference is considerably more pronounced for women with two live births than for those with three. Of course, a woman who has lost a child has at least one fewer living children than a woman with the same number of live births whose children are all living. It is thus interesting that although the average number of additional children wanted is greater

Table 7.1. Fertility Desire, by Number of Live Births or Living Children and Experience with Child Mortality, Unadjusted and Adjusted Statistically for Current Age, Region, and Rural-Urban Residence, as Reported by Currently Married Women Aged 15–44

	Two live births		Three live births	
	All living	One or two died	All living	One or more died
Percent wanting more children				
Unadjusted	32	75	16	39
Adjusted	32	70	16	39
Number of additional children wanted[a]				
Unadjusted	0.51	1.26	0.29	0.58
Adjusted	0.51	1.11	0.29	0.57

	Two living children		Three living children	
	All living	One or two died	All living	One or more died
Percent wanting more children				
Unadjusted	32	38	16	19
Adjusted	32	39	15	20
Number of additional children wanted[a]				
Unadjusted	0.50	0.56	0.29	0.28
Adjusted	0.50	0.61	0.36	0.41
Preferred number of children				
Unadjusted	2.6	2.9	3.1	3.3
Adjusted	2.6	2.9	3.1	3.3

Source: CPS3.

Note: The number of live births and living children include anticipated births for pregnant women when the analysis refers to desire for more children or number of additional children wanted, since the question on desire for additional children referred to desire for children after the expected birth. Statistical adjustment is made through Multiple Classification Analysis.

[a] Including women who want no more children.

for women who have lost a child, the difference is less than one child. This indicates that the extent of desired replacement of dead children is less than complete. Statistical adjustment for background characteristics reduces the difference even further for women with two live births but has little effect for women with three live births.

Women with the same number of living children are more likely to want additional children, want a larger number of additional children, and indicate a higher preferred family size if a previous child has died than if all children were still alive. Although the differences are not very pronounced, this finding suggests that some women who have had a child die may wish to insure against future loss of children. Moreover, data relating fertility desires to a couple's own experience with child mortality cannot shed light on whether or not couples attempt to insure against child loss because of perceived risks based on the experience of others in the community. The possibility of such an additional effect must remain an open question, especially given the ambiguous results from the focus-group sessions. The quantitative data from CPS3 do suggest, however, that at present in Thailand there might be some interrelation between fertility desires and mortality experience at the individual couple level.

The Perceived Rise in the Cost of Living and Child Rearing

Time and again, when participants were asked why the younger generation wants smaller families than the older generation had, they responded that nowadays everything is expensive and that earning an adequate living is difficult. A multitude of examples were cited pointing out how much more costly virtually every item is today compared with the past when it was either far cheaper or was home produced, homegrown, or available for free in nature. The increasing cost of raising children is seen as an important part of the rising cost of living, and although it was not stated explicitly, expenditures on children are likely to be competing with the expanding array of other expenses deemed necessary to conduct a satisfactory life. Thus, bringing up children is viewed by both generations as a far greater economic burden now than in the past. Limiting family size is seen as an important means for the younger generation to keep their expenditures within reasonable bounds.

"Before when things were not expensive, there were plenty of children. Now when things are expensive, there are fewer children. If you have many children, you need to spend a lot. If you have fewer children, you spend less." (older Buddhist woman, south)

"Right now everything is expensive, and there's also education for your children. Earning a living is also very hard. To have many children is to be poor." (younger Buddhist woman, south)

More children, more expense; fewer children, less expense. Parents can't earn enough money to serve their children's needs." (older woman, northeast)

Survey evidence from SOFT indicates that in Thailand men in both rural and urban areas appear to be acutely aware of the financial burden of raising many children. Nearly two-thirds of the men interviewed in the husband survey spontaneously mentioned the financial cost of children as a disadvantage of having a large family, which indicates high awareness of such concerns. A series of closed-ended questions were also asked about whether raising a fam-

ily of two, four, and six children respectively would be fairly easy economically, somewhat of a burden, or a heavy burden. Although only 6 percent felt
two children would be a heavy economic burden, over half (55 percent) thought
four children would be and almost all (96 percent) thought raising six children
would be a heavy economic burden. There was almost no difference between
rural and urban husbands. Thus, according to these survey results, the perceived economic burden of raising children is as high in rural as urban areas
(Arnold and Pejaranonda, 1977). The Value of Children Study in Thailand
also indicates the importance of economic concerns in attitudes about family
size. Men and women in each of the several socioeconomic groups studied
gave financial costs as their principal reason for not wanting more than their
desired number of children (Arnold et al., 1975).

Market Penetration, Monetization, and Consumer Aspirations

Objectively, it is unlikely that the majority of people are worse off economically now than they were in the past. Real per capita income has increased
substantially over the last few decades (World Bank, 1980). Most Thais probably live more comfortably in the sense that they are healthier, better fed,
better educated, better clothed, and own more consumer durables nowadays
than a few decades ago. However, young parents feel they need to spend more
on their children than was true for the older generation because they believe
they need more education than in the past and because child-care practices
and views of the legitimate needs of children have changed. Moreover, their
own perceived "need" for a whole range of consumer goods is undoubtedly
far greater now than it was for their parents a generation ago.

The crucial process underlying the perceived increase in the general cost of
living is the rapid expansion of the cash economy through widespread market
penetration of goods purchased outside the local community and the conse-
quent increased monetization of daily life. The availability of durable goods
and specialty-food products in rural areas has increased substantially through
an expanding network of village shops and increased access to urban stores
and markets due to expanded public transportation. This has led not only to
substitution of store-bought items for those previously produced at home or
gathered in nature but also to aspirations for goods previously unavailable
or unfamiliar to the average villager. In addition, the declining proportion of
households engaged in farming means that a smaller share produces their own
food. Mass-media penetration has surely contributed to a greater awareness
of the availability of goods and to the spread of consumer values affecting the
aspirations of both parents and children for a whole range of products. Although only two decades ago radios were rare and television virtually unknown in the countryside, now radios are commonplace in rural households

and in the large majority of villages, there is at least one television set (see chapter 3).

Another important source of increased expenses for rural families is the rising costs of production as more modern agricultural practices are adopted and crops are diversified. Although this was rarely specifically mentioned in the focus-group sessions themselves, retrospective data from the IPS Village Survey make clear that there has been a substantial increase in the use of fertilizers and insecticides as well as in the mechanization of agricultural production, all of which require cash outlays or their equivalent in the form of credit. For example, in only 39 percent of the villages was it reported that fertilizer was used in 1969 compared to 91 percent reporting that fertilizer was used in 1979; insecticides were used in only 31 percent of the villages in 1969 compared to 84 percent in 1979; and the percent of villages in which at least some farms used mechanical equipment increased from 31 percent to 69 percent. The sweeping extent of changes over the last quarter century in agricultural production and the extent to which such changes involve additional expenditures is nicely illustrated in a recent case study of a village in the central region (see Ingersoll and Ingersoll, 1985).

The increased need for money both to cover the costs of raising children and to meet a couple's other needs and desires has undoubtedly made these costs far more salient. Moreover, the increasing availability and awareness of consumer items and the desire to acquire them create a situation in which having another child and purchasing goods may be perceived as alternatives.

"These days we need to spend money to raise children. We can't have many." (younger woman, north)

"Before, parents used rice to raise children. Now they use money." (younger woman, Bangkok construction site)

Participants were keenly aware of the extent to which monetization pervades their lives, frequently discussing the expenses that confront them just to meet their everyday needs. Moreover, the older-generation groups made clear how rapid the change has been, identifying a variety of differences between just a generation ago and now. Participants no longer view themselves as self-sufficient home producers but rather as consumers in a cash economy. Numerous examples were cited: rope made from jute has been replaced by nylon rope; bowls made from coconut shells have been replaced by plastic, aluminum, stainless steel, and glass bowls. Fish, fruit, and vegetables formerly were either far less expensive or could be acquired without purchasing. Clothes and fabrics that were commonly woven and sewn at home have now been replaced by factory-manufactured products. Moreover, focus-group participants mentioned a range of goods that were simply not available or thought not necessary before that now have to be bought. The heightened perceived need for consumer goods among the rural population, as well as the urban poor, is undoubtedly fueled by the demonstration effect of conspicuous consumption by the urban elite and emerging middle class. Awareness of such consumption patterns is facilitated by increasing mass-media exposure and increased mobility to urban centers made possible by the "transportation and communications revolution" described in chapter 3. Participants clearly feel that a major change has occurred in production and consumption habits with the result that money is more needed nowadays than was true a generation ago.

"Before, you made it at home, but now you buy it in shops." (older Muslim man, south)

"When you wake up, you start to pay. . . . You brush your teeth with toothpaste. When you go down from the house you have to pay, you have to wear shoes or sandals." (older man, northeast)

"Today we've got to buy everything. In the past we didn't have to spend money on these things. We didn't spend much money like nowadays." (older woman, north)

The pervasive sense of economic hardship today is understandable when interpreted within a framework of rising expectations. As Freedman (1979) points out, the increasing awareness of and availability of modern consumer goods, including a whole host of items such as radios, sewing machines, bicycles, motorcycles, motorized pumps, and television sets, affect the lives of not only those who have them, but also the large number who want them but may not be able to afford them. Comparison with more affluent peers may distort the sense of improvement between now and the past. Easterlin's concept of relative income, defined as the ratio of anticipated earnings to aspirations, seems relevant (Easterlin, 1980). Even if real income is higher now for those in the early stages of family building than it was for the older generation when they were starting their families, higher consumer aspirations, higher anticipated costs of adequate child rearing, and the greater extent to which these require monetary payment result in a lower sense of relative income.

Medical Costs and Child Care

The modernization of medical care is seen as contributing to the rising cost of living. Although traditional and modern medicine still coexist in Thailand, the greater effectiveness of modern medicine is increasingly recognized by both the older and younger generations (Riley and Sermsri, 1974). The cost of modern treatment, however, is considerably higher than that of traditional services and often involves additional transportation costs. Even when the treatment is provided at subsidized prices at government health outlets, the cost can be significant to the average villager.

The increasing resort to modern treatment affects costs both for the parents' own medical care and for their children's, thus contributing to the perceived increased cost of child rearing. Focus group participants felt that health services were a significant part of the cost of raising children, as did the villagers Lauro (1977:106) studied. In addition, the increasingly common practice of giving birth in a hospital or health center rather than at home attended by the traditional midwife or relatives has increased the cost of childbearing. For example, the proportion of women under age 50 who reported being assisted for their most recent birth by a medical doctor, nurse, or government midwife increased from 5 percent in 1969 to 28 percent in 1979 for rural women and from 15 percent in 1970 to 92 percent in 1979 for urban women (based on LS1 and NS). By 1982 the percent of births to all women that were delivered in either a hospital or clinic was 45 percent (ESCAP, 1984).

"Raising children was easier [in our generation]. No need to see the doctor. No troubles like today. We had traditional medicine." (older woman, northeast)

"When [children] get sick, you have to spend all your money. You have to pay for medicine." (younger woman, central region)

"[Nowadays], if a child is a bit sick or hurt, you take it to the hospital. . . . Just going once [to the hospital] means money for traveling, food." (younger woman, north)

Some participants stated that nowadays people are more concerned about the health needs of their children and take better care of them than in earlier times. This may largely be due to an awareness of the availability of health-care facilities and a conviction that parents can now exert a greater influence on their children's health than in the past. In several groups, however, there were suggestions that children are now the subject of more concern and attention, not only in terms of health needs but other needs as well, and that parents indulge their children more today than in the past. For example, a number of participants indicated that children were watched more carefully and were no longer left to crawl in the dirt, and that parents were more concerned about providing proper clothes for a child. To the extent that these changes in child-care practices have occurred, they are undoubtedly in part a product of other changes, such as a better understanding of hygiene and ready availability of cheap store-bought clothes. Thus, it is difficult to judge the extent to which the participants' comments reflect a change in attitudes toward children, but it does seem to indicate children require more parental attention than in the past.[2]

2. The anthropologist who studied the northeastern village in our focus-group sample indicates that, in his view, considerable change in attitudes toward child rearing has taken place between the older and younger generations currently living in the village and that information conveyed through the mass media has played an important part in this regard (Podhisita, personal communication).

Some participants seemed to feel that the wishes and demands with which children confront parents are accorded more attention today. Remarks indicated that children now request, and apparently receive, small amounts of money to buy candy and other treats, whereas previously such requests would have been considered out of place. Participants also commented that children are permitted to play more now. There were hints that parent-child relations may be shifting because, with the spread of schooling, a fairly young child often has more formal education than his parents, potentially undermining parental authority and increasing the legitimacy accorded children's demands and wishes.

"They haven't got out of bed before they ask for money. 'Mom, one Baht please.' " (younger woman, north)

"[Nowadays], kids just run away to play because kids from this house and kids from that house do it. Everybody then does it." (older man, northeast)

"If you ask your child to help you with your work, he will answer he cannot and hurry off to practice sports saying the teacher told him to practice hard. Before, whatever parents said, the children would do." (younger man, central region)

Increasing Educational Costs and Aspirations

In Thailand, although public education at the primary level is nominally free, there are real costs associated with it, given that students must provide their own uniforms, supplies, and so on. These costs can be quite a significant consideration for a poor family. Beyond primary education, moderate tuition charges, which nevertheless can represent a substantial proportion of an average villager's income, are levied in public secondary schools and the amount increases for higher levels of education (Arnold and Pejaranonda, 1977). In addition, if the school is not in the village, there are travel costs involved and, if the distance is too far for daily commuting, boarding costs as well. There are also indirect costs, because school attendance may interfere with the contribution children make by helping parents with household, farm, or other chores, particularly if the school is not within commuting distance. In the focus-group sessions both generations identified a variety of reasons for the increasing cost of raising children, but expenses associated with schooling were probably most consistently mentioned and considered the most significant. Most groups mentioned spontaneously that the cost of education played an important part in the younger generation's desire for smaller families. Everyone seemed to believe that education is more important today than in the past and that only by having fewer children can a couple afford the appropriate education for each.

"[People want fewer children] because now things are expensive and because they want their children to get a higher education. If there are many children you cannot send them to school, but if you have only one or two children, you can manage. Nowadays education must come first." (younger Muslim woman, south)

"We can afford our children's education if we've got just a few. But if we have more, it would be a big burden." (younger woman, north)

"Having more or less children is related to education. Now with two or three children you can afford to send them to school. If there are ten [children], it will not be possible, it will be troublesome." (older man, northeast)

The perceived financial burden of educating children is compounded in Thailand by the feeling today that all children, whether sons or daughters, first or last born, should be given an opportunity for education. In the past, sons were more likely to receive an education than daughters, a fact which came up in the discussions. As evident from the statistics in chapter 3, sex differentials in education have diminished considerably. Significantly, there was no indication in the focus-group discussions that younger-generation participants planned to favor their sons in terms of providing an education. Rather, participants spontaneously mentioned that if they had many children and only gave some an education, the others would feel disappointed or resentful.

"If you have many children and you send [only] some to school, you feel very sorry for the others. If you have fewer, such as two or three children, you can send them all to school." (older Buddhist woman, south)

"If we have too many children, parents won't have the money to send them to school. If we [only] send the older child to school, the second child will ask why we do that and we will quarrel. If we send only one child, it will mean we love that child and do not love the other." (younger man, north)

This does not mean that they expect all children to receive an equal education. A number of comments were made recognizing differences in aptitude and willingness to study. But there seems to be a strong feeling that all siblings should have the opportunity to study and that how far they go should depend on their ability to learn and not be hampered by the parents' inability to pay. Several participants mentioned that older siblings who complete their education should help pay for younger siblings' studies, a not uncommon occurrence in Thailand. For some, this seemed to mitigate the need to limit family size.

The increased need for education is seen as emanating both from an increasing need to find nonagricultural employment, because of the perceived diminishing opportunities to make a living off the land, and from the attraction of jobs that require some education as a way to improve one's standard of living. There is considerable concern among participants that their landholdings will not be adequate for their children if they are divided up among them. An important strategy for dealing with this problem is to prepare at least some children for jobs outside of farming by providing them with adequate schooling. For many parents, education has come to be seen as a replacement for land. This was particularly evident when inheritance was discussed. Children who went furthest in school would receive less land than their lesser-educated siblings, perhaps even receive no land at all.

"We send children to school thinking that they will not come back to take the land." (younger man, northeast)

"Having higher education is the same as owning rice fields. Without education there's no job." (older woman, northeast)

"Some people do not have land for their children so they want them to get education, to be civil servants, to be a soldier or policeman, things like that." (younger man, central region)

Schools are now more accessible and available than before. As indicated in chapter 3, the educational infrastructure in Thailand expanded considerably over recent decades while compulsory education has been increased from grade 4 to grade 6. The expansion of the educational system itself helps to increase the level of educational attainment needed to have a good prospect for modern sector employment. Furthermore, schools, especially beyond the primary level, are more accessible, both because more are being built and because improved transportation makes travel to them easier. Data from the CPS3 Village Survey, for example, indicate that the percentage of rural villages with at least a primary school increased from 53 to 70 percent by 1984. Other data from the IPS Village Survey revealed that of the sixty-four villages surveyed, the number within 5 kilometers of a secondary school increased from thirteen to seventeen during the decade between 1969 and 1979 (Chayovan, Hermalin, and Knodel, 1984a). Probably even more important with respect to increased access to secondary schools is the improving public transportation system (see chapter 3). With better roads and more frequent buses, it is now increasingly possible for children to attend a school 10 or even 15 kilometers away and continue to live in villages by commuting daily. The greater accessibility of schools was mentioned a number of times in the focus-group sessions. Thus, as education has come to be viewed as more desirable, increasing numbers of rural Thais also see education for their children as more readily within their grasp.

"Back in our time we did not think about [education being necessary]. The school was very far away. But nowadays you can walk to the main road, and see the school." (older Buddhist woman, south)

"Now the school is close to our homes. Most of the children now finish secondary school." "To study in our village is very convenient because we don't have to buy food for the children [since they can come home to eat]." (two older men, north)

Higher educational aspirations are interwoven with hopes for upward social mobility so that the children can live a more comfortable life and will be in a better position to provide financial support for their parents later in life. Participants generally perceived farming (in which most were engaged themselves) as an arduous and precarious occupation. They viewed making a livelihood this way as subject to considerable risks, dependent on circumstances beyond their control, particularly the weather, and thus as yielding an uncertain and unstable income. Many indicated that they did not want their children to experience the same difficulties as they had. An anthropological study of two Thai villages notes similar negative attitudes toward farming as a means of earning a living and widespread aspirations for children to take on occupations that free them from the difficulty of farm life (Mizuno, 1978a). Interestingly, a fear of periodic adversity over which the individual has little control is cited as a reason why parents in an area in South India wish their children to get more education and thereby be able to get nonagricultural employment (Caldwell, Reddy, and Caldwell, 1984b). This may be a fairly common force toward change in developing countries. Younger Thai focus group participants most frequently mentioned government service occupations as most desirable for their children. Such jobs are seen as secure, providing steady income, social-welfare benefits, and prestige. Children who obtain such jobs are thought to be able to live comfortably themselves and be able to help their parents as well, especially through financial contributions.

"We are in difficult times as farmers. I don't want my children to do this type of work. I want my children to have knowledge, to do work sitting in a chair, like other people." (younger Buddhist woman, south)

"Children who have an education will sometimes make their parents comfortable, but those without an education will depend on their parents. Those with education will use their education to earn a living." (older Muslim woman, south)

"I want [my children] to be civil servants because it's so hard to work like us, their parents. We have to work in the sun. Now I have two children. When I have money I'll send them to school. If they become civil servants, I'll be relieved." (younger woman, north)

"To be a government employee is good both for them and us." (younger man, central region)

In most villages there are already examples of farmers' children who have been successful in attaining the types of positions many parents wish for their own children, thus making such aspirations seem realizable. Mass media also fuel such hopes by providing abundant examples of relatively affluent urban life-styles along with stories of upward social mobility. Thus, a combination of necessity and hope has led parents to reorient their aspirations for their children and increasingly to feel a need to provide them with an education as a way to achieve social and economic betterment.

An intensive anthropological study of the northeastern village in which we conducted our focus groups comes to a similar conclusion about the critical role of rising educational aspirations for children in exerting considerable downward pressure on family size. According to this study, parents' concern about "establishing" their children later in life in positions favorable for their making an adequate living, as defined by local life-styles and aspirations, is a "driving force" behind the desire to limit family size. Parents see education as an important strategy that can divert the pressure from the land and prepare children to make a proper living. They refer to education, and the non-agricultural jobs that it presumably leads to, as "other rice fields," that is, as a substitute for providing them with land (Podhisita, 1985a).

Several surveys provide information on the educational expectations and aspirations for children. In most cases, substantial differences in the questions asked make comparison between surveys inappropriate. However, data from LS1 and NS, presented in table 7.2, provide some indication of increasing expectations during the decade of the 1970s. Although the subset of respondents asked about expectations in each of the surveys differed from each other, as specified in the table footnotes, similar questions were asked about how far they expected a child currently enrolled in school to study. The most pronounced changes evident are in the increased proportions of respondents, both in the rural and urban samples, who indicate they expect their children to complete at least twelve years of education and in the increased proportion who say they want their children to go as far as their ability will permit. Both at the beginning and at the end of the decade there are marked rural-urban differences, with urban parents expressing substantially higher educational expectations. Nevertheless, it is clear that even rural parents are increasingly expecting their children to obtain a high-school education or beyond.

Husbands' views of the minimum education necessary for boys and girls "to get along in the world these days" were elicited in SOFT in 1975. Results, summarized in table 7.3, indicated that in both rural and urban areas, substantial proportions believed at least a high school education is a necessity, although the proportion was considerably higher among urban husbands. The distributions are in sharp contrast to the actual educational levels achieved by the parents themselves (see chapter 3). Even among rural respondents, only a minority believe a lower (fourth-grade) or even an upper primary (sixth- or

Table 7.2. Percentage Distribution of Educational Expectations for Youngest Son Still in School, as Reported by Household Heads with a Son Still in School, 1969–79

Highest grade thought child will reach	Rural		Urban	
	LS1 1969	NS 1979	LS1 1970	NS 1979
0–3	0	0	0	0
4–6	46	48	5	3
7–9	15	5	2	0
10–11	16	10	12	5
12+	15	23	38	45
As far as can or depends on ability	7	14	31	45
Depends on money	1	0	12	1
Total[a]	100	100	100	100
Number of respondents	328	312	498	75

Sources: LS1 and NS.

Note: Excludes responses do not know, no answer, not sure, and not classifiable in above categories.

Results for LS1 are limited to male household heads with at least one son aged 6–12 still in school. Results for NS include responses from both male and female heads with at least one child under 18 still in school; in the case of the NS, respondents were asked about the youngest son still in school unless there was no son still in school, in which case they were asked about the youngest daughter still in school, if any.

[a] Sum of categories may not add to exactly 100 because of rounding.

seventh-grade) education would be sufficient today, despite the fact that the vast majority of adult Thais at the time of the survey had themselves only a lower primary education. Most husbands (63 percent) thought that boys and girls need the same amount of education. Of the remainder, most thought that boys needed more education (Arnold and Pejaranonda, 1977). Thus, the mean number of years of schooling thought necessary is higher for boys than for girls but only by a modest amount.

Responses to a similar question about the minimum amount of education necessary to earn a comfortable living, included in the Thailand phase of the Asian Marriage Survey in 1978–79, yield similar results. About three fourths of women interviewed in a general sample of Bangkok felt that at least a high school education was necessary, as did over 40 percent of those interviewed in a sample of a Bangkok slum and a rural area in the central region. Most agreed a boy and girl need similar educations but, on average, boys were said to need a modestly higher education.

Table 7.3. Percentage Distribution of Views on Minimum Education Needed for Boys and Girls and the Financial Burden of That Amount of Education as Reported by Married Men, 1975

	Total		Rural		Urban	
	Boys	Girls	Boys	Girls	Boys	Girls
Educational level thought necessary						
Lower primary	13	24	14	26	3	6
Upper primary	15	18	17	20	4	6
Lower secondary	32	28	33	28	24	29
Upper secondary or beyond	40	30	36	26	69	59
Total[a]	100	100	100	100	100	100
Mean number of years	10.2	9.0	9.9	8.7	12.8	12.1
Extent to which providing necessary education would be a financial burden						
No burden	11	16	11	16	13	16
Somewhat	49	52	48	52	58	59
Heavy burden	40	32	41	33	29	25
Total[a]	100	100	100	100	100	100

Sources: SOFT; Arnold and Pejaranonda (1977).

[a] Sum of categories may not add to exactly 100 because of rounding.

Each husband was also asked how much of a financial burden it would be for a family in his circumstances to educate his sons and daughters to the level he felt was necessary. Results, also shown in table 7.3, indicate that almost all felt it would be at least somewhat of a burden and a substantial proportion, especially in rural areas, felt it would be a heavy burden. In addition, in response to an open-ended question on the advantages and disadvantages of having a large number of children (six or more), the costs of educating children was often singled out as a disadvantage (Arnold and Pejaranonda, 1977). Thus, focus-group and survey results agree quite well in underscoring changing educational aspirations for children and the costs associated with fulfilling those aspirations as an important source of pressure for reducing family sizes to well below the number of children that prevailed a generation ago.

The most critical change that is occurring in terms of educational aspirations and achievement is probably the extension of schooling from the primary to the secondary level. This is generally consistent with the fact that, realistically, secondary education is the minimum level needed for most of the jobs parents nowadays want their children to have. In terms of both direct and indirect costs, this change represents a qualitative and not just a simple quantitative departure from the past, especially for rural parents. Primary school is free and typically located within the community. In contrast, secondary school involves tuition fees and commuting or lodging costs if the school is not nearby. Moreover, the opportunity costs of lost labor are considerably higher for children of secondary-school age than those of primary-school age. Thus, what is taking place is not simply a continuing rise in the average number of years of schooling, but a qualitative shift with significant implications for both parents and children.

Although urban and nonagricultural jobs are undoubtedly expanding in Thailand, opportunities are nonetheless limited. During recent years, growth in government employment has not kept pace with the growth in the number of university graduates, which, as noted in chapter 3, is increasing rapidly due to the recent expansion of the university system. Certainly, the number of government service jobs likely to be available in the coming years will come nowhere close to being enough to meet the aspirations of most rural parents for their children. The frequent mention of civil service positions as the desired job for their children may reflect a lack of familiarity on the part of villagers of the wider range of jobs available outside agriculture for which education is important. Villagers are more likely to have contact with civil servants than with most nonagricultural professionals. Moreover, in the past, some form of government employment has been the traditional path to social mobility. It seems clear at present, however, that many of today's young parents have unrealistic hopes for their children. There is, of course, a wide range of nonagricultural private sector employment available, although it is more vulnerable to economic fluctuation and more subject to judgments based on performance than government work and hence less secure. In addition, a variety of less remunerative, less secure, and less prestigious jobs can also be found or created in the informal sector and no doubt many of the participants' children will have to turn to such work regardless of how well educated they are.

The possibility of an impending widespread disillusionment with the potential of higher education as a sure road to social and economic betterment is reflected in a song titled roughly "Higher Education, Higher Deception" (*Mahalai Mahalok*). Very popular in 1985, and played repeatedly on the radio, it tells of rural boys and girls who come to study at the university in hopes that higher education will be the key to a good job, but when they graduate they discover such jobs are few and that they lack the connections needed to get them. Indeed, there was some recognition expressed by focus-group participants of both generations that education does not always guarantee a "better" job for their children.

"Sometimes children with an education still cannot find any jobs. . . . Before [the children] acquire a job or complete their schooling, parents have to sell their land. It seems like we spend money for nothing." (older woman, northeast)

The focus-group discussions support the point made recently by Caldwell (1980) that at the onset of fertility transition, the changing educational level of children is a more important stimulus to fertility reduction than the changing educational level of the parents. As indicated in previous chapters, not only is the adult rural population fairly homogeneous with respect to low educational attainment, but also, educational differentials in fertility goals and contraceptive practice are weak. Thus, it seems unlikely that changes in the parents' education have played as important a role in encouraging a smaller family size as changes in the perceived need for and cost of education for children. It is possible, however, that increasing educational levels of parents heightens their concern for providing better education to children and in this way plays an important part in the process leading to increasing educational aspirations for children. In addition, although the average educational attainment of the current parental generation is low, literacy is widespread and probably facilitates exposure to a number of the influences in aspirations for themselves and their children.

The importance of educational aspirations for children as a force encouraging limiting family size is also evident in quantitative data from several studies. For example, data for a rural area in the central region, collected in the Thailand component of the Asian Marriage Survey in 1978–79, indicates an association between desired family size and the minimum amount of education thought necessary for children to make a comfortable living: women who thought less than ten years of education was necessary desired an average of almost four children compared to an average of less than three children for women who believed ten or more years were necessary.

In another study, including both Buddhists and Malay-speaking Muslims in a southern province, a clear inverse relationship emerged for Buddhists between the number of years of schooling thought necessary for either a son or a daughter and the preferred number of children. For example, after statistically adjusting for marriage duration, education, occupation, and sex of the respondent, the average preferred number of children of Buddhists who thought only a primary education was necessary for a son was almost four, compared to only slightly more than three for those who thought more than a high school education was necessary. For Muslims, a relationship in an opposite direction was found: the preferred number of children was almost five for those who thought a college education was necessary for a son, compared to slightly more than four for those who thought only a primary education was needed. For both religious groups, the relationship between preferred family size and the amount of education thought necessary for a daughter was similar to results relating preferred family size and the amount of education thought necessary for a son.[3]

More thorough analyses of expected schooling for children and fertility have been done based on data for households in thirty-four villages in two provinces in the central region. The conclusion reached in one such study, after an elaborate regression analysis incorporating a variety of other variables, was that expected completed family size was negatively related to the expected school level of children. Moreover, "the child schooling variable performed better empirically than did a variable for mothers' years of school, and this result supports the thesis that parents interested in higher quality (i.e. education) expect to have lower numbers of children" (Dyck, 1979:iv). A different analysis of the same survey concluded that "farm families living in the Central Plain Region of Thailand made a trade off between . . . expected schooling and the number of children they wished to have. . . ." (Ron, 1980).

Land Availability and Concern over Inheritance

The rate of expansion of agricultural land not only has not kept pace with population growth but also appears to be slowing in recent years (see chapter 3). In many localities, land formerly readily available for those who wished to clear it is now a scare resource. Interviews with leaders in the sixty-four villages included in the IPS Village Survey indicated that for about 60 percent of the villages, it was virtually impossible to find new land in the surrounding vicinity by the end of the 1960s. This was the situation for over 90 percent of the villages by 1979. Concern about the increased shortage of land at the present time compared to former days has been noted by several anthropologists (e.g., Foster, 1977; Mizuno, 1978a; Podhisita, 1985a).

The focus-group seminars reveal that parents no longer feel they can provide each of a large number of children with significant amounts of land for the children to live comfortably; they also feel it is unlikely that their children can acquire individual land on their own. Participants often spontaneously raised the problem of limited land availability when discussing why couples nowadays want fewer children. Many indicated the amount of land and its present productivity was not sufficient to support many children. This shortage of land and the limited opportunities in agriculture were often cited as the reason why there was an increased need to provide an education for their children. Conversely, plentiful land in the past was often given as a reason why the older

3. These results are based on an MCA analysis of data provided us by Chavalit Siripirom from a survey he conducted in 1982 interviewing approximately 2,000 heads of households in Pattani Province.

generation had large families. Many participants stated that their present land-holdings are inadequate. Whereas in former times holdings could be expanded simply by clearing forests, this is no longer seen as possible. Instead, the primary means of acquiring more land is through purchase, but for most participants prices are prohibitive. The problem of land availability was particularly prominent when people discussed inheritance and the difficulty of providing sufficient funds for their children's future.

Other studies confirm concern among village families over scarcity of land and the implications this has for the welfare of children when the time comes for them to inherit property. Concern about limited land availability, coupled with the subdivision associated with the prevailing system in which both sons and daughters share inheritance, was a primary motivating factor leading to adoption of fertility-control practices and reduced family size (Mougne, 1982; Potter, 1976). This is seen as a critical force underlying the acceptance of family-size limitation (Podhisita, 1985a). The concern about the sufficiency of land among farming households in general is documented by several surveys. Results from LS1, LS2, and NS consistently indicate that close to half of the heads of farming households regarded the amount of land they had as not sufficient to support themselves at present and less than one in five felt their land was sufficient to support both their children's households in the future and their own household at present.

Traditionally, land is seen as the main asset parents pass on to children. Inability to acquire additional land has forced parents to reassess not only the need for education but also the way to subdivide the family's land among their children. The tradition of dividing the land equally threatens the viability of individual holdings under conditions of rapid population growth. Parents are concerned with the problems their children or grandchildren will have to confront when the land must be subdivided once again. Many feel that unless family size is limited, their children will be unable to make a living from the land. Participants also mentioned that their control over other natural resources important to their sustenance, such as fisheries and forests, was declining.

"Back then if we wanted more land in the morning we could carry our axe and clear some [by the evening]. We could get as much as we wanted. But now if we want just one rai [about four-tenths of an acre], we will have to spend money in the tens of thousands of Baht. To be able to get land without money is not possible." (older Muslim man, south)

"If people had many children [nowadays] they would starve. They got very little [land] from their parents because there were four or five children. They could get only small shares and if there were more children it would be terrible." (younger woman, north)

"I don't have enough land. It's not like earlier times. There are more people now so I don't want to have many children." (younger woman, northeast)

"During our parents' time there was plenty of land. For example, my mother got twenty rai. I have six brothers and sisters, so we each got a little. Now in my time I have to divide [my share] for my children. For many children it is not enough. So you just have two or three children at most. Like me, I had two and then got sterilized." (younger man, central region)

"Even during our parents' time we only got two or three rai. By our grandchildren's time there won't be anything left." (younger woman, central region)

In brief, rural Thais perceive the traditional means of making a living through farming, which has served so many well in the past, to be increasingly threatened now by limited land availability. They anticipate the situation will become quite untenable in the future if family size remains large and alternative sources of employment are not found. To cope with this problem, people in the younger generation plan both to limit the number of children they will have and to provide their children with the education they see necessary for finding nonagricultural jobs.

Contributions of Children to Household Economic Activities

So far we have dealt only with the effects of recent social change on the costs of children. Also important are changes in the benefits provided by children, since it is the net balance of costs and benefits—broadly defined to include both economic and noneconomic dimensions—that determines family-size preferences. For Thailand, it is useful to distinguish between contributions children make while they are still young and support provided once the children become adults. Although participants largely agreed that the help children provide while growing up has declined, expectations of support for parents by adult children remain substantial. Since the latter is a deeply rooted cultural expectation, discussion of the support provided by adult children is deferred until the following chapter. In the present chapter, consideration is limited to the contributions children make while they are growing up. Moreover, our analysis of costs has concentrated primarily, although not exclusively, on economic dimensions and our analysis of benefits does likewise. This is in part because economic concerns were more salient in the focus-group discussions and in part because they seem more easily identifiable.

In agricultural countries such as Thailand, virtually all members of the household except infants contribute some labor both to productive activities and to household chores. Older focus group participants confirmed that in their youth they helped their parents plant rice, take care of buffaloes, fetch water, cook food, and perform other work that contributed to the economic sustenance of the household. Survey results from SOFT in 1975 indicate that about half of all husbands interviewed felt that there was a conflict between sending children for education and the family's need for them to help on the farm (Arnold and Pejaranonda, 1977). Nevertheless, the reduction in land availability, as well as the changes in agricultural technology, have probably resulted in a decreased need currently for children to help actively in the family economy and thus may facilitate the trend to keep children in school longer. At the same time, the increased period of time that children spend on education, as well as other school activities, has correspondingly decreased the child's ability and willingness to contribute to the family's work. Thus, the trends toward more education and fewer contributions by children are mutually reinforcing.[4]

When asked how much children help their parents nowadays compared with the past, the consensus in most groups, both younger and older, was that children currently help less, in part because children now spend more time at school, study more, and play a lot more than previously. Moreover, the content of the schooling is not seen as useful for teaching children how to do needed chores. Although parents complain about the decline in the help children give to them, they seem to accept it as part of the cost of educating children today.

"[Nowadays, children] do not help very much because they all go to school. Only the parents are left at home." (younger Buddhist woman, south)

"[Children back then] worked in the field, in the garden, did everything. Whatever the parents did, the children would do the same. But today they only study, they don't help their parents. Only study and the parents have to earn money to support them." (older woman, north)

"Children nowadays are not like children before. Before they helped mother and father but now all they want to do is have fun. They have a lot of friends." (younger woman, central region)

"The school teachers support the children in playing sports so everyone plays. We thus cannot blame the children. It has to do with the surrounding social environment." (older man, northeast)

Quantitative information on the extent to which children help around the house and in family enterprises as reported by husbands is available from SOFT. Husbands thought that sons begin to make useful contributions at an average age of 12 and daughters at about 11, although many felt that even by age 7 or 8, useful contributions were being made (Arnold and Pejaranonda, 1977). Married men with children aged 8 or over were asked if their children actually do help out around the house as well as in the family business or on the farm. As reported in table 7.4, almost all, whether rural or urban, re-

---

4. Nag and Kak (1985) provide a vivid description of how socioeconomic and technological changes have reduced the need for child labor in an Indian village.

Table 7.4.　Percentage Distribution of Extent of Children's Help around the House and in the
　　　　　Family Enterprise, as Reported by Married Men, 1975

	Total	Urban areas	Rural areas
Help around the house (for families with children aged 8 and over only)			
A great deal	20.2	12.9	21.1
A moderate amount	53.6	60.1	52.7
Only a little	18.2	18.7	18.2
None	8.0	8.3	8.0
Total	100.0	100.0	100.0
Number of cases	1,815	192	1,623
Help on the family farm or in the family business (for families with a family enterprise and children aged 8 and over only)			
A great deal	23.8	10.7	24.8
A moderate amount	37.2	28.4	37.9
Only a little	10.2	9.0	10.3
None	28.8	51.9	27.0
Total	100.0	100.0	100.0
Number of respondents	1,604	115	1,489

Source: Based on SOFT as reported in Arnold and Pejaranonda (1977).

ported at least some help with housework. Overall, a large percentage (71) of
those with a family enterprise reported some help from children. Moreover,
the degree of help was usually rated as at least moderate. A considerably higher
proportion of husbands in rural areas indicated their children help in the family enterprise than did husbands in urban areas.

　　Although data from SOFT make clear that nonadult children can and do
provide a substantial amount of help to parents, including contributions to the
family's economic activities, especially in the countryside, a comparison of
the 1970 and 1980 censuses suggest that such help is on the decline. For
example, the proportion of children aged 11–14 reported as economically
active during the week prior to the census declined from 48 percent to 31 percent between 1970 and 1980. It should be noted that economic activity is
broadly defined in the census and includes unpaid family workers. Since the
vast majority of economically active 11-14-year-olds are in this category, the
decline in economic activity presumably reflects declining help in the family
enterprise. This trend is undoubtedly related to increased school attendance
among this age group as documented in chapter 3.

　　At the same time that children appear to be providing less help to their families, the need for child labor may be declining, at least in rural areas, as farming technology changes and opportunities for expanding holdings through clearing new land disappears. In addition, in some places, such as the northeastern village where we conducted focus-group discussions, diminishing farm size probably leads to less demand for child labor. Podhisita (1985a), however, concluded, on the basis of his anthropological study of the village, that the declining demand for children's labor had little influence on the desire to have small families. In our focus groups, participants rarely related the decline in help from young children to the fact that people now want to have fewer children. Unlike education, which is seen as involving direct and continued monetary cost and thus as an obvious economic burden for the parents, the decline in children's help, which is often a matter of degree, is seen more as an inconvenience than as a serious hardship. The net result is that parents' perception of children is changing from a view of their being an integral part of the division of family labor to being recipients of the family's resources.

Conclusion

In chapter 3, a variety of statistical indices were reviewed documenting the changing social and economic circumstances of the Thai population. A picture emerged of a society experiencing the broad array of changes typically associated with what social scientists conventionally label modernization. The present chapter has presented evidence from focus-group discussions and selected survey results to portray how these changes and the perceptions of them have influenced reproductive behavior and attitudes. The picture that emerges is one of multiple but interrelated forces that have increased both the real and perceived costs of children, particularly in monetary terms, for parents. Especially crucial in this respect is the increasingly felt need to provide children with a sufficient education to enable them to function effectively in the newly and rapidly emerging socioeconomic environment.

Changes in the nature and extent of the benefits of children are less clear, although it seems likely that the economic contributions of younger children have decreased, in large part because of increased time spent in school. Discussion of one of the very most important benefits of children, their contribution as adults to the care and upkeep of older-aged parents, however, is deferred to the next chapter. Nevertheless, the evidence is clear that whether or not there have been major changes in the benefits of children, their increased costs have resulted in an almost universal perception among Thai couples that large families are not affordable under present-day social and economic conditions. To adjust to these conditions, Thai couples have turned en masse to the limitation of family size through deliberate means of birth control. Their ability to do so is greatly facilitated by the cultural context of Thai society, the topic of the next chapter.

8

The Cultural Context of Reproductive Change

In any society, the impact of social and economic change on reproductive behavior is mediated through the cultural setting. To be sure, the features that characterize that setting are also affected themselves by those same social and economic changes. Nevertheless, many cultural dimensions are likely to show continuity and a fair degree of persistence even when social and economic change is rapid and thus can be discussed in terms of the extent to which they predispose or inhibit change, at least over the intermediate run. Although it is also possible to raise questions about the ultimate economic and historical factors that have shaped the cultural context from the start, this is an issue far beyond the scope of our own study. Thus, for the purposes of our analysis, we take culture as a primary determining factor.

This chapter explores those dimensions of Thai culture that seem particularly relevant to understanding the rapid change in reproductive behavior. In important ways, Thai culture is conducive to the limitation of family size and the adoption of birth control as ways of adjusting to changing socioeconomic circumstances. In addition, several pronatalist props or barriers to fertility decline characteristic of many Third World cultures are notably absent in Thailand. The following discussion covers parent repayment expectations, the locus of reproductive decision making, the extent of female autonomy, and the influence of Theravada Buddhism. In addition, the contrasting reproductive

143

attitudes and behavior of Buddhists and Muslims are considered in terms of their implications for evaluating the importance of cultural influences on fertility decline in Thailand.

The Persistence of Parent Repayment

The expectation that children, when economically active adults, will provide comfort and support to their parents, particularly when parents are too old to work or care for themselves, is shared by all segments of Thai society. Indeed, it is a common expectation in virtually all Third World countries and is often cited as a major incentive for high fertility. The general lack of effective government and private pension systems providing more than very limited coverage in Thailand and most of the developing world ensures that the majority of couples will look to family members, and particularly their children, for support in their later years.

In Thailand, this support takes both economic and social forms and is viewed as repayment to parents for having borne, cared for, and raised the child (Rabibhadana, 1984; Phillips, 1965:158–59). It is a tradition deeply rooted in the secular and religious culture and firmly linked to the broad normative structure. Temporary service in the Buddhist monkhood by sons, a common occurrence in Thai society, is seen as part of this repayment since it confers merit on the parents as well as the son.[1] As part of a traditional rite frequently performed prior to ordination, explicit reference is made to the obligation that a son has to repay his parents and ordination is seen as part of this process. In elementary school, a commonly read excerpt from a classical text deals with the strong obligation a child has to repay his parents for their care.[2]

Many observers have commented on the pervasiveness of the patron-client relationship as a predominant mode of social interaction in Thai society (Kap-

1. "Merit" (*bun*) refers to the Thai belief derived from the Hindu-Buddhist doctrine of Karma that all one's good conduct earns spiritual credit (merit) and brings positive rewards; one's evil conduct results in spiritual demerit and yields negative rewards both in the present life and in subsequent incarnations (Pfanner and Ingersoll, 1962:352–53; Suebsonthi, 1980:159). Throughout their lives, individuals maintain a relative store of merit that represents the accumulated balance between merit and demerit (Kirsch, 1977:246).

2. We are grateful to Fern Ingersoll and Jasper Ingersoll for calling our attention to these points. In the preordination rite, specific reference is made to the fact that parents take total care of their children, including cleaning up the child's feces and urine. The idea of cleaning up after one's elderly parents as part of the obligation of repaying parents was spontaneously mentioned in one of the focus group's sessions. Apparently the task of cleaning up feces and urine or assisting in matters related to bodily elimination, because of their unpleasant nature, are used to symbolize the extent of care parents give children and children must return to parents later in life. Moreover, the fact that most Thais live in residences without indoor plumbing contributes to the salience of this concern.

lan, 1981). Accordingly, social relations are often guided by a model in which the socially or economically superior patron will confer benefits on the inferior client with the expectation and understanding that the client will reciprocate with loyalty and deference and by providing needed services at appropriate times and in appropriate ways. In a sense, parent repayment epitomizes this deeply entrenched model of social relations. Moreover, helping support parents and providing them comfort is also viewed as a way a person can accumulate merit, thus conferring a religious significance on a tradition that is firmly rooted in the secular culture (Podhisita, 1985b:38–39).

Parent repayment in Thailand is a process that begins when children are old enough to be useful and continues through the child's adult years as long as the parents live. Indeed, even after parents die, children are expected to pay respects to the deceased parents. It encompasses the help young children provide parents discussed in the previous chapter. It is the later stage of the process, however, when parents are no longer able to work or care for their own needs, that is seen as the essence of parent repayment. The discussion of repayment to parents, therefore, focuses on contributions made during the children's adult years.

Focus-group participants of both generations agreed that parents expect and are entitled to support from their adult children as repayment for, or as an obligation created by, the care parents provided children during infancy and childhood. The discussions made clear that repayment encompassed both economic and noneconomic dimensions. Contributions of money, material goods, and labor assistance to the parents' economic activities were cited as well as social and moral support.

The most frequently mentioned expectation was assistance during illness, primarily in the form of physical care and psychological comfort, but also financial help in purchasing medicine and paying for medical services. Children are also expected to be responsible for arranging and paying for funeral ceremonies, often a significant expense in Thailand, and for "making religious merit" on behalf of deceased parents. Other common examples included provision of food and clothes, donations of money on a regular or irregular basis, social visits, help around the house, and help with cooking. The form of repayment is seen as varying with the stage of both the parents' and the adult children's life cycles, in essence balancing need and ability. Parents anticipate a reduction in monetary and material contributions once adult children start to raise families of their own.

Discussions during the focus-group sessions made clear that the expectation of help and support is perceived as a fundamental reason in Thailand for having children. Both the older and younger generations view children, at least ideally, as a form of security and comfort in old age.

"If my children don't come [to look after me] when I am old, I don't know why I had children." (younger woman, northeast)

"I hope for everything from my children but I don't know if they will do it all for us . . . to help us in work, get money for us, help the family, things like this." (younger man, northeast)

"When we are sick, when we are old, we expect our children to cook and get food for us, to get water for us. We are not strong enough to fetch water, so we want to depend on them. If we do not have any strength to work, have no money, we will depend on them." (older woman, central region)

Although there seemed to be nearly universal agreement that it is important for children to help support and comfort parents in old age, there was some recognition that it does not always work out that way. Several participants stressed the need for at least several children in case some turn out not to be dependable.

While expectation of old-age support from children clearly persists, it is difficult to assess whether the extent of support has changed, in part because the form of support appears to be shifting. Many participants observed that monetary remittances from wage labor or nonagricultural jobs outside the village are replacing help in activities requiring labor. Thus, parent repayment is becoming monetized along with other aspects of villagers' lives. Both generations appear to be aware of this change. While some see it as an improvement and even as an increase in the extent of support provided to parents by adult children, this viewpoint is not universal.

The monetization of support is tied in with many of the changes discussed in chapters 3 and 7. The increasing scarcity of farmland and the greater rewards of wage-earning jobs mean more children seek their livelihood away from home. It is often difficult to leave a job elsewhere to return to the home village when labor is needed, such as during planting or harvesting time, although this still occurs with some frequency. Older parents are faced with the same monetization of daily life as everyone else but may have greater difficulty earning cash incomes of their own. Hence, the shift from labor assistance to cash remittances may be convenient for both parents and children. Moreover, many elderly parents probably have access to each form of support, since often some children remain home or near the village while their siblings have nonagricultural jobs elsewhere.

"Back then [children] helped with labor. Now they help with expenses." (older Buddhist man, south)

"The kind of help which children give to their parents has changed from working in the rice field to sending things or money to their parents because the children always work outside the village." (older Muslim woman, south)

"Those who stay at home help us to cook. Those who are far away send us money." (older woman, north)

"It's changed for the better. They make money for us, that's better. Before there was no place to earn money. Today there are lots of places. In the past children only helped growing rice. . . . [Today] they both grow rice and make money for us. [Before] I didn't know where to go. After the rice growing season, we stayed at home. Now after growing rice, they go to earn some money. It's better than before." (older woman, northeast)

Survey data on expectations and hopes for help from children during the parents' older years are available from several sources. A substantial amount of information was collected in SOFT based on interviews with married men. In response to open-ended questions on the advantages of a large family and disadvantages of small families, Thai husbands showed considerable interest in the help that children provide when the parents are old or when the parents become ill. This was true for both rural and urban men (Arnold and Pejaranonda, 1977). Husbands were also asked what means of support they expected in old age and to what extent they expected to rely on their children. Three-fourths of all husbands spontaneously mentioned children as a means of old-age support. This was a far larger percentage than for any of the other possible means. For example, only 39 percent spontaneously mentioned savings, the second most commonly mentioned means (Arnold and Pejaranonda, 1977).

When asked specific questions in SOFT about help expected from children, as shown in table 8.1, 88 percent thought they would depend at least in part for economic assistance from children during their older years. On the other hand, only 28 percent expected a great deal of financial support. Rural men are somewhat more likely to indicate reliance on children for such support than their urban counterparts. The substantial degree of economic and emotional reliance on children in the later years is evident from the finding that 85 percent of rural husbands and 77 percent of urban husbands said they expected to live with their children during old age.

As indicated above, expectations of repayment to parents generally extend over most of the productive life of children. Adult children with a job are often expected to contribute income to the family, especially if unmarried. This is evident from the responses of married men interviewed in SOFT to questions about their expectation of receiving income from unmarried and married adult children. The questions referred to adult children in general and not to the respondent's own children. The results indicate that most husbands, both in rural and urban areas, expect parents to receive income from adult children, but primarily from unmarried children. Rural husbands especially appear to feel that once their children are married, the burden of caring for their own families will prevent them from sending income to their parents. Among the

Table 8.1. Attitudes toward Assistance from Children during Old Age, by Residence and Age Cohort

	All ages			Age cohort (rural and urban combined)			
	Total	Rural	Urban	Under 30	30–39	40–49	50+[a]
Percent of married men in 1975 (SOFT) who expect:							
To rely on any financial support from children when old	88	89	78	89	89	87	87
To rely on a great deal of financial support from children when old	28	29	19	27	27	28	34
To live with children when old	85	86	75	85	86	84	81
Unmarried children to give part of income	63	64	56	61	62	64	70
Married children to give part of income	18	17	27	15	16	20	24
Percentage distribution of responses to question "Can you rely on your children to take care of you in your old age?" 1979 (NS)							
Household heads							
Yes	80	81	68	76	78	78	83
No	7	5	16	5	7	7	6
Uncertain	14	14	16	19	15	14	11
Total[a]	100	100	100	100	100	100	100
Ever-married women							
Yes	74	75	67	72	71	74	81
No	4	4	4	3	3	5	6
Uncertain	22	21	29	25	27	22	13
Total[b]	100	100	100	100	100	100	100

Sources: SOFT and NS.

[a]For SOFT, results include a small number who did not know their age.
[b]Sum of categories may not add to exactly 100 because of rounding.

subset of husbands who had children who actually earned money, the large majority (77 percent) of unmarried children contributed income at least occasionally compared to slightly less than one-third of married children (Arnold and Pejaranonda, 1977). Thus, expectations appear to conform well to the actual pattern.

Data from NS in 1979 also confirm high levels of expectation of support from children when parents are old. Respondents with children were asked if they thought they could rely on their children for support in old age. The wording of the question referred to support of any kind, not necessarily financial support. Results are also shown in table 9.1 and indicate that the large majority of both rural household heads, most of whom were male, and rural ever-married women thought they could rely on their children for support in old age. Most of the rest said they were not sure and only a modest proportion of either group indicated they believed they could not rely on their children for support. Although expectations of support were lower for urban respondents, still about two-thirds of both urban household heads and urban ever-married women thought they could rely on their children in old age. Again, most of the remainder were uncertain.

Although the focus-group results indicate that expectations of parent repayment are widespread among both older- and younger-generation participants, they cannot serve as the basis for judging in any precise manner either the extent to which such expectations have been changing over time or if generational differences exist. The quantitative data from surveys also make clear that expectations of support of parents by adult children are very prevalent. Unfortunately, however, there is a lack of series of comparable data from different surveys to permit a direct assessment of trends. Although not directly a measure of change, age-group comparisons of attitudes toward support in old age from a single survey can at least indicate if there are cohort differences at a given time. For this reason, the findings in table 8.1 are also shown according to the age group of the respondent.

Results from both SOFT and NS indicate modest age cohort differences in some attitudes toward assistance from children during old age and almost no difference in others. To the extent that differences are evident, they generally indicate that expectations were more prevalent among the older cohorts. For example, according to the results from SOFT, there is almost no difference in the percentage of married men under 30 and those over 50 who expect to rely on at least some financial support from children during old age. For all age groups, such expectations are very prevalent. Expectations to live with children during old age are also very prevalent among younger men. However, a higher percentage of the older men expect a great deal of support compared to the younger men. There is also a somewhat higher proportion of older than younger men who expect unmarried and married children to give part of their income to parents. Questions about giving part of the income to parents did not refer specifically to old-age support. Thus, the fact that there are greater cohort differences in responses to these questions than to those that referred specifically to old age may indicate that the latter are more resistant to change, possibly because they represent the essence of parent repayment.

Responses based on NS about reliance on children for assistance in old age indicate a slight increase with successive age cohorts in the proportion who think they can rely on children. This is entirely a result of a decrease in the proportion of the older cohorts who are uncertain about assistance, however, rather than a decrease in those who say that they do not think they can rely on their children. Possibly the age-cohort differences in the percentage who are uncertain about assistance reflects the fact that the older respondents are already at an age when they would be receiving such assistance. Thus, there is little uncertainty in their situation. In contrast, for the younger respondents, such assistance is still at a considerable distance in the future.[3]

The persistence of parent repayment expectations over a period when fertility changed rapidly is consistent with data indicating stability in expectations about another related basic familial value, namely, preference concerning postnuptial residence of children. As was mentioned in chapters 3 and 6, there is a strong cultural expectation, particularly in the northeast and north, that newlyweds will reside initially with one of the spouse's parents, usually the bride's. Survey data from LS1 and NS, presented in table 8.2, indicate that attitudes toward desired postnuptial residence have changed little among rural Thais.

The overall pattern of the survey results show that substantial proportions of ever-married women want a son or daughter to reside with them right after marriage and that far more prefer their daughter to take up coresidence than their son. A substantial number also indicate that the choice is up to the child. Of particular interest is that the results of the two surveys, taken a decade apart, show very similar patterns. Anthropological evidence generally indicates that coresidence is usually only temporary, from a few months to a few years, dependent in part on how long it takes the newly-wed couple to accumulate sufficient resources to construct a house of their own. Most children eventually live neolocally. This may help explain why attitudes toward postnuptial residence have not changed greatly during a period of substantial societal change in other areas, since social and economic development is generally thought to lead toward neolocal residence as the predominant form. Results from Taiwan suggest that the extent to which development affects coresidence

3. The case of Taiwan, where fertility has fallen even further than in Thailand and where the level of economic development is considerably higher, provides an interesting comparison. Survey data for Taiwan permit direct analysis of trends and indicate that although expectation of support from children in old age has remained high in the course of the fertility transition, it has nevertheless decreased. The Taiwan results caution against relying on age-cohort differences to reflect trends accurately since changes in attitudes of the same cohort over time were found to be greater than differences between older and younger cohorts at any given time period. In general, it was found that although many family values, including obligations of old age support by children, have been changing in the course of social and economic development, these changes have lagged behind other attitudinal and behavioral changes taking place in Taiwan, particularly those supporting personal control of the childbearing process, the massive adoption of contraception, and the rapid fall in fertility (Coombs and Sun, 1981).

Table 8.2. Attitudes toward Children's Postnuptial Residence, Ever-Married Women, 1969–79

	For son			For daughter		
	Rural		Urban	Rural		Urban
	LS1 1969	NS 1979	LS1 1970	LS1 1969	NS 1979	LS1 1970
Desired residence after marriage						
In same household	29.9	28.1	36.9	50.4	55.4	27.9
In same compound but separate house	5.7	8.2	1.5	5.5	6.4	1.4
In separate location	26.9	28.6	18.6	12.8	9.6	28.1
As child wishes	33.1	30.4	41.0	29.8	26.4	40.1
Other	4.3	4.6	2.0	1.5	2.2	2.5
Total percent[a]	100.0	100.0	100.0	100.0	100.0	100.0
N	1,430	2,139	2,141	1,435	2,142	2,148

Sources: LS1 and NS.

[a] Sum of categories may not add to exactly 100 because of rounding.

patterns may be more limited than originally thought (Freedman, Chang, and Sun, 1982).

There is a considerable rural-urban contrast in attitudes toward postnuptial residence. The most common preference among urban women is for neolocal residence for both the son and daughter. In addition, a larger percentage indicate a preference for coresidence with the son than with the daughter, probably reflecting the strong representation of ethnic Chinese in the cities. Regional differences among ethnic Thais may also contribute, given the high proportion of the urban population that lives in the central region (including Bangkok), where the preference for newlyweds to live with the bride's parents rather than the groom's is less pronounced (Limanonda, 1979).

In brief, cultural expectations of parent repayment have remained strong and attitudes toward postnuptial residence have remained stable during a period when rapid reproductive change has taken place. This suggests the ability of deeply entrenched cultural features to persist in the face of rapid social and economic change supporting the view expressed by Freedman (1979) that abandonment of traditional familial values is not necessarily a prior condition for large-scale adoption of contraception and a substantial reduction of fertility.

Given the persistence of the parent repayment norm and the continuing anticipation of dependence on children for support in old age by older and younger generations alike, we were particularly interested in how focus-group participants reconciled this with the younger generation's desire for a smaller number of children. Old and young participants alike were evenly divided as to whether or not having few children threatened security in old age.

The most common view was that a trade-off is involved between maximizing the economic security and psychological comfort to be gained in old age by having many children and minimizing the economic hardships and burdens of child rearing by keeping family size small.[4] Parents today opt for small families because they judge that the additional benefits to be gained later in life from many children are not worth the hardships that raising a large family would involve. Some simply feel there is in fact no choice to be made, since under current social and economic circumstances they could not possibly afford raising many children.

"I want many children after they have grown up. But right now I want only a few because I have no time to raise them." (younger Muslim woman, south)

"In principle, having a lot of children will make you comfortable when you are old, but when they are young it will be difficult to find the money to raise them." (younger man, north)

"When children have grown up, the one who has many is more comfortable than the one who has few. But if the children are still small, the one with many children will not be as comfortable as the one with few." (older man, northeast)

Nevertheless, a number of focus-group participants believed that the only persons on whom one can truly depend are one's own children and that a couple with few children runs the risk that there might not be anyone around to help later in life. There were also a number of participants who expressed uncertainty about whether children can truly be depended upon in old age. Lauro (1979:111) noted a similar uncertainty among the central Thai villagers he studied. This uncertainty may mitigate to some extent the sense of conflict felt between reduced family size and a need for many children later in life.

One view among participants who did not feel that having few children jeopardized old-age support was that support in later years does not depend on

---

4. A survey in two northern provinces in 1976–77 included a question asking if the better strategy for ensuring support for old age is to have three or fewer children and give them a better start in life or to have as many children as possible. The vast majority of respondents chose the former (Shevasunt and Hogan, 1979). This seems inconsistent with the fact that many focus-group participants indicated a conflict between small families and old-age support. The response pattern in the survey may result from the extreme and somewhat biased wording of the question. Especially in the north, where fertility has exhibited early and very rapid decline, having as many children as possible is not an attractive alternative nor was it a *deliberate* reproductive strategy even prior to the start of fertility decline. Moreover, not to choose the option stating a preference for giving one's children a better start in life may be perceived by the respondent as implying that he or she does not want the best for his or her children.

the number of children but rather on their upbringing. A small number, if properly raised, would still be sufficient to provide parents with security. Given the norm that only one child, typically the youngest daughter, will reside permanently with the parents and hence carry the bulk of the burden of responsibility for parental care, having a single child should be sufficient to be reasonably assured of support in old age (Lauro, 1977).

There were also participants who believed that the relationship between the number of children and economic support later in life has changed and that a simple association between more children and greater economic security in old age no longer holds in today's changing social and economic environment. They felt that fewer but better educated children would be more favorably situated to obtain desirable non- agricultural jobs and thus would be better able to provide economic support to their parents, especially in terms of cash remittances. Since the cost of providing an adequate education for many children would be prohibitive, the economic prospects of both children and parents are improved by limiting family size to a few children.

"[Support in old age] depends on how you raise and bring up your children. To have a small number of children but to raise them well is better than to have many children but not to raise them well." (younger Muslim man, south)

"[Parents will still be supported well] because education has progressed. Now children get a higher education. Repayment of parents will go according to the level of education. Before not too many studied, but for those who got a high education, they repaid their parents well. The needs and expectations of parents with two or three children will be greater but the children will receive more care. Two children with education can repay parents better than ten [without]." (older man, northeast)

"[Children should study a lot.] That's good. They'll be able to find jobs. We'll be able to rely on them. There will be a future for them." (older woman, north)

"I think it is important [to have children take care of you when you are old]. That's why now I try to send my children to school. I expect that in the future I will depend on them." (younger man, central region)

In brief, both the focus-group discussions and survey data clearly indicate that younger couples still have strong expectations that their children will support them during their later adult years even though they wish to have only a few children. Although many see having few children as conflicting with maximizing support in old age, other considerations favoring small families override these concerns. Others see no conflict since they believe that a few children are sufficient for support. Some even argue that couples with small families will be better off, since they will be better able to educate their children and, given the societal changes underway, more highly educated children will be in a more advantageous economic situation to provide the expected repayment to the parent.

The Locus of Reproductive Decision Making

Discussions of the persistence of high fertility in some Third World societies have recently emphasized the importance of the influence of kin, particularly the couple's parents, on the reproductive decisions of the couple. Such influence is typically pronatalist, in accordance with the kin group's own interests, and serves as an important prop supporting high fertility (e.g., Caldwell, 1982:117–18). In Thailand, however, this is clearly not the case. Decisions with respect to the establishment of a conjugal unit, and hence the initiation of reproduction, as well as decisions concerning the number of children to have, are generally defined as being primarily the responsibility of the couple themselves.

In Thailand, both the choice of spouse and the timing of marriage are largely decisions for the individual couple themselves. As discussed in chapter 6, participants in the focus group sessions emphasized maturity and responsibility as important prerequisites for marriage. At the same time, however, they also indicated that ultimately the timing of marriage depends on the individuals themselves.

"They can get married at whatever age they want to." (younger woman, north)

"Some say it's good but some say it's bad to marry when you are young. It really depends on the individual." (younger man, northeast)

"It depends on whether the boy would like to be ordained or to enter the military service. If he doesn't want to wait he can marry." (older woman, Bangkok construction site)

"Above 20 years [it is good to get married]. At that age they can take good responsibility for a family. But then, it depends on the individual." (older Buddhist man, south)

Questions about who makes decisions concerning mate selection were not discussed in the focus-group sessions. But there is a considerable body of sociological and anthropological literature indicating that for some time the norm has been that individuals have freedom to select their own mate. Arranged marriages, among the Buddhist majority at least, are relatively rare, although they may have been more common in the past. Parents or other kin play mainly an advisory role (Limanonda, 1983; Henderson et al., 1971:69). As Lauro (1979:270–72) points out, despite the formal structure of some marriage arrangements involving negotiations over bride price and ceremonial visits between respective households, in actual practice the decision to marry is a prior one made almost completely by the marriage partners themselves. Various mechanisms for couples to circumvent parental disapproval exist and appear to be commonly used, particularly elopement and occasionally abduction (Riley, 1972). Although bride payment is common, it does not sig-

Table 8.3. Attitudes toward Children's Mate Selection, Ever-Married Women, 1969–79

	For son			For daughter		
	Rural		Urban	Rural		Urban
	LS1 1969	NS 1979	LS1 1970	LS1 1969	NS 1979	LS1 1970
Who chooses mate						
Parents must choose	13.7	13.0	10.6	13.5	13.7	11.9
Child chooses on own	68.3	71.0	68.6	68.2	69.1	64.5
Child chooses with parental approval	9.8	10.3	14.4	10.0	10.7	16.6
Parents choose with child's approval	7.7	5.6	5.0	7.6	5.9	5.5
Other	0.5	0.1	1.4	0.7	0.5	1.5
Total percent[a]	100.0	100.0	100.0	100.0	100.0	100.0
N	1,434	2,104	2,128	1,436	2,140	2,130

Sources: LS1 and NS.

[a] Sum of categories may not add to exactly 100 because of rounding.

nify corporate family involvement in the marriage contract and the payment is not returned in case of divorce as is common in societies emphasizing an extended-family structure. In addition, there is little family involvement in cases where couples decide to divorce. Essentially, marriage and divorce are matters for the couple itself to decide. Other family members have minimal influence.

Survey data on attitudes toward mate selection, presented in table 8.3, are available from both LS1 and NS for the rural sample covering the decade 1969 to 1979. These data confirm the predominant view that both sons and daughters should exercise considerable freedom in their choice of a spouse. Consultation between parents and children is expected but only a small proportion of respondents felt that the parents should select a child's spouse. No significant shift in attitudes toward this aspect of family life among rural Thai women is evident during a decade when substantial social change, including a major transformation of reproductive behavior, was taking place. This probably reflects the fact that the preexisting pattern already favored the mode of mate selection toward which social and economic development are usually assumed to lead. It is interesting that there was little difference at the time of LS1 in attitudes concerning mate selection between rural and urban women.

As discussed in chapter 4, both survey and focus-group evidence suggests that in Thailand, family size has changed from being perceived as a matter over which little deliberate control was exercised to being a matter of conscious choice. Under the latter circumstances, cultural influences on who makes decisions about the number of children become potentially important determinants of family size. Childbearing decisions in Thailand are generally defined as being primarily the responsibility of the couple themselves. Focus-group participants of both older and younger generations were largely in agreement on this matter. When asked whether they sought advice from anyone about how many children to have, younger participants rarely mentioned parents. They either stressed that the marriage partners themselves decide or they mentioned the advice of friends and siblings. Moreover, when they discussed such matters with others, they were simply seeking informal advice and were not being given imperatives from persons with deeply felt vested interests. The older generation also rarely mentioned discussing reproductive matters with their own parents. When asked whether they had advised their children on such matters, many older respondents indicated they had not.

The advice that was given typically encouraged the use of contraception and advocated having few children. This encouragement of small families by the couple's parents is justified primarily in terms of the couple's own benefit. Occasionally, older-generation participants indicated that small families for their children were also in their own best interest, since grandparents might have to help to ease the burden of raising many children. The two generations agreed that whatever advice is offered, ultimately it is for the younger couple to decide whether or not to follow it.

"The husband and wife consult only each other. Nobody else should have an opinion. Other people don't help raise the children." (younger woman, northeast)

"I never discussed [how many children to have] with my children. They never asked me for my advice. I never give advice." "I told my children to have two is enough." (two older women, Bangkok construction site)

"It's not related to anyone else. The husband and wife decide together." (older man, northeast)

"We don't talk with anyone else. If we want, we get two. . . . We wouldn't listen to what other people advise. We listen to ourselves." (younger woman, north)

"[I advised them] not to have many children because not only they but we will also be in difficulty." (older man, northeast)

The focus-group results in this respect are quite consistent with findings reported from a nationwide rural survey conducted in 1975. The vast majority interviewed (91 percent of husbands and 79 percent of wives) indicated they had not received advice from other family members about the number of children to have. Among the few who did receive advice, a third of the men and almost half of the women said they did not follow it (Deemar Company, 1975).

Hence, both survey and focus-group evidence agree that there is a notable lack in Thailand of a pronatalist influence of the older generation. The relative independence of couples in decisions about marriage and subsequent childbearing is consistent with a general and pervading theme in the Thai value system (which will be discussed later in connection with the influence of religion), stressing individual responsibility for one's own actions and destiny. It is also consistent with the views of a number of observers that kinship ties beyond the immediate nuclear family are relatively weak and that even among the nuclear family the sense of duty and obligation may be less pronounced than in many other Asian cultures (Lauro, 1979: 79–84; Siripirom, 1983; Embree, 1950). Thus, even though the initial period of reproductive activity for a young couple may take place within a coresidential extended-family household, the parents would still be likely to define their appropriate influence on such decisions as minimal. In addition, it is also consistent with the relatively weak emphasis on family lineages among Thais (discussed later).

The lack of influence of parents and kin over the reproductive decisions of their children, including both the establishment of the conjugal family and subsequent childbearing, fits in with the prevailing expectation, discussed in chapter 6, that each conjugal unit will be largely responsible for the support of its own children. Even during the initial coresidential period following marriage, the younger couple may contribute more to the upkeep of the household than does the older couple (Yoddumnern, 1983). Moreover, the young couple is often striving to accumulate sufficient resources to construct their own house. This is in considerable contrast with the situation thought to typify many developing countries, whereby shared resources associated with coresidence in a joint household free the younger couple from the direct economic responsibility of rearing children and permit an earlier start to childbearing than would be the case if they had to depend primarily on their own resources alone (Davis, 1955).

The absence of strong parental and kin pressure to have large families means that a prop considered important for the continuance of high fertility in many other societies is absent in Thailand. Moreover, the relative economic independence from an extended-family grouping makes Thai couples particularly sensitive to socioeconomic changes that lead to increased costs of raising a family. Since reproductive decisions are considered to be almost entirely the responsibility of couples themselves, they are free to adjust their fertility to fit their own perceived interests, thus facilitating rapid reproductive change.

Female Autonomy

Another important feature of the Thai cultural setting that facilitates rapid fertility decline is the relatively favorable status of Thai women. Compared with women in many parts of the Third World, Thai women rank relatively well in several important respects affecting female status (Safilios-Rothschild, 1985). For example, literacy among Thai women currently in the reproductive ages is close to universal and labor-force participation rates are high (see chapter 3; Curtin, 1982; Meesook, 1980; Debavalya, 1983). Relations between husband and wife are also relatively egalitarian (Hanks and Hanks, 1963; Henderson, 1971:69).

Several features of Thai culture and social structure support, reflect, and enhance the position of women in Thailand. As indicated in chapter 4, there is not a strong gender preference for sons, as there is in many other societies. Families in rural areas are traditionally organized around female members. Even though authority rests with the senior male, it is usually passed through the female line, especially in the north and northeast. Ideally, property is shared equally between sons and daughters, but the family home is typically allotted to the one who takes care of the parents in old age, customarily the youngest daughter. The postnuptial residence pattern emphasizing coresidence with the bride's parents means that at marriage the man joins the ritual, economic, and social group of his wife. Both men and women are expected to contribute to the household's productive activities without a sharp dividing line between the tasks that men and women carry out. Within the family, the wife has considerable power and typically controls family finances (Phongpaichit, 1982; Mougne, 1984; Bunnag, 1971:7; Henderson, 1971:72–73; Muecke, 1984). According to Lauro (1979:273), in the village he studied major family economic decisions were likely to involve consultation between husband and wife, but often the wife had the greater say. The importance of women in trading is a related feature of women's economic roles (Mougne, 1984).

It is often pointed out that Theravada Buddhism in theory ascribes an inferior status to women (Thitsa, 1980; Aneckvanich, 1979). Ordination into the monkhood is reserved for men. Moreover, monks are forbidden any physical contact with women. This prohibition is not necessarily a sign of female inferiority, however, but rather a reflection of a fear that female sexuality may distract monks from their spiritual path. It is by no means clear that Buddhist culture in practice relegates women to a religiously inferior status relative to men (Keyes, 1984). Women are more frequent contributors of food and other items of daily charity to monks than are men and hence their moral prestige is high (Henderson, 1971:70).

The high degree of female autonomy (i.e., the ability to manipulate one's personal environment) that characterizes Thai culture extends into the area of decisions regarding reproductive behavior.[5] In a recent article, Dyson and

5. When discussing influences on reproductive behavior, it is useful to distinguish the concept of autonomy, which refers to the ability to manipulate one's personal environment, from the

Moore (1983:45) suggested that societies in which there is a high degree of female autonomy are characterized by at least several of the following features: freedom of movement and association for adolescent and adult females; postmarital residence patterns that permit continued social contact between the bride and her natal kin; the ability of females to inherit and dispose of property; and some independent control in choice of marriage partners. Thailand clearly passes each of these tests. In general, Thai women act more independently in many spheres than women in most other Third World societies.

The focus-group discussions make clear that Thai women nowadays believe they have considerable influence over reproductive decisions. Participants were asked their opinions about whether the husband or wife should decide about the use of birth control, as well as who had the ultimate say in deciding on the number of children to have. The most common opinion expressed was that reproductive decisions were the joint responsibility of husband and wife. Since younger-generation participants often shared the same reproductive goals as their spouses, the question of who should prevail was sometimes seen as irrelevant.

"You must discuss [the number of children] between both husband and wife." (younger Muslim man, south)

"We have to decide [on the number of children] together." (younger man, north)

"There has to be a consensus. We must first ask the child's mother whether to control or not in order to see how willing she is." (younger man, central region)

"Both sides should be satisfied, the husband and the wife . . . [the number of children] can usually be agreed upon." (younger man, northeast)

When participants did not stress the joint nature of reproductive decisions, they often indicated that they themselves had the dominant influence or ultimate say. Men usually held that the husband, as head of the household and the primary provider for the family, should be the one who ultimately determines such matters. In contrast, women stressed that wives had more at stake, inasmuch as they experience the pain of giving birth and most of the burden of child rearing. Some men agreed with this view. Obviously, the issue is a matter of dispute among Thais.

"The man [should be the one to decide on birth control] because the man is the one who supports the family and everything depends on him." (younger man, northeast)

---

broader and more diffuse concepts of female status and social position, since female autonomy is of more direct relevance (Dyson and Moore, 1983). However, as the preceding discussion indicates, the favorable position of women in Thailand is not related to autonomy, but also includes their ability to exert influence in decisions involving the couple and not only matters concerning themselves exclusively.

"[The wife decides on the number of children because] after we give birth, we are responsible for housework, raising children. The men . . . are always away from the house. . . . We are at home with all this work and difficulty. We have to raise the children and the buffaloes as well." (younger woman, northeast)

"We decide [on family planning] ourselves. Our husbands don't know anything about it. We don't ask them. . . . We are women. We have to protect ourselves first. . . . If we want two, we'll have two. I cannot have three as my husband wishes. He does not carry the child. He does not give birth with us." "I consulted with my husband by telling him two are enough. [He said] nothing. If I want two, he gets two." (two younger women, north)

"Usually the husband doesn't say [how many children to have] but the wife will think about it for herself. She will buy the pill." (older woman, Bangkok construction site)

The focus-group results make clear that Thai women commonly take an active part in deciding on reproductive goals and in implementing them through their decision to use birth control. Although some participants of each sex stressed their own dominance over the reproductive decision-making process, more weight should probably be given to the woman's role, since women argue convincingly that they have special interests in limiting family size and in controlling childbearing. In contrast, men who argue they have the major say in reproductive matters do so mainly on the basis that they occupy the titular role as family head and hence may simply be reluctant to admit in front of others, or even to themselves, the importance of their wives' views. At least one study of a central Thai village noted that women act independently of their husbands with regard to use of contraception. In addition, husbands frequently indicated that practicing contraception was completely up to their wives, since the women are burdened by giving birth and raising the children (Lauro, 1979:273). Perhaps most significantly, as indicated in chapter 5, survey data make clear that the vast majority of Thai couples currently practicing contraception rely on female methods and thus in a very real sense contraception is under the woman's direct control.[6]

A number of surveys in Thailand have included questions about family decision making (e.g., National Council of Women of Thailand, 1977; Siripirom,

6. One reason cited as important in explaining the shortfall in some countries between predicted demand for contraception, based on surveys gauging contraceptive knowledge, attitudes, and practice (KAP), and actual subsequent use once family-planning programs have been established has been the assumption inherent in the surveys that reproductive decisions were primarily controlled by the couple, especially the wife (Warwick, 1982:115–17; Caldwell, 1985b:47). This criticism of KAP surveys may be valid in some contexts, but it is worth noting that not only does the assumption seem valid in the case of Thailand, but also that KAP surveys showing considerable built-up demand proved to be quite good predictors of the subsequent massive surge in contraceptive use once the national family-planning program was established.

1982). In general, they yield results consistent with the impressions provided by the anthropological literature. Many decisions tend to be made jointly. For example, women tend to have an important say in financial matters. When asked about family finances in LS1, the most common view among both rural men and women was that the wife controlled them. A recent intensive study of households in a number of northeastern villages confirms that women are the more important custodians of all cash income (Palmer, Subhadhira, and Grisanaput, 1983).

With respect to reproductive decisions, survey results are generally consistent with the findings based on the focus-group discussions. The most common opinion, among both male and female respondents, is that both spouses should decide on such matters together. Among those who do not indicate that reproductive decisions should be jointly made, men are more likely to emphasize the husband's role and women the wife's role. For example, results from the rural phase of LS1 in 1969 indicate that, among those who expressed an opinion, 55 percent of men and 60 percent of women said decisions about the number of children were joint decisions. Among the remainder, the majority of each sex indicated it was they who make the decision. Interestingly, unusually large proportions did not express an opinion in response to this particular question, perhaps reflecting the fact that at that time, family size was not yet truly a matter of deliberate decisions.

In a later, large-scale survey of the rural population in 1975, respondents were asked whose responsibility it was to plan the number of children and to practice birth control. The proportion with no opinion was reasonably low. Of those with an opinion, the majority of both sexes (56 percent of men and 58 percent of women) felt it was the responsibility of both husband and wife. Again, most of the rest felt it was the responsibility of the spouse of their own sex (Deemar Company, 1975). In contrast, the majority of both men and women with an opinion (57 and 79 percent respectively) agreed that contraception was the woman's responsibility. The question may have been interpreted by some to mean who actually uses the method rather than who should decide on whether or not to practice and thus reflected the predominance of female methods.

The relative autonomy of Thai women not only means that women have an important say in matters related to childbearing but also that women as well as men are exposed to the societal forces, discussed in chapter 7, that encourage smaller family sizes. Women now receive almost the same amount of education as men and are likely to participate in the labor force, including jobs outside the home in the case of urban women (see chapter 3). Perhaps of particular importance is the relatively free access of women to the rapidly expanding communications and transportation networks. As has been documented by several surveys, there are only modest differences between rural men and women in the frequency with which they visit towns and are exposed to mass media.

A series of questions on visits to markets and towns outside the village were asked of rural household heads in LS1 (1969) and rural ever-married women in LS2 (1972). The results indicate that 46 percent of women said they visited the district marketplace at least once a month or "often," compared to 56 percent of men in 1969; about one-fourth of the women visited the provincial capital at least once a month or "often," compared to one-third of male household heads; and about half of the women have ever visited either the regional urban center or Bangkok, compared to about seven out of ten men. Another survey of the rural population, conducted in 1975, found that 46 percent of women said they went to "town" at least once a month, compared to 65 percent of men (Deemar Company, 1975). Thus, although rural women are not as frequently in contact with urban settings as men, they are far from secluded.

Information on exposure to mass media is also available for household heads from LS1 and for ever-married women from LS2 and indicates similar or only modestly different levels of exposure to mass media. For example, about two-thirds of both rural men in 1969 and rural women in 1972 indicated they listened to the radio frequently ("often, daily, or almost daily"). Because of the lack of television in rural areas at that time, only 6 percent of rural men and 7 percent of rural women indicated they were frequent viewers. Data from the urban phase indicated that 63 percent of urban men in 1970, compared to 58 percent of urban women in 1973, listened frequently to the radio and 37 percent of urban men, compared to 45 percent of urban women, viewed television frequently. Data from a large rural sample in 1975 indicated that 72 percent of rural women, compared to 82 percent of rural men, said they listened to the radio frequently (Deemar Company, 1975). Results both from LS and the 1975 rural survey, however, indicate considerably more frequent newspaper reading among men, perhaps reflecting, in part, the higher male literacy rates in the older age groups.

Religion and Related Cultural Values

Much of the dominant Thai value system and its associated behavior patterns derive from Theravada Buddhism, the religion of the vast majority. This is true despite the influence and practices of Brahminism and animism, which are still evident and are intertwined with Buddhism as practiced in modern Thailand. The teachings of this school of Buddhism are absorbed from early childhood and major precepts are recited in primary school. Many Thai males, especially in rural areas, spend a short period (typically three months) as monks during early adulthood; this experience reinforces both Buddhist concepts and behavior patterns (Mole, 1973).

The only other religion in Thailand with any significant number of followers is Islam. As indicated in chapter 3, Muslims represent only 4 percent of the Thai population (compared to 95 percent who are Buddhists) and thus do not have a large national demographic influence. Only in the south, where they represent a fourth of the population, is their impact substantial. Nevertheless, because of the considerable differences between the two religious groups in reproductive attitudes and behavior (see chapters 4 and 5), a comparison between the two with respect to the extent and nature of influence that religion has on such matters is instructive and serves to underscore the importance of Buddhism and its associated cultural values in facilitating Thailand's fertility decline.

In some societies, implicit or explicit pronatalism or proscriptions on birth control are part of the predominant religious ideology or associated folk beliefs and can serve as a powerful cultural barrier to reducing fertility. This is by and large not the case in Thailand. Thai Buddhism not only poses no major barriers to the use of contraception or to reduced family size but in some respects facilitates them. There are no scriptural prohibitions against contraception, nor is Buddhist doctrine particularly pronatalist. Only abortion is opposed on religious grounds, because of the Buddhist proscription against taking life (Ling, 1969; Fagley, 1967:79). In contrast, Islam tends to exert pronatalist pressures on couples and discourages use of specific methods of birth control. Although scholars of Islam hold differing views about whether Islam explicitly encourages people to have large families, many observers agree that institutional pressures related to Islam, such as the Islamic conception of women's roles and its implication for the status of women, exert pronatalist influences. Moreover, Islamic religious authorities strongly oppose abortion and sterilization, although temporary methods of contraception, particularly withdrawal, are not generally opposed (Nagi, 1983; Fagley, 1967:81).

It was notable that religion was almost never mentioned in our focus-group sessions in connection with discussions of family size or fertility control. In one session with Buddhists, in response to a direct inquiry by a resident anthropologist, the participants indicated that they felt it would be inappropriate to discuss family planning with monks, since it had nothing to do with Buddhism. This is consistent with the Buddhist principle that religious matters and worldly matters should be separated; birth control clearly falls in the latter category (Suebsonthi, 1980). In sharp contrast, Islam is an all-pervasive religious system which makes little distinction between the sacred and the secular (Sadik, 1985).

Although religious reasons for opposing small families or fertility regulation did not surface in the focus-group sessions in the Muslim village we studied, considerable opposition to modern contraception was expressed in the Deemar focus-group sessions conducted with southern Muslims. Some of the opposition was general and some was with reference to specific methods, particularly sterilization.[7] The opposition was almost always on religious grounds and typically stemmed from a rejection of the idea that couples should limit the number of children they have. Doing so was viewed as attempting to preempt God's will. This is consistent with the general belief held by Muslims that only God knows and determines the future and that to try to determine the future oneself is equivalent to acting against God's will (Suebsonthi, 1980:119; Fagley, 1967:81). The opposition to birth control did not appear to extend to the idea of deliberately spacing births, nor did it include use of traditional methods such as withdrawal, which were viewed as ways of "controlling by yourself" and hence consistent with Islam.

We can't [practice birth control] because it is against religion. To do so would be to act in advance of God's will. It means we don't trust in God. God has already determined how many children you should have. Not to trust in God is bad." (Malay-speaking young Muslim man, Deemar focus group)

"We are not allowed to [get sterilized], we have to control by ourselves. The religion tells us to control by ourselves." (Malay-speaking middle-aged Muslim woman, Deemar focus group)

"[My husband] never thought about [family planning]. He thought of Allah and how it depends on Him how many children we have." (Malay-speaking middle-aged Muslim woman, Deemar focus group)

7. There are several possible explanations for why the Deemar focus-group sessions detected clear indications of religious opposition to modern birth control, although such opinions were not expressed by focus-group participants in the Muslim village in which we conducted our own focus groups. The most likely reason is that we never explicitly asked if birth control was related to religion; such a question was included in the Deemar discussion guidelines. In addition, the selection criteria were quite different; we purposely selected younger-generation participants who wanted small families, whereas the Deemar groups purposely included some groups of nonusers of contraception. Nevertheless, our older-generation Muslim participants, who were selected for having a substantial number of children, also did not condemn modern contraception. It seems likely that our Muslim village was truly more liberal than most, since, as was indicated in chapter 2, it was probably more integrated into Thai society than of Muslim villages generally are. A 1980 survey of the local district in which the village is located indicates relatively liberal attitudes with regard to matters of birth control among Muslims. Over 90 percent of both Muslim and Buddhist women said they agreed with the use of some method to prevent or postpone childbearing. Moreover, although disapproval among Muslims was higher than among Buddhists, only a small minority indicated they did not use a method because it was a sin. Although the survey did not explicitly ask if contraception was against religion, the results are suggestive of more tolerance of birth control among this particular group of Muslims than among Thai Muslims generally (Porapakkham, Pramanpol, and Knodel, 1983).

"[The religious leaders] say we shouldn't practice contraception because it is against the religion." (Malay-speaking middle-aged woman, Deemar focus group)

Although there are differences in the socioeconomic situation of Thai Muslims and Buddhists, both are subject to many of the same societal forces discussed in chapter 7 that make large families seem disadvantageous to the majority of Thai Buddhist couples. It is clear that many Thai Muslims feel these pressures. Indeed, it is difficult to distinguish comments made in the focus-group sessions we conducted in the Muslim village from those made in the Buddhist villages about the difficulties of raising many children. The resistance to secular education on the part of a large proportion of southern Thai Muslims, based on religious reasons, may lessen to some extent the degree of conflict between educational aspirations and large families (Prachuabmoh, 1980; Suthasasna, 1985). For example, in a survey conducted in 1982 in a predominantly Muslim province in the south, the average amount of education thought appropriate for a son or daughter was distinctly lower for Muslims than for Buddhists (Siripirom, 1983). In addition, some Muslims may feel that discrimination against them precludes their children's access to many of the government service jobs that so many Buddhist parents hope education will bring their children. Nevertheless, it is evident from comments in the Deemar focus groups that religious views are an important force impeding adjustment of fertility to the changing socioeconomic circumstances. A number of participants explicitly indicated that they felt a conflict between their religious views and what they perceived to be their secular needs, especially in light of the changing socioeconomic environment.

"I don't know how to make the right decision. If I think only about comfort, I would practice birth control. But that would mean I flee from God's commandments. If we believe in our own ability, it means we are running away from God." (Malay-speaking young Muslim man, Deemar focus group)

"If you don't think in terms of religion, birth control is good. But since it is related to religion, I have to ask those who are knowledgeable about religion first." (Malay-speaking young Muslim man, Deemar focus group)

"I would agree with family planning if it were not against the religion." (Malay-speaking middle-aged Muslim woman, Deemar focus group)

"[Birth control] is against the religion but is compatible with the condition of life nowadays." (Thai-speaking young Muslim woman, Deemar focus group)

Survey evidence suggests that both Buddhist religious leaders and laypersons alike generally approve of contraception. Among a sample of almost 2,000 monks, 83 percent indicated they were supportive of the government's pro-family-planning policy (Muangman and Hirunraks, 1980). Surveys of the general population indicate overwhelming approval of contraception and a widespread disapproval of abortion. Interpretation of results from earlier surveys concerning attitudes about contraception is complicated because a number of respondents were unaware of contraceptive methods. However, in all major surveys taken since the mid-1970s, by which time familiarity with contraception was close to universal, the large majority of respondents, typically over 80 percent, expressed favorable attitudes toward the use of birth control (Knodel et al., 1982).

One of the major topics for investigation in CPS3 in 1984 was religious attitudes toward marital-fertility control and contraceptive methods.[8] The results, summarized in table 8.4, indicate pronounced differences in the attitudes of the two religious groups. Because most Muslims live either in the south or in Bangkok and the surrounding central region, separate results are shown for each. Overall, the findings are reasonably consistent with those of the focus groups.

Among women who reported never using contraception, two-thirds of the Muslims mentioned religious objections as a reason for nonuse, compared to only 13 percent of the Buddhists. This difference is all the more impressive given that almost half of Muslim women had never used a contraceptive method, compared to only one in eight Buddhist women. Opposition to spacing and limiting births among married women in general is quite low for the Buddhists. Although more Muslims than Buddhists oppose birth spacing, Muslims show far more tolerance of spacing children than they do of limiting family size. Only about a third of Muslims indicated that they thought spacing was contrary to Islam, whereas four-fifths thought limiting family size was objectionable on religious grounds. Attitudes toward specific contraceptive methods are consistent with this general view of spacing and limiting. Again, only a small minority of Buddhist women expressed religious opposition to the methods shown. Muslims were more likely to object to all three of the methods but opposition is far less to withdrawal and the contraceptive pill, both temporary methods that could be used for spacing, than to female sterilization, a permanent method. Interestingly, southern residence bears little relationship to the percentage disapproving of birth control, both in case of Muslims and Buddhists.

Additional survey evidence of religious opposition to birth control among Muslims is available from a fairly large-scale survey of Muslims in the southernmost area of Thailand, conducted in 1977 by Thailand's National Economic and Social Development Board. Only a minority of respondents (44 percent of men and 40 percent of women) explicitly agreed that contraception

---

8. Because a special supplemental sample of Muslims in the southern region was interviewed, in contrast to most other national surveys, a sufficient number of Muslim respondents was included to permit reasonably reliable comparisons to be made between Muslims and Buddhists.

Table 8.4. Religious Attitudes Regarding Fertility Control, by Religion among Currently
Married Women Aged 15–49

	Buddhists			Muslims		
	Whole country	South only	Central and Bangkok	Whole country	South only	Central and Bangkok
Percent citing religious reasons for nonuse of contraceptives among those who never used	13	12	9	67	67	67
Percent believing the following is against their religion						
Deliberate spacing	11	7	12	36	35	41
Limiting family size	15	11	13	79	80	69
Percent believing specific method is against their religion[a]						
Withdrawal	8	4	6	38	41	23
Pill	12	7	12	40	39	44
Ligation	14	10	12	83	85	73

Sources: CPS3 as reported in Kamnuansilpa and Chamratrithirong (1985) and original
tabulations.

[a] Limited to women who said they were familiar with the specific method.

was not contrary to their religion. Interestingly, a majority (64 percent of men
and 60 percent of women) indicated approval of contraception in response to a
question about their own attitude, suggesting, as did comments from the
Deemar focus-group sessions, that a number of Muslims feel a conflict between secular considerations and religious values (Rachapaetayakom, 1983).

A full analysis of the difference in Buddhist and Muslim reproductive attitudes and behavior in Thailand would need to involve consideration of a variety of issues beyond the scope of the present discussion. Of particular concern
would be the extent to which the minority status of Thai Muslims affects reproductive patterns independently of or in interaction with religion. Moreover, the position of Thai Muslim women, and probably Southeast Asian
Muslim women generally, is considerably more favorable than women in most
other Muslim societies. For example, Thai Muslim women play a significant
and probably dominant role in the household economy, managing family finances in much the same way as Thai Buddhist women (Prachuabmoh, 1985).
In addition, married Muslim women (but not single women) are quite active
in trading and thus appear frequently in public markets. This is quite contrary

to the practice of secluding women, common in South Asian and Middle Eastern Muslim societies (Dixon, 1976). Nevertheless, Thai Muslims and Thai Buddhists maintain fundamentally distinctive cultural identities stemming from their different religions and reinforced by their different historical heritage, different clothing, and, in much of the south, by different languages (Prachuabmoh, 1985; Suthasasna, 1985). Although some of the differences in reproductive attitudes and behavior may be attributable to differing socioeconomic circumstances, the conclusion that much of the contrast is due to cultural differences associated with religion seems inescapable. In particular, Thai Buddhism is considerably more conducive than Thai Islam to the practice of contraception and the limitation of family size as a way to adjust to the pressures created by the ongoing process of socioeconomic change currently affecting both groups.

In contrast to approval of contraception among the general population, survey findings reveal close to universal disapproval of abortion. In the 1964 study of the Potharam district, more than 90 percent of women interviewed indicated disapproval of abortion in response to a question that did not specify particular circumstances (Hawley and Prachuabmoh, 1971b). The most recent findings from a national sample come from NS and indicate that only 6 percent of either urban or rural women approved of abortion if the reason for seeking the abortion was simply contraceptive failure. A large majority, however, indicated approval under special circumstances, such as danger to the mother's health or rape (Institute of Population Studies, 1982). Objection to abortion is basically on religious grounds. Most Thai Buddhists when asked about their view on abortion will immediately reply it is a sin. One survey of Buddhist monks found 98 percent perceived abortion as being against religious doctrine (Kanchanasinith, Kolasartsenee, and Bennett, 1980).

The lack of public approval of abortion, as indicated by opinions elicited in surveys, seems to be inconsistent with indications that the practice of abortion is rather widespread (see chapter 5). Several anthropological studies have commented on this. Lauro (1979: 267) points out that the moral issue of abortion is confounded by the general Buddhist notion that the seriousness of taking a life increases with the size and complexity of the life being taken and by the general cultural tendency, discussed below, for leaving decisions to individuals. Riley (1972: 227) is of the opinion that although inducing abortion is theoretically considered a moral wrong, it is also recognized as a practice that might be carried out by a reasonable person under certain circumstances. This agrees with survey findings showing that approval of abortion is highly dependent on the severity of the circumstances described in the question (Population Council, 1981; Institute of Population Studies, 1982). Moreover, the same set of circumstances when confronted in reality by the respondent herself may well be more likely to be perceived as sufficiently severe to justify an abortion than when posited in an abstract question in a survey.

In several indirect but important ways, Buddhism as practiced in Thailand may facilitate rapid reproductive change as a response to the changing socio-economic environment. Values and behavior reflecting individualism and freedom of action are common in Thai culture and are largely traceable to religious roots. Buddhism stresses the role of the individual in seeking spiritual liberation and generally emphasizes the primacy of individual action and responsibility (Lauro, 1979; Mole, 1973:65–68; Phillips, 1967:363–64). A variety of Buddhist teachings point to the need of individual effort to achieve desired goals. The attainment of Nirvana (release from the suffering incurred in the recurrent cycle of birth, death, and rebirth), the ultimate goal of Buddhism, is brought about through each person's individual efforts. There is no transcendent savior or deity to help. The way to Nirvana differs for each individual, depending on the balance of merit and demerit accumulated during present and past lives. Although precepts are offered on how to attain Nirvana, these are viewed as guidelines to be followed according to the individual's wishes rather than as rigid rules to which the individual must adhere (Mole, 1973:34).

A frequently repeated secular saying, not derivative from Buddhism but consistent with the emphasis on individualism, is that "to do as one pleases is to be genuinely Thai" (Podhisita, 1985b:82–83). As Embree (1950:182) has pointed out, Thai culture sanctions considerable variation in individual behavior. This sense that individuals are largely responsible for their own fate and that they should follow their own wishes probably is quite consistent with the concept that couples should limit their family size in their own interest. Combined with the lack of proscriptions on contraceptive practices, Buddhism's emphasis on individualism provides a normative context permissive of rapid reproductive change. The Buddhist stress on individual responsibility is in sharp contrast to the emphasis in Islam on the importance of God's will in determining an individual's fate.

Buddhist ideology, as popularly perceived, can also be seen as contributing to the general flexibility and tolerance often associated with Thai culture. Interference with the affairs of others in most circumstances is thought inappropriate (Mizuno, 1978b; Lauro, 1979; Mole, 1973:66–67). Remaining calm ("cool-hearted") and indifferent in situations that might provoke social condemnation or intervention elsewhere is a prevalent value (Podhisita, 1985b). Generally, the value system requires relatively little commitment or obligation toward other individuals or institutions, which is consistent with Buddhist teachings regarding the individual's responsibility for achieving spiritual liberation (Mole, 1973:60–61; Embree, 1950). In this respect, Buddhist culture contributes to the relative ease with which modern tastes, attitudes, and behavior, including changing reproductive patterns, can be adopted with only minimal social pressures surfacing against such changes. There are probably fewer barriers to the influence of the mass media in spreading "Western" lifestyles and consumer aspirations than in many other cultures.

There are also other aspects of the Thai cultural setting that may have facilitated the decline in fertility, although they are more difficult to specify. There
is relatively little stress on the importance of family lineage or the need to
have ancestors. As Lauro (1979:81) notes, in the village he studied, most villagers were unable to trace their genealogies back for more than a couple of
generations. The unimportance of lineal descent is underscored by the fact
that most Thais did not have surnames until they were required by a royal decree from the king in 1916.

That pragmatism and expediency are prized values within Thai culture is
no doubt also of relevance and fits the general view that Thais show considerable flexibility in their behavior (Wijeyewardene, 1967:83; Mole, 1973:83–
84; Rosenfield et al., 1982). This flexibility and pragmatism, characteristic of
Thai culture and manifest in the relative fluidity of interpersonal relations, has
struck Western observers for some time and led to the somewhat controversial
depiction of Thai society as "loosely structured" (Embree, 1950; Evers, 1969).
Although there have been objections both to this specific terminology and the
general characterization (see, e.g., Potter, 1976), many Thai cultural traits
seem consistent with this overall impression.

One anthropologist has noted that Thais have an unusual ability to imitate
and thus to adapt themselves readily to alien cultural influences from the West
or from Japan (Bunnag, 1971:20). In a study of the maintenance of ethnic
boundaries focusing on Thai Muslims, another anthropologist contrasts Islam
and Buddhism as practiced in Thailand. This anthropologist points out that
unlike Islam, Buddhism does not provide either the sources of ethnic identity
or the mechanisms for maintaining sharp ethnic boundaries to any substantial
extent. Thus, Buddhism has little influence on regulating interaction with out-
siders (Prachuabmoh, 1980:267). This is not to deny that Thais have a strong
sense of ethnic identity and a clear view as to what constitutes being a Thai.
Still, the net result appears to be a relative openness on the part of Thais to the
diffusion of ideas and practices initially exogenous to Thai culture, provided
they are seen as meeting an individual's perceived needs. Such a characterization is consistent with the rapid adoption of modern means of contraception
as well as with the rapid acceptance of and aspirations for modern consumer
goods. It might also contribute to the speed at which the small-family norm
has taken hold.

Conclusions

The importance of indigenous cultures in conditioning reproductive behavior
is often acknowledged but rarely given more than cursory consideration outside the anthropological literature. Demographic transition theory, for example, focuses almost exclusively on the role of mortality and socioeconomic

change as the major factors involved in fertility decline. The tendency to ignore the role played by the cultural context has been reinforced by the emphasis on exclusively quantitative analyses of fertility change in the demographic literature, given the difficulties of quantifying cultural variables in a satisfactory manner that would capture both their subtleties and complexities. We believe, however, that it is essential to take Thai cultural traits into account when interpreting the response in reproductive behavior that Thai couples have made to the evolving socioeconomic environment and to the organized efforts to promote and provide family planning by the government and private agencies (see chapter 9).

In the case of Thailand, a deeply entrenched sense and practice of parent repayment involving the provision of both economic and non-economic support to parents in their older ages when the children themselves are adults has not prevented a major reduction in fertility from taking place. Some Thais who opt for small families see this choice as eventually detracting from the amount of support they will receive in their later years but believe that it is a trade-off necessitated by the current socioeconomic environment. Many others, however, believe parent repayment is a function of the quality rather than the quantity of individual children and some even argue that fewer children will be able to provide better financial support, since it will be possible to educate them better. Thus, a potential major cultural barrier to fertility decline has not proven to be the deterrent that many social scientists would have expected it to be.

In a number of ways Thai culture is conducive to reproductive change as a means of adjusting to changing socioeconomic circumstances. Parents and kin exert only minimal influence over the reproductive decisions of younger couples. This is true with respect to mate selection and the timing of marriage, and, more important, with respect to marital reproductive decisions. Thus, a potentially important pronatalist prop to continued high fertility is largely absent. The considerable degree of autonomy accorded women in Thai culture has also facilitated fertility reduction. Women have considerable influence over contraceptive practice and, when decisions are made affecting their reproductive activity, are able to take account of their own interests as the bearers and primary rearers of children. Theravada Buddhism, the predominant religion, and the associated value system stressing the primacy of individual action and responsibility are also conducive to a pragmatic and flexible attitude toward reproductive behavior.

9

The Role of Organized Family-Planning Efforts

As was documented in chapter 5, in terms of proximate determinants, the rapid transition to lower fertility taking place in Thailand can largely be accounted for by the recent dramatic increase in the use of modern contraceptives. Both quantitative and qualitative data make clear that the change in reproductive behavior has been accompanied by a substantial increase in knowledge of contraception and a growing preference for small families among broad segments of the Thai population. The two previous chapters examined the socioeconomic forces behind these trends and the cultural context in which they took place. At issue still is the timing, suddenness, and rapidity with which much of reproductive change occurred. Although some of the socioeconomic changes have been quite rapid, many of the pressures toward reducing family size were already emerging prior to increased contraceptive use and the resultant fertility decline. Moreover, there appears to have been a considerable latent demand for family-size limitation for at least some time prior to major changes in reproductive behavior.

This chapter deals with these issues by focusing on the particular channels through which the diffusion of deliberate birth-control practices spread. Although attention is focused primarily on the formal channels of diffusion, in particular on the organized efforts of the National Family Planning Program, some consideration is also given to the informal mechanisms through which knowledge and acceptance of birth-control methods spread. An explanation of the timing and rapidity of reproductive change, and hence a fuller understanding of Thailand's reproductive revolution, require taking into account the role these mechanisms played in promoting contraception and the nature of the diffusion process through which knowledge and practice of contraception spread.

The role of the National Family Planning Program, which encompasses both governmental and private efforts to promote the use of contraception, is of general interest, both because this type of program is the major means of intervention by which many Third World countries seek to lower their population-growth rates and because of the ongoing debate about whether these programs represent an effective approach to doing so (Simmons and Farooq, 1985; Ness and Ando, 1984). At the heart of the controversy, which has continued virtually since family-planning programs were first instituted in the Third World, are fundamental issues concerning fertility and its determinants. Of particular concern is the extent to which deliberate interventions to provide the means for fertility limitation and encourage their use can have an impact on reproductive behavior independent of the socioeconomic conditions that encouraged greater fertility control and smaller family sizes. At the one extreme are those who believe that the motivation to limit family size can only come about with sufficient socioeconomic development and that once such motivation does arise, the means to control fertility would be found by most couples even in the absence of an organized family-planning program. Their position can be summarized by the slogan raised at the 1974 Bucharest World Population Conference: "Development is the best contraceptive." In contrast, others argue that provision of contraceptives and organized efforts to promote their use can and will have a considerable impact on population change even before the onset of substantial development in other areas. It is increasingly being recognized that the validity of either position may vary with the particular setting and thus understanding the role of organized family- planning efforts within the Thai context is of some importance.

Thailand's National Family Planning Program

During most of the present century, Thailand's official stance on population was pronatalist. As recently as 1956, the government offered bonuses for large families. Following a report by a World Bank economic mission in 1959 recommending that the government seriously consider the adverse effects of high population growth on economic development, officials started to reconsider the government's position. Pressures for a change were reinforced by the interest of several key health officials as well as several influential Thai scholars who had studied demography in the United States. Study committees were appointed and several national population seminars were held to discuss the issue; the first one took place in 1963. In 1964, a pilot project was initiated in the rural Potharam district, approximately 80 kilometers (50 miles) from Bangkok. Results from this project showed considerable receptivity to the practice of contraception among the study population (Institute of Population Studies, 1971a).

In 1968, a unit concerned with population issues was established in the National Economic and Social Development Board and was assigned the task of making a final recommendation to the Thai Cabinet concerning the population issue. Their recommendations, along with efforts of the Ministry of Public Health and the National Research Council, finally led to the adoption by the Thai Cabinet in 1970 of a formal population policy aimed at slowing population growth. An important part of this policy was support to voluntary family planning through an official government program (United Nations, 1979; Rosenfield et al., 1982; Krannich and Krannich, 1980). During this same period of the 1960s and early 1970s, profound shifts in official government positions from pronatalism to antinatalism were taking place in many other countries as well, particularly in Asia (Ness and Ando, 1984). Undoubtedly, policy developments in Thailand were influenced by the changing international climate and can be more fully understood within this broader international context rather than as strictly a national phenomenon.

Despite changes of government, the antinatalist policy remained continuously intact. When a new constitution was drafted in 1974, it explicitly recognized the importance of population matters for the nation's welfare. This recognition was reinstated in the subsequent constitution drafted in 1978. Ever since the official policy was adopted, each successive five-year economic plan of the government has set specific population-growth rates. Each successive target was lower than the previous one. The relative political stability in Thailand has undoubtedly contributed to the continuity of population policy and has been an important condition contributing to the effective functioning of the family-planning program.

With the declaration in 1970 by the Thai Cabinet of an official policy to reduce population growth, the National Family Planning Program was formally established under the auspices of the Ministry of Public Health. A number of steps had been taken prior to 1970, however, that in effect constituted the beginning of a government-sponsored program to promote family planning. In 1965, four major government hospitals in Bangkok opened family-planning clinics. In 1967, the Family Health Research project was started in the Ministry of Public Health and served as the direct predecessor of the National Family Planning Program. As a result of this project, by the time the national policy was declared in 1970, many public health personnel, including doctors, had been trained in family planning. This included personnel in almost all provinces. Thus, an operative program was already in place by the official start of the program and could be rapidly expanded shortly thereafter (Krannich and Krannich, 1980). Since family-planning activities under the jurisdiction of the Ministry of Public Health are integrated into child- and maternal-health services, the program was able to take advantage of the existing extensive infrastructure available for government health services in general.

The Thai program has been unusual both in its willingness to include new methods of contraception and in the development of an innovative distribution system (Rosenfield et al., 1982). For example, since 1966, injectable contraceptives have been used in Thailand. Initially, injectables were dispensed primarily through a missionary hospital in northern Thailand, but starting in 1975, this method was offered by all government hospitals and subsequently offered by some lower-level health outlets as well. The "minilap" sterilization technique was pioneered in Thailand and also utilized in the program. The technique has the advantage of being relatively simple to perform and requiring minimal special equipment. Thus, it can be carried out in areas where physicians have neither the elaborate equipment nor the training needed for other techniques of female sterilization, such as laparoscopy. More recently, a long-acting subdermal contraceptive implant has been introduced into the program on a trial basis (Satayapan, Kanchanasinith, and Varakamin, 1983).

Important innovative concepts have also guided distribution of contraceptives. A postpartum program for providing contraception, namely IUDs and sterilization, to women immediately after they had given birth was instituted in 1966 in Bangkok and later in a number of provincial hospitals and regional maternal and child health centers. The most significant innovation in terms of distribution, however, has been the use of paramedics to dispense methods provided only by physicians. A policy allowing nurses and auxiliary midwives (who in Thailand must be high school graduates with two years of midwifery training) to distribute birth control pills was instituted early in the program and widely implemented by the end of 1971. This had the effect of expanding the number of outlets from which oral contraceptives were available from about 350 doctor-operated government clinics to more than 3,500 health stations, mostly supervised by auxiliary midwives. This expansion occurred primarily in rural areas where health stations staffed by midwives already existed. Thus, not only condoms, which were unpopular among married couples, but also birth-control pills became widely available throughout rural areas by the end of 1971. Pill-resupply functions have since been extended to village health volunteers thus further expanding the network through which rural villagers can have access to modern and effective contraception. In 1983, the Ministry adopted a policy allowing auxiliary midwives to administer injectable contraceptives and started a training program for this purpose. Even before this, however, some provincial-level medical officials had already instituted a similar policy on their own initiative. Paramedics have also been trained to insert IUDs and even to perform sterilizations, but so far on a much smaller scale.[1]

Although the policy to allow paramedics to distribute the pill was a primary factor in expanding the availability of oral contraception, the decision in 1976 to provide the pill free of charge apparently also boosted oral-contraceptive use and ultimately contraceptive prevalence (Knodel, Bennett, and Panyadilok, 1984). Prior to the last quarter of 1976, the Ministry of Public Health had been charging acceptors 5 Baht per cycle of oral contraceptives, 20 Baht for an IUD insertion, 50 Baht for a vasectomy, and 150 Baht for tubal ligation (20 Baht equaled one U.S. dollar at that time). Although these charges were officially voluntary, the vast majority of acceptors paid them. Starting with the last quarter of 1976, a new policy of providing the pill free at all government health outlets and the IUD and sterilization free of charge at all rural outlets was instituted. After that, a marked and sustained increase in the number of pill acceptors occurred without a compensating decline in acceptors of other methods or in commercial sales. Although the policy was not always implemented as stipulated, independent survey evidence indicates that most women who obtain oral contraceptives from a government source do in fact obtain them free, and of those who have to pay, the charge is often less than the former charge of 5 Baht. Rates of contraceptive continuation among pill users increased slightly following the elimination of charges, although the continuation rates have subsequently declined. This decline does not appear to be the result of the free-pill policy since the highest continuation rates were among women who received the free pill.

An extensive international comparative study of national family-planning program effort in Third World countries has recently been carried out by Lapham and Mauldin (1984; 1985). Each country was rated by several knowledgeable persons on thirty items grouped into four general areas: policy and stage-setting activities, service and service-related activities, record keeping and evaluation, and availability and accessibility of services. The ratings refer to the status of the program as of 1982. The Thai program was rated as moderate in terms of overall effort. It ranked relatively high, however, with respect to the availability and accessibility of services, undoubtedly reflecting the innovative approaches that have been used toward distributing services.

Trends in Clients and Program Impact

The particular mix of methods practiced in Thailand as well as the trends in the prevalence of different methods are undoubtedly associated with develop-

---

1. The process is continuing, however. A pilot study conducted during 1979–83 concluded that nurse-midwives can be successfully trained to perform postpartum tubal ligations. As a

ments in the National Family Planning Program. For example, the fact that survey data on prevalence indicate that in rural areas the pill was the most popular method for much of the duration of the program is no doubt related to its wide availability, especially through outlets of the Ministry of Public Health, and, as shown in table 9.1, coincides with the fact that during the last decade the majority of new clients reported by the National Family Planning Program chose the pill (Knodel et al., 1982).[2] The unusually large increases in pill use during seven years following 1976 are probably influenced by the free-pill policy implemented in 1977. The high rates of female sterilization and the fact that it has recently become the most common method are probably related to the increasing emphasis given this method in the national program, especially in more recent years (Thai/U.S. Evaluation Team, 1980; Rosenfield et al., 1982). At the same time, it probably also reflects the maturing of the program: couples who have used temporary contraceptive methods earlier in their reproductive career may more readily accept permanent methods.

The number of new family-planning clients officially attributed to the program (which includes most acceptors to affiliated private programs) has grown annually since its inception almost without exception, increasing from about 225,000 during 1970, the year it was established at full scale, to over 1 million each year since 1979. The figures are somewhat inflated in the sense that persons classified as *new* clients include those switching methods as well as several other categories of persons who were in fact previously using contraception. Nevertheless, these statistics imply that a large proportion of contraceptive users obtain their method from the national program.

A number of studies using different methodologies have attempted to estimate the quantitative impact on fertility of the National Family Planning Program. Although the results vary with the methodology and the assumptions of the particular study, in general they indicate that much of the fertility decline is attributable to the contraceptive practice of program clients. For example, one analysis assessed the impact of the national program on fertility by estimating the number of births averted through use of program-supplied contraception (Khoo, 1979). The range of estimates depended on different assumptions made about potential fertility, the actual amount that fertility was assumed to decline, and the contraceptive continuation rates incorporated

---

result, in 1983 the Cabinet issued a decree permitting the use of trained nurse-midwives for postpartum sterilization services, to be performed under medical supervision (Dusitsin and Satayapan, 1984).

2. The temporary decline in new pill clients in 1973 is probably attributable to a change in the brand of oral contraceptives supplied by the program. The new brand reportedly had more side effects associated with it and, although the problem was quickly corrected, negative rumors about the pill were thought to have taken some time to dissipate (Rosenfield et al., 1982; Research and Evaluation Unit, 1978).

Table 9.1. Number of New Clients (in 1,000s) in Thailand's National Family Planning Program, 1965–84

Year	Total	Pill	IUD	Injectables[a]	Sterilization Female	Sterilization Male[b]	Other[c]
1965–67[d]	129	7	86	n.a.	36	n.a.	n.a.
1968	57	10	35	n.a.	12	n.a.	n.a.
1969	130	61	54	n.a.	15	n.a.	n.a.
1970	225	132	74	n.a.	19	n.a.	n.a.
1971	405	295	86	n.a.	24	n.a.	n.a.
1972	457	328	90	6	33	n.a.	n.a.
1973	422	269	93	10	47	3	n.a.
1974	495	305	90	19	74	7	n.a.
1975	562	345	75	25	83	8	26
1976	665	377	72	73	95	10	38
1977	830	489	75	69	107	19	71
1978	941	558	78	87	124	44	50
1979	1,040	615	78	118	139	35	55
1980	1,121	654	79	150	152	31	55
1981	1,126	635	80	170	149	28	63
1982	1,116	622	84	178	144	23	65
1983	1,183	598	127	206	146	27	79
1984	1,316	582	190	250	165	45	85
1985	1,420	587	185	374	160	37	77

Sources: Rosenfield et al. (1982) and Ministry of Public Health.

Note: In the Thai program, a person is considered a new client if she is obtaining a method from a government outlet for the first time, is switching methods, or has returned after a pregnancy for postpartum contraception. Private-sector organizations submit summaries of new clients, which are incorporated into the NFPP monthly achievement report.

[a] Not officially counted until 1972; McCormick Missionary Hospital in Chiang Mai had a total of 28,000 new users of injectables between 1965 and 1971.
[b] Not officially counted until 1973.
[c] Not officially counted until 1975. These are primarily condom users.
[d] The categories include only women obtaining a contraceptive method at four Bangkok hospitals with postpartum contraceptive programs.

n.a. = not available.

into the model. The results suggest that a reasonable estimate of the national program's effect on births averted would account for close to 80 percent of the decline in the total fertility rate between 1964 and 1975.

Another analysis also based on calculations of births averted but using a somewhat different methodology indicated that about three-fourths of the amount that marital fertility was suppressed in 1975 compared to the 1970 level was attributable to family-planning program clients (Leoprapai and Piampiti,

1982: 192). Both analyses assume no substitution of program methods for non-program methods. Allowance for substitution would reduce the estimated impact of the program. It is not possible, however, to estimate with any certainty the extent to which substitution occurred. At the same time, the estimates also ignore the possibility that new acceptors may be self-selected for higher-than-average fertility and that some birth-control use outside of the program might have been stimulated by program activities. Allowance for these factors would increase the estimated program effect.

A quite different methodology, based on multivariate regression analysis, is employed in yet another study (Chao and Allen, 1984). The approach followed is intended to measure the net impact of the program after nonprogram factors have been simultaneously included, and thus in effect controlled for, in the analysis. Rather than using the number of clients as input data to represent the role of the program, family-planning program expenditure per capita is used. According to the results, 53 percent of the decline in the total fertility rate during 1962 to 1980 and 68 percent of the decline during 1972 to 1980, the period when the program had attained national coverage, are attributable to program activities.

The Sources of Contraception for Current Users

The series of Contraceptive Prevalence Surveys conducted in Thailand are useful in assessing the extent of the government's contraceptive services, independent of the government's official program statistics. Results summarized in table 9.2 show that the large majority of users report a government source as the provider of their current method of contraception. In each survey, more than three out of four women indicated they obtained their method from a government outlet. As might be expected, given the more extensive commercial network and concentration of private clinics in urban areas, the importance of the private sector is greater for urban than for rural women. According to CPS3, the most recent survey, over four out of five rural women and almost two-thirds of urban women reported relying on the government for provision of family-planning services.

The source of contraceptive supplies or services differs considerably according to the method being used, as is evident from table 9.3, which presents results from CPS3. The township (tambol) health stations are clearly the most important source of oral contraceptives for rural women, with more than half obtaining their supply from them. In contrast, urban women are most likely to report buying contraceptive pills in a drugstore. Female sterilization, now the most common method in Thailand, is typically performed in a government hospital for both rural and urban women. District hospitals, which themselves are located mostly in areas classified as rural, play a significant role for rural

Table 9.2. Percent of Current Users of Contraception, by Source of Supply or Service, 1978–84, and by Residence, 1984

Source of contraceptive supplies or service	National			By residence, 1984 (CPS3)	
	1978/79[a] (CPS1)	1981 (CPS2)	1984 (CPS3)	Rural	Urban
Government	77	78	79	83	63
Private	23	22	21	17	37
Total	100	100	100	100	100

Sources: Knodel et al. (1982), Kamnuansilpa and Chamratrithirong (1985).

[a] Excluding provincial urban.

women along with other government hospitals, primarily located in urban places.

Although government outlets are clearly the major source of contraception in Thailand, the private sector also plays a significant secondary role. The importance of the drugstore and other private channels has already been pointed out for pill users, especially in the urban areas. Almost half of rural condom users and the large majority of urban condom users also obtain their supplies through the private sector, particularly drugstores. Private-sector sources account for almost one-fourth of vasectomies in rural areas and almost one-half in urban areas. This is likely related to an incentive program for providers through which private physicians receive a government bonus for each sterilization procedure they perform, whether ligation or vasectomy (Thai/U.S. Evaluation Team, 1980; 1984). Thus, a large number of private-sector sterilizations are, in effect, government subsidized and in some sense, part of the government effort.

Survey results about the source of contraception are likely to reflect some degree of error inasmuch as some respondents may not correctly identify their source. In addition, where responses are imprecise, additional error may be introduced through coding.[3] The problem may be particularly severe in distinguishing some types of private from some types of government sources or in distinguishing drugstores from some other private sources. Thus, the contribution of the category "other private sources" is probably understated.

The best-known private organization providing contraception is Community Based Family Planning Services (CBFPS), now a division of a larger par-

3. Although it is tempting to conclude that the sterilizations attributed to township health centers, which are normally not staffed by doctors, must be errors, this is not necessarily so. Mobile sterilization teams sometimes conduct their procedures at local health centers.

Table 9.3. Percent of Current Users of Contraception According to Source of Supply or Service, Residence, and Method, 1984

	All methods[a]	Pill	Condom	Injectable	IUD	Sterilization Female	Sterilization Male
RURAL							
Government	*83*	*78*	*53*	*74*	*93*	*91*	*77*
Township health station[b]	27	58	34	41	11	1	14
District hospital or station[c]	30	11	14	22	58	44	26
Other government hospital[d]	22	1	4	6	21	46	24
Village health volunteer	2	6	1	0	0	0	0
Other government	3	2	0	4	3	0	13
Private	*17*	*22*	*47*	*26*	*7*	*9*	*23*
Drugstore	7	16	43	1	0	0	0
Clinic or hospital	10	4	2	24	6	9	21
Other private	1	1	2	1	1	0	2
URBAN							
Government	*63*	*37*	*16*	*69*	*91*	*83*	*53*
Township health station[b]	2	5	0	0	4	0	1
District hospital or station[c]	13	20	7	34	17	5	14
Other government hospital[d]	48	11	7	34	69	77	38
Other government	1	0	2	1	0	1	0
Private	*37*	*63*	*84*	*31*	*10*	*17*	*47*
Drugstore	18	49	81	0	0	0	0
Clinic or hospital	17	12	2	31	10	17	29
Other private	2	2	1	1	0	0	18

Source: Kamnuansilpa and Chamratrithirong (1985).

Note: Total percentages for government or private sources may differ slightly from sum of individual categories because of rounding.

[a] Excluding methods not requiring a source of supply or service.
[b] Including midwifery centers.
[c] Including Bangkok metropolitan health center.
[d] Including regional MCH centers.

ent organization, the Population and Development Association (PDA). This organization has received considerable international attention, largely because of its charismatic and publicity-oriented director, who has been a vigorous promoter of family planning in Thailand.[4] The CBFPS program began officially

4. The founder and director of CBFPS and PDA is Meechai Viravaidya. His promotional activities, which have involved public distribution of colored condoms to various visiting dignitaries, and contests to blow up condoms, have been well publicized. As a result, condoms are becoming known as "meechais" among many urban residents.

in 1974 and quickly established a network of village-based agents covering approximately a third of the Thai population (Duhl, 1984). Their agents act as distributors of condoms and oral contraceptives, which they sell at subsidized rates. The distributors retain a small profit from the sales. In Bangkok and several other urban areas, PDA also has family-planning clinics or shops. Besides providing pills and condoms, and in a few urban clinics, injectables, PDA distributors are also instructed to act as referral agents to potential clients who may desire or be suitable for other methods, particularly sterilization. Moreover, PDA has also been active since 1979 in performing vasectomies from a mobile unit, especially in and around Bangkok, and in holding well-publicized vasectomy fairs.

PDA's contribution to the increase in contraceptive use is of interest because of the many accounts in the popular press and family-planning literature attributing a major role to PDA and its director in bringing about Thailand's reproductive revolution (see, e.g., Duhl, 1984; Gupte, 1984; Wirtz, 1981; McBeth, 1984; Krannich and Krannich, 1980).[5] A reasonably accurate estimate of PDA's contribution as a provider of contraception can be derived from the service statistics of the National Family Planning Program (see appendix D). Based on these data, PDA is estimated to account at most for about 5 percent of all users. Thus, PDA has played only a minor role in the provision of contraception within the overall national program, despite popular accounts to the contrary. All evidence available makes clear that the government, particularly through Ministry of Public Health outlets, and not private organizations, is the major provider of contraception on the national level.

Although their direct contribution is small, there are less tangible contributions that have potentially been made by PDA and the other private associations affiliated with the national program, particularly in terms of publicizing birth control, increasing its acceptability both among the general public and within government circles, and perhaps in motivating couples to practice family planning. Although these contributions are more difficult to measure, they should neither be ignored nor overestimated. As discussed in previous chapters, there has been little opposition to contraception among the general public from the start. Its widespread acceptability is rooted in the Thai cultural context, whereas motivation to limit family size arises both from powerful forces of social and economic change currently underway and from a number of conditions that were conducive to creating a latent demand before modern contraceptives were widely available. In addition, informational activities

5. Judging from the results of CPS3, it would seem that few respondents utilize PDA distributors or any other private outlets as their primary source of contraceptive supplies or services. The category "other private" accounts in total for only 1 or 2 percent of pills or condoms in either rural or urban areas; only for vasectomies in urban areas is a larger share attributable to this category. As discussed in appendix D, this is undoubtedly an underestimate.

of private organizations probably have been far more limited than those of the government, which operates through the vast network of health-service facilities, extending all the way down to the pervasive township health station. In the case of PDA, by the time it became fully operational in the mid-1970s, at least some familiarity with contraception was close to universal (see chapter 5). Two methods particularly advocated by PDA, the condom and vasectomy, have been and continue to be relatively unpopular among married couples, but the publicity efforts of PDA have probably improved the public's view about them. Thus, these indirect contributions of private family-planning organizations, although not insignificant, are probably fairly limited. One possible but important exception may be their contribution to fostering acceptability within the government, where reservations and even opposition to promoting family planning have been present among some circles, especially during earlier stages of the national program.

Another private-sector source of contraceptive services deserving comment is the family-planning program associated with the McCormick Christian Hospital in the northern province of Chiang Mai. Limited family-planning services were started in 1963 and were expanded substantially by the end of the 1960s when mobile services, covering much of the province, were initiated. The program is best known for the dominant role played by injectable contraceptives, which were accepted and used successfully by large numbers of women. Even during the first half of the 1970s, after the government program was implemented, the McCormick program accounted for the majority of new acceptors in Chiang Mai Province. The program has also received attention because of the early and rapid fertility decline that occurred in Chiang Mai. There are divergent opinions about the role the McCormick program played in bringing about the fertility decline, though, since fertility appears to have been declining at a substantial pace even when the program was operating on a limited scale during its initial years (Baldwin, 1978; Pardthaisong, 1978, 1986).

Access to Contraception

One result of the National Family Planning Program is that within a relatively brief period of time, contraception became readily accessible to the large majority of the Thai population. In urban areas, the commercial sector, including numerous drugstores, private clinics, and hospitals, combines with government facilities to create high accessibility. In rural areas, commercial channels are far less significant, but accessibility of the rural majority to contraception through government outlets is nevertheless quite favorable. In particular, the program's policy of providing oral contraceptives through township (tambol) health stations and midwifery centers has meant that at least one effective

Table 9.4. Village-Level Indicators of Accessibility to Government Outlets for Contraceptive
Supplies and Sources in Rural Areas, 1971, 1979, and 1984

	1971	1979	1984
Mean distance in kilometers to:			
Nearest health station of any type	6.4	3.5	2.5
Nearest hospital[a]	39.5	36.8	14.4
Mean travel time in minutes to:			
Nearest health station of any type	55	25	n.a.
Nearest hospital[a]	159	96	n.a.
Percent of villages for which nearest health station is:			
Within 5 kilometers	69	83	90
More than 10 kilometers away	19	6	3
Within 30 minutes	53	80	n.a.
More than one hour away	23	8	n.a.
Within 5 kilometers or 30 minutes	72	94	n.a.

Source: 1971 and 1979 data are from the IPS Village-Level Survey as reported in Chayovan,
Hermalin, and Knodel (1984b); 1984 data are from the CPS3 Village-Level Survey and are
unweighted.

Note: Results for 1971 and 1979 are based on a total sample of 64 villages; results for 1984 are
based on 208 villages.

[a] The question about the nearest hospital did not differentiate between government and private
hospitals. However, it is unlikely that more than a very few, if any, of the villages were nearer to a
private than a government hospital.

n.a. = not available.

modern contraceptive is reasonably conveniently available. Moreover, in most
cases, oral contraceptives are provided free of charge at local health stations,
so there is little problem with affordability (Kamnuansilpa and Chamratrithirong, 1985:57). At the district level, besides pills and condoms, health stations often provide IUDs and injectables, and, if a district hospital exists,
male and female sterilization will also be available. Provincial and most other
government hospitals provide the full array of methods at the provincial level.

   Results from the IPS and CPS3 Village-Level Surveys illustrate the remarkable degree of accessibility to government-provided contraception for the
rural population and the improvement in accessibility during the 1970s. Retrospective reports for 1971 and 1979 collected during the IPS survey and contemporary reports for 1984 from the CPS3 survey of that year are summarized
in table 9.4, which includes several selected indicators of accessibility defined
in terms of distance and, when available, travel time to the nearest government outlet of any type through which contraceptives are available.

Even in 1971, the average village was only between 6 and 7 kilometers distance and less than an hour's trip from the nearest outlet. Because of the construction of new health-service outlets during the 1970s and improvements in transportation, by 1979 the nearest government outlet for contraceptives was only 3.5 kilometers away on average and involved less than half an hour's travel time. By 1984, the average distance was reduced to only 2.5 kilometers. The very high accessibility of at least some modern methods of contraception by 1979 is indicated by the finding that well over nine out of ten villages were either within 5 kilometers *or* thirty minutes' travel time from a government outlet by that year. Moreover, even in 1971, only a modest proportion of villages appear to have been relatively inaccessible to government outlets, judging either from the proportions that were more than 10 kilometers distant or the proportion that were more than one hour's travel time away. This high level of accessibility is all the more striking considering it does not take into account either CBFPS village distributors or the recent program of distribution through government village-health volunteers.

In most cases, the nearest outlet is a township health station (or midwifery center), which is usually limited to dispensing pills or condoms. As indicated earlier, a variety of other methods are made available through government outlets at higher levels. Thus, accessibility to a full-service outlet is also of interest. Indicators of access to the nearest hospital are also shown in table 9.4 since all methods, including the IUD, injectables, and sterilization, are generally available at hospitals. Although the nearest hospital is considerably further away than the nearest health center, by 1979 travel time to a hospital from the average village was only slightly more than an hour and a half and thus clearly within a day's round trip. The rapid expansion of the district-hospital network taking place in Thailand in recent years is reflected in the sharp drop in the distance to the nearest one between 1979 and 1984, by which time the average village was within less than 15 kilometers distance. Given that the methods typically sought after at a hospital either require no revisits or revisits at less frequent intervals than is the case with pills, the longer distance and greater time involved in obtaining them are unlikely to be a serious deterrent.

It seems reasonable to assume that the high degree of accessibility to contraception that has characterized Thailand recently has been an important factor facilitating the rapid increase in contraceptive prevalence. There is some quantitative evidence indicating that couples living in villages more accessible to a government outlet for family planning are more likely to practice contraception than couples living in villages that are less accessible, thus indirectly supporting this contention. Information collected in the IPS Village Survey permit the construction of indices representing at least several important dimensions of accessibility (Chayovan, Hermalin, and Knodel, 1984b).

Table 9.5. Percent of Currently Married Women Aged 15–44 Currently Using Contraception,
           by Two Measures of Accessibility to Sources of Contraceptive Supplies or Services,
           1972 and 1979

Measure and degree of accessibility	1972	1979
Index of weighted travel time		
Higher accessibility	22.4	54.7
Medium accessibility	22.6	50.7
Lower accessibility	12.5	37.5
Index of weighted distances		
Higher accessibility	22.7	59.8
Medium accessibility	24.1	45.5
Lower accessibility	11.0	38.1

Source: Chayovan, Hermalin, and Knodel (1984b).

Note: The indices weigh either the distance or travel time from each village to the nearest township and district health station and the nearest hospital by 1, ½, and ⅓, respectively. The
cutting points to determine the three categories under each index for each of the two years were
guided by attempting to have roughly equal numbers of cases in each category. Because of
changes in both distance and travel time between 1972 and 1979, different cutting points were
used for the two years.

Table 9.5 shows the relationship between two of the indices of accessibility,
measured at the village level, and contraceptive prevalence in 1972 and 1979.
One index refers to accessibility as measured in terms of distance; the other
refers to travel time. In both cases, an attempt is made to take into account the
different ranges of services offered through various types of outlets by weighting either the distance or the travel time to the nearest outlet of each major
type (township health station, district health station, and hospital) in a way
that reflects the increasing range of services provided at each higher level of
services.

In both 1972 and 1979, contraceptive prevalence is distinctly lower for
women living in villages that are least accessible to a government service for
contraception than it is for other women, regardless of whether accessibility is
defined in terms of time or distance. In 1972 there was little difference between the higher and medium accessibility categories, but in 1979 both the
distance and time indices show a direct, monotonic relationship with prevalence. These associations do not take into account factors other than differences in accessibility that might be responsible for the observed relationship.[6]

6. A complex multilevel analysis based on a variety of measures of accessibility yielded somewhat puzzling results. For 1979, interactive models showed that several measures of accessibility
had significant effects on contraceptive use among younger women. In an additive mode, all ac-

Nevertheless, they do at least suggest that accessibility facilitates contraceptive practice in Thailand and indirectly support the suggestion that the generally high level of accessibility has been important for the spread of contraception since the start of the government family-planning program.

The Process of Diffusion

The importance of the National Family Planning Program lies not only in the provision of contraception but also in increasing the awareness of the possibility of controlling family size through effective and acceptable means. As survey and focus-group results discussed in chapters 5 and 6 indicate, knowledge of birth-control methods was quite limited prior to the start of the government's efforts to provide contraceptive services. The rapid increase in knowledge of contraception, coincident with implementation of the national program, suggests that information dissemination by the program was probably of considerable significance, whether it occurred through activities explicitly intended to provide information or indirectly through a demonstration effect set in motion by users who obtained their method at a program outlet. In this connection, it is interesting to note that word-of-mouth communication was effective as a way to recruit family-planning acceptors during the early phases of the government's program, when public informational activities were severely restricted (Rosenfield, Asavasena, and Mikhonorn, 1973). For example, in the course of the experimental Potharam project in the mid-1960s, many acceptors learned about the services from friends. Similarly, soon after Chulalongkorn Hospital in Bangkok started providing an IUD service in 1965, thousands of women from three-fourths of all the provinces in Thailand came for IUDs even though the program made no promotional efforts outside the hospital. Many of them chartered local buses or trucks as groups. The informal passing of information person-to-person was apparently responsible (Fawcett, Somboonsuk, and Khaisang, 1967).

The program also attempted to legitimate a preference for fewer children. A number of spontaneous comments were made in the course of the focus-group sessions acknowledging, with approval, the government's policy to promote smaller families and provide contraception. Given the general lack of normative resistance to smaller families among Buddhists, even on the part of the older generation as evident from the focus-group sessions, the legitimation provided by the program's activities may not have been crucial. In the case of the Muslim minority, there appears to be considerably more normative

cessibility measures appeared to have a sizable effect on use for older women but the effects were reduced when other village characteristics, particularly level of electrification, were added to the equations (Chayovan, Hermalin, and Knodel, 1984a).

resistance. It is unclear, however, whether messages from government sources will have much influence on Muslims given their pervasive distrust of a government and their association of the government with Buddhism (Suthasasna, 1985).

Comments by focus-group participants shed light on the shifting source of diffusion of birth-control knowledge. As discussed in chapter 6, most older-generation participants indicated they first learned about birth control through some source connected with the official program. Although many younger-generation participants also cited a government health outlet or worker as their initial source of information, mass media and particularly informal channels of communication were mentioned noticeably more often by them than by older-generation participants. Friends and siblings were a particularly common source of initial knowledge of birth control for younger-generation participants. In a number of instances, they also mentioned that they learned through observing or hearing of someone else obtaining or using birth-control methods.

"[We first learned about birth control] from doctors, hospitals. . ." "and from villagers who got it in hospitals or learned about in hospitals and told us here in the village." (two older men, central region)

"[I first learned about birth control] from the doctors at the hospital. Health workers told us to take pills. Someone had an IUD inserted and told others." (older woman, northeast)

"[I first learned about contraception] when I was just married. I did not dare to consult any other persons [i.e., health personnel] so I consulted my friends first. . . . Those who used to take [pills] told us." "I saw my sister taking pills. I was 19 then. I asked her [what they were]." "We got to know about [birth control] as time passed. . . . Before marriage we saw others taking pills but we didn't know how [to take them]. They said taking these birth control pills would prevent childbirth but I was still ignorant. I saw the midwife give them out. After marriage there was a problem of how to take the pills so I want to ask friends. I went to see the doctor and he gave me the pills." (three younger women, north)

"I heard about contraception from my mother. She had me buy pills for her." (younger man, north)

"I heard about it when [my friend's] mother went to get an IUD. During that time many in the village went to do it." "[That was] a long time ago, about 10 years. The radio station was just being built and the health center began to announce it. It spread to the village. People went from every house." (two younger men, northeast)

"It seems that we learned about [birth control] from inside the village. Most of the time people will talk about it and tell others." (younger woman, central region)

The contrast between the older and younger generation's description of how they learned about birth control illustrates the process by which modern birth-control practice can be rapidly transformed from an innovation emanating from outside the community to a well-established, institutionalized pattern of behavior learned from persons inside the community. The comments made by focus-group participants also indicate how the diffusion process can occur far more rapidly today than it did in the past. With the establishment of the national program, which operated primarily through existing health stations and hospitals, modern contraceptives were introduced throughout rural Thailand. Mass media, particularly the radio, had permeated the countryside by the early 1970s when the program became fully operational, and helped spread the message to virtually every village.[7] Moreover, compared with the initial stages of sustained fertility decline in the West, when withdrawal, abstinence, or clandestine abortion were the major methods, modern methods today are much more visible to others in the community. Users can be seen openly going to obtain services and, in the case of oral contraceptives, may be observed possessing a packet or actually taking their pills. Thus, the potential for a demonstration effect is great and awareness of modern contraceptive methods can diffuse at a very rapid pace compared to the past. If there is sufficient receptivity, as existed in the case of Thailand, use can spread quickly.

Conclusions and Discussion

In Thailand, and indeed in a number of other Third World countries, the abruptness, rapidity, and pervasiveness of recent fertility decline is almost as challenging to explain as the occurrence of the decline itself. Although important shifts have been occurring in the social and economic environment during the period of fertility decline, reproductive change has been so rapid that it would appear to have outpaced most measurable changes in socioeconomic conditions during the equivalent period. The abrupt and rapid increase in deliberate marital-fertility control, at least in much of rural Thailand, can be seen as the result of the sudden introduction of an extensive system of contraceptive distribution within a context where substantial latent demand already existed but where there was little traditional store of knowledge of effective and acceptable means of birth control. Indeed, prior to the recent changes in reproductive behavior, the notion of deliberate family limitation appears not to have been a well-articulated component of the prevailing views held by

---

7. Commercial advertisements in the public mass media of any potentially dangerous medicines or drugs such as oral contraceptives is prohibited by Thai law. Nevertheless, the national family-planning program was permitted to launch a radio campaign throughout the country starting in the early 1970s to explain different methods of modern contraception available through the program. Provincial radio stations frequently played prepared tapes as a public service. Moreover, before this campaign, news-type broadcasts probably contributed information about the development of the government's policy and programs.

most Thais concerning their own reproduction (see chapter 4). In this connection, it is useful to distinguish between the diffusion of information (e.g.,
about modern methods of contraception and the possibility of controlling fertility through their use) and the diffusion of other attitudes and behavior bearing on the other "costs" of fertility regulation—such as approval of the use of
such methods. The potential for rapid diffusion of information would seem to
be considerably greater, given that it requires no change in values. In Thailand, it appears that an important hindrance to fertility decline, at least during
the immediate period prior to organized family-planning activities, was lack
of knowledge of appropriate means of contraception; thus, the potential for
very rapid change in reproductive behavior existed. Moreover, the relatively
homogeneous nature of Thai society probably facilitated rapid diffusion of the
concept of family limitation and knowledge of specific means of contraception once such a process began. This, in turn, permitted the rapid adoption of
birth control practice given the preexisting receptivity to limiting family size.
Such a process can easily outpace social structural change.

Just how fast contraceptive prevalence can rise at the village level once
acceptable means are made known and available is illustrated by the well-
documented case of the northern Thai village of Ban Pong. In 1966, the
village was selected for a pilot project to assess the potential for mobile
family-planning services in rural areas of Chiang Mai Province by McCormick
Hospital, which had recently started offering contraception. A baseline survey determined that only 10 percent of married women in reproductive ages
could mention a modern method of contraception and only 5 percent were
practicing contraception. In 1968, two years after a mobile family-planning
unit started to provide oral and injectable contraceptives in the village, almost
90 percent knew of contraception and prevalence had risen to 37 percent
(McDaniel and Pardthaisong, 1973; Mougne, 1982). This proved to be a
rather accurate harbinger of the very rapid increase in contraceptive use that
characterized the province in subsequent years (Shevasunt and Hogan, 1979).

The coincidence between the timing of the implementation of a nationally
organized family-planning program and the occurrence of both increased contraceptive prevalence and sustained fertility decline in rural Thailand is consistent with the interpretation that the program played an important role in precipitating and facilitating reproductive change. Even in urban areas where
substantial proportions of women reported themselves as already using contraception in 1970, before the program was officially launched, many were
undoubtedly availing themselves of the family-planning services provided by
government hospitals that predated the establishment of the national program.
In rural areas, survey data are quite clear in indicating that only minimal contraceptive use predated the onset of the national program.

It is also significant that despite the powerful forces of social change leading to widespread deliberate limitation of births, no general upsurge occurred in the use of traditional methods, with the possible but unknown exception of massage abortion. In a number of countries in Europe, where withdrawal had been a traditional form of birth control, its practice persisted long after modern methods became available, which indicates that modern methods are not automatically preferred over nonmodern ones (Leridon, 1981). Thus, the lack of any substantial increase in the use of withdrawal in Thailand, despite the strong interest in limiting family size, is probably not simply a consequence of more effective alternative methods being available. Rather, it confirms the lack of awareness and acceptability of the method, as was discussed in chapters 5 and 6. In view of the absence of any tradition of effective nonmodern methods, except among restricted segments of the population, it seems improbable that overall prevalence could have risen to the present level, especially within such a short period of time, solely through the use of such methods, had modern methods remained unavailable.

Whether, in the absence of the national program, the limited number of commercial outlets providing modern contraception to the rural population would have expanded sufficiently to generate a prevalence level equivalent to the level currently prevailing seems unlikely. Obvious constraints would have existed because most modern methods require either trained personnel or licensed drugstores for their provision, and because the monetary costs of contraception affect levels of use among the rural poor, as illustrated by the response to the free-pill policy. Moreover, although increases in induced abortion might have been greater, moral reservations about its acceptability among many in the population and the common perception that abortion, especially when carried out by traditional methods, involved serious health risks would probably have served as important constraints to its widespread use. It is thus unlikely that fertility would have fallen as fast as it did in the absence of the organized efforts to provide modern contraception methods through the National Family Planning Program, despite the considerable socioeconomic changes that pressure couples to want small families.

In brief, any adequate understanding of the timing of Thailand's fertility transition must take into account the crucial role played by the establishment and implementation of the National Family Planning Program. At a minimum, the program has been an important source for the provision of contraceptive supplies and services. Most contraceptive users obtain their methods through government-sponsored outlets and some of those who do not are served through private organizations affiliated with the program and in varying degrees supported by the program. Also important, if more difficult to assess, is the role that the National Family Planning Program played in the spread of information about the possibility of limiting family size through effective and acceptable means of birth control. The family-planning activities of the program have undoubtedly served to increase the observability of what appears initially to have been innovative birth-control behavior, thereby speeding up the diffusion process (Retherford and Palmore, 1983:297–98).

The program can thus be seen as generally facilitating the fertility decline where it had already begun and, in the cases of many individual villages, as probably initiating the widespread use of effective contraceptives that resulted in the curtailment of births. Nevertheless, in the search for an explanation of Thailand's reproductive revolution, an attempt to assess separately the impact of the program divorced from the socioeconomic forces encouraging small families and the cultural milieu within which reproductive decisions are made would be inappropriate. The establishment of a large and efficient family-planning program might not have been possible, for example, without the supportive setting provided by substantial socioeconomic development within a relatively stable political setting and a receptive cultural context. In the real world, all these aspects coexisted. It is the interaction of the program with societal change operating within a particular cultural setting conducive to reproductive change that has resulted in the rapid increase in fertility control and rapid decrease in fertility in Thailand. Recognition of this interplay among all these factors is necessary if a fuller understanding of the changing reproduction of Thai couples is to be achieved.

10

Synthesis and Conclusions: Toward an Understanding of Thailand's Rapid Fertility Decline

Thailand is among a growing number of developing countries that have moved in recent years from an early stage of demographic transition characterized by falling mortality in the presence of high, relatively stable fertility to a later stage in which fertility has also started to decline. In the case of Thailand, the fall in birthrates has been both rapid and pervasive. The available evidence suggests that mortality has been declining since the early decades of this century with a probable interruption associated with the events of World War II. It is also difficult to date precisely the onset of the fall in fertility. Most evidence indicates that the fertility decline started to gain momentum only during the 1960s and, for the rural majority, probably dates largely from the latter part of that decade.

The decline of fertility is primarily attributable to reduced reproductive rates among married couples, with a rising age at marriage contributing only modestly to the change. The reduction in marital fertility was brought about by a massive increase in the practice of birth control among married couples and was accompanied, with some delay, by a substantial, if not proportionate, reduction in family-size preferences. Within only a decade, between 1969 and 1979, marital fertility fell by approximately 40 percent while contraceptive prevalence among married women in their reproductive ages increased from under 15 percent to approximately 50 percent. By 1984, contraceptive prevalence had risen further to approximately 65 percent and, although information

193

on fertility trends during the early 1980s is not completely consistent, most evidence points to a continuing decline. At the same time, the mean preferred family size expressed by reproductive-aged married women fell from almost four to under three children. The momentous scale of the reproductive revolution taking place is apparent in the contrast between the six to seven live births and five to six living children experienced by the average couple only a generation ago and the two-to-three-child families that, according to recent survey evidence, are almost universally preferred by newly married women today. Given the widespread use of contraception, the actual fertility of recently married couples in Thailand is likely to conform reasonably closely to these expressed preferences for small families.

One of the most striking features of Thailand's recent reproductive change has been its pervasiveness. Almost all major segments of Thai society have participated. During the last decade or so, fertility decline and increased use of contraception have been substantial, both in rural and in urban areas, as well as among couples at all levels of educational attainment. Although regional differences have been apparent in the timing as well as the extent of fertility decline, all areas of Thailand had at least started to participate in the fertility transition by the early 1980s. Moreover, differentials in fertility desires and contraceptive use by educational attainment and family income are only modest, reflecting the full participation of the least-educated women and the poorest couples in the move toward smaller families. The one readily identifiable group that appears to be relatively resistant to the changing reproductive patterns is the small Muslim minority, many of whom live in southern Thailand where, to a lesser extent, fertility decline has also lagged among Buddhists. Since Muslims constitute only a very small proportion of the total population, however, their impact on national trends is minimal.[1]

Major Factors Underlying the Reproductive Revolution

An adequate explanation of the timing, pace, and extent of Thailand's fertility decline involves four major interwoven components. First, rapid and fundamental social changes have been taking place that have caused couples increasingly to view large numbers of children as an economic burden. Second, the Thai cultural setting is relatively conducive to the acceptance of deliberate fertility regulation and limitation of family size as adaptations to changing circumstances. Third, a latent demand for effective and acceptable means to

1. There is also some evidence indicating that the fertility of several other groups, also of minor demographic importance, such as the populations living in the most remote areas of the northeastern region and hill tribes in the northwest, was falling more slowly than the rest of the population (ESCAP, 1985a).

control fertility was present among a sizable proportion of couples for at least a generation before the fertility transition began. Fourth, organized efforts to provide modern contraceptive methods, especially through the government's National Family Planning Program, resulted in a pervasive increase in awareness of and accessibility to effective and acceptable means of fertility regulation. Each of these four components is reviewed below.

Social and Economic Change

Interrelated fundamental social and economic changes that intimately influence both the daily lives of Thai villagers and their future plans for themselves and their children have been underway for some time. These changes can be seen as having been responsible, in part, for the latent demand for fertility control that apparently existed prior to the onset of fertility decline and, far more so, as underlying the current desire for small families among couples currently in the reproductive ages. The net result of these changes has been to increase directly or indirectly the monetary cost of raising children, thus making large families far more of an economic burden than in the past. Discussions with older and younger Thais reveal that both generations believe the cost of living in general and the cost of raising children in particular are far greater now than before and that the average couple can no longer afford to have many children. The perceived increase in the general cost of living appears to result from the closely related processes of the spread of the cash economy through extensive market penetration, monetization of daily life, and changing consumer aspirations. Changes in agricultural technology, such as the greater use of fertilizers and pesticides and increased mechanization, have likewise increased the monetary costs of production among the large farming population. Although most Thais probably are experiencing a higher standard of living than in the recent past, they probably feel under even greater financial pressure because of higher expectations and the greater need for money to satisfy what they now consider the basic necessities of work and daily living.

Particularly salient for the perceived increase in the cost of raising children is the cost of education. The cost involved in sending a child just for elementary schooling is felt to have risen, but more significantly, many couples also feel a need to send children for higher levels of education than considered necessary in the past. Providing children with more schooling is seen as the primary mechanism through which families can cope with limited land availability and reduced prospects for making a satisfactory living through agricultural pursuits, not only for themselves but, more important, for their children. Education is seen by most Thais as the main vehicle for social mobility and by the rural majority as a prerequisite for more secure and prestigious jobs outside of agriculture. Moreover, expanded availability of schooling has made the possibility of educating children to higher levels than before an increasingly realistic option.

Changes in what is normatively considered appropriate child care and legitimate needs and demands of children may also have contributed to the perceived increase in child-rearing costs. Rising consumer aspirations, the perceived need for increased education for children, and changing views on child care have all undoubtedly been reinforced by expanded mass media penetration. At the same time that the perceived cost of raising children has risen, children are generally perceived to be less helpful in doing household chores and contributing to the family's economic activities while they are growing up. This is seen in large part as a result of the trend toward increased schooling. It is now common to think in terms of monetary costs when contemplating raising children. The idea that the more children a couple has, the more costly it will be, has come to be an accepted way of thinking.

There remain, of course, a variety of both economic and noneconomic reasons, including both social and psychological ones, why couples still want children even if in limited numbers. Among the most important is the persistence of expectations of what in the Thai context can aptly be called parent repayment, especially in the form of providing comfort and support during the parents' later years. Some shift toward greater monetization of this type of support is occurring. Many Thais currently in the process of family building view a reduction in the amount of support they expect to receive as a necessary price for avoiding the hardship of raising many children. Not all couples, however, see a direct relationship between the number of children they have and the amount of support they will receive later in life. Some perceive the amount of support to be more dependent on how well, rather that how many, children are raised. Others even feel that there is more to be gained with respect to parent repayment from few but better-educated children than from many less well educated ones.

Caldwell (1982) has argued recently that the fundamental issue in demographic transition is the direction and magnitude of intergenerational wealth flows, broadly defined to include cash, goods, services, and a variety of intangibles. Sustained fertility decline is brought about when the net flow reverses from a situation favoring the parents to a situation favoring the children. It is difficult to determine from either the qualitative or quantitative data presently available when, or even whether, such a reversal occurred in Thailand. The focus-group results do make clear that the perceived (and undoubtedly real) monetary costs of raising children have significantly increased while some benefits have decreased. Thus, the results are consistent with a reversal of the wealth flow, at least while the children are still young. However, it remains to be determined if the net flow was upward from children to parents even for earlier generations. Moreover, the views expressed by some focus-group participants that parents will gain better returns in the current socioeconomic setting from having fewer children whom they can afford to educate well than from having more children who are less well educated suggests that even if the wealth flow remained upward, there would still exist a basis for reducing fertility.

The Cultural Setting

In any society, the impact of social and economic change on reproductive behavior is mediated through the cultural setting. Although culture also is not static, there are a number of important and relatively persistent aspects of Thai culture that facilitate the adoption of family-size limitation as a means of adjusting to changing socioeconomic circumstances: the locus of reproductive decisions is largely confined to the couples themselves; female autonomy is relatively high; and Buddhism, the majority religion, is largely silent with regard to reproductive behavior and is associated with an outlook on life that emphasizes individual responsibility.

One of the more important pronatalist props and hence barriers to fertility decline characteristic of many Third World societies is the control or influence over reproductive decisions of younger couples by parents and kin. In Thailand, the influence of parents and kin is notable for its relatively minor extent. Reproductive decisions are generally defined as the domain of the couple themselves with only minimal influence exerted by others. Moreover, a deeply embedded large-family-size norm is absent and older-generation Thais, despite their own high fertility, are generally supportive of the lower-family-size goals now professed by younger couples. The lack of extensive influence of parents and kin over the reproductive decisions of couples fits in with the prevailing expectation that each conjugal unit is largely responsible for the support of its own children. Whereas in some Third World countries, the erosion of patriarchal authority and emerging emotional and economic nucleation of families may be critical for the onset of fertility decline (Caldwell, 1982), nuclear families in Thailand have been relatively independent for at least several generations.

The considerable degree of female autonomy in Thailand has also contributed to the extent and pace of fertility decline. Women have considerable influence over birth-control practice and family size, enabling them effectively to take into account their own stake as the bearers and rearers of children. Indeed, most birth-control methods practiced in Thailand depend on the woman's initiative. Moreover, women's autonomy in many other spheres of life exposes them almost as fully as men to the forces of social and economic change that are now underway.

Buddhism, as practiced in Thailand, also poses no major barriers to the reduction of family size. Although abortion is opposed on religious grounds, there is little opposition to contraception. More generally, Thai Buddhism emphasizes the primacy of individual action and responsibility, thus contributing to the general flexibility and tolerance associated with Thai culture. In such a cultural setting, modern tastes, attitudes, and behavior, including changing reproductive patterns, can take hold with relative ease. Moreover, the relative cultural homogeneity of Thai society as manifested by a common religion and language shared by the vast majority facilitates the rapid diffusion of ideas made possible by modern mass-media and transportation systems. In the case of family-planning practices, an extensive government-service network also contributes to this process. The fact that Thailand's reproductive revolution encompasses a broad social and economic spectrum is undoubtedly related to this cultural homogeneity.

In contrast, both the religious views and some associated cultural traits of the Thai Muslim minority are considerably less favorable to the practice of birth control and the small-family norm. Their notably lesser participation in the reproductive change taking place is possibly in large part attributable to these cultural differences, including the fact that a substantial proportion of Muslims speak a Malay rather than a Thai dialect. While minority status and differences in socioeconomic conditions may also play a role, the distinctive reproductive behavior of the Thai Muslims helps underscore the importance of Thai Buddhist culture in facilitating the ongoing fertility transition among the Buddhist majority.

Prior Latent Demand for Fertility Control

Evidence from surveys, focus-group research, and observations by a number of anthropologists indicates that effective means of birth control were by and large neither known nor practiced among the large majority of rural Thais until recently. An exception may be awareness of abortion by traditional massage, a potentially effective method but one probably limited to extreme circumstances because of its lack of moral acceptability and the perceived dangers to physical health involved. Withdrawal and lengthy or periodic abstinence are largely alien concepts to Thai culture and, to the limited extent known, considered unsuitable as methods of birth control except among Thai Muslims and some southern Thai Buddhists.

Despite the absence of effective practice of birth control in the past, there appears to have been considerable interest in limiting family size and spacing children for at least a generation prior to the onset of fertility decline. The existence of a latent demand for fertility regulation can be deduced from comments to this effect made by older-generation Thais in the course of focus-group discussions and from their reports of having tried unsuccessfully to control fertility through ineffective means, particularly traditional herbal medicines. Many older Thais say that fertility was high in their generation because the means of effective birth control were unknown or lacking. These ineffectual attempts to control fertility may have preconditioned couples with respect to the adoption of modern effective methods once the latter became known and accessible. Such latent demand for effective birth control arose out of concerns that couples, and particularly women, had about the burdens inherent in childbearing and child rearing as well as from some of the same social forces that became more pronounced during the subsequent period of fertility decline. In addition, reductions in infant and child mortality during the decades preceding the onset of fertility decline increased the number of surviving children and thus, in effect, raised family size above what had traditionally been the case.

Organized Promotion of Family Planning

The existence of considerable latent demand for fertility regulation helps explain why organized efforts to provide contraception to couples throughout the country met with such immediate success. The development of these efforts began during the mid-1960s. By 1972, following implementation of a policy to distribute oral contraceptives and condoms through the existing system of local-level health stations, the program had in effect penetrated the entire countryside. Information-dissemination activities associated with the program helped spread awareness of birth-control methods, legitimized concern over large numbers of children, and reinforced desires for fertility control. The onset of the fertility decline in the rural areas coincides with the development of the National Family Planning Program, the major supplier of contraceptive methods to rural Thais. The establishment of organized activities to promote family planning thus helps explain the timing and extent of fertility decline in rural Thailand. Although some reduction in rural reproductive rates may have preceded such organized efforts, it is unlikely that the same massive and rapid increase in awareness and practice of effective means of birth control could have occurred in their absence.

All four factors are interrelated and thus are best understood in conjunction with, rather than in isolation from, each other. The socioeconomic changes played an essential role in creating the initial and continued receptivity to limitation of births. The organized efforts to promote and provide contraception facilitated, and in some localities helped initiate, the widespread use of birth control. The effect was often immediate because of the existing latent demand for effective fertility-control methods and the absence of cultural barriers to reproductive change. Thus, it is the interaction between socioeconomic change and an organized program, both operating within a cultural setting conducive to reproductive change in which a latent demand for birth control already existed, that resulted in the rapid and extensive decline of fertility. Under such circumstances, the conventional debate over the relative importance of family-planning programs versus socioeconomic development in bringing about a fertility reduction poses an inappropriate question.

Implications

Many of the socioeconomic forces discussed in connection with the ongoing fertility transition in Thailand are operating in varying degrees throughout the Third World. Other countries have also mounted organized efforts to promote and provide contraception. Given the success of the Thai family-planning program, it is legitimate to ask if there are operational lessons to be learned from the Thai experience for other countries where organized efforts have met with less success. More generally, given the various commonalities between Thailand and other developing countries, it is interesting to consider the extent to which the dynamics of the Thai fertility transition are relevant for understanding reproductive behavior elsewhere.

With respect to the family-planning program, the most important features seem to be the availability of a wide selection of methods and the extensive distribution system made possible by allowing paramedical personnel to provide oral contraceptives and, to a limited extent, other methods that more typically are reserved for distribution by physicians. Compared to most other countries in the Asian and Pacific region, the Thai program is notable for the full range of modern contraceptive methods it offers (Economic and Social Commission for Asia and the Pacific, 1985b). The low cost or free provision of methods to clients, and, in the case of sterilization, the modest subsidies to the provider, may also have contributed to the program's success. Any of these aspects should be advantageous to programs elsewhere as well.

As we have stressed, however, both the effects of socioeconomic change on reproductive decisions and behavior and the impact of the family-planning program are mediated through a cultural setting particular to Thailand. In addition, relative political stability has facilitated the effect of and continuous operation of the program. Moreover, latent demand for fertility control appears to have been unusually strong prior to the establishment of the program.

Given the importance of these other, nonprogrammatic factors to the success of the family-planning program, it would be unrealistic to assume that duplication of the specific features of the Thai family-planning program, when applied in a different cultural or political context, will necessarily meet with equally successful results. Thus, expectations about the achievements that can be attained by applying the lessons of the Thai program are best kept modest. For example, in cultures where female seclusion is the norm and where, unlike Thailand, women cannot move freely beyond the family compound or village, a clinic-based family-planning program would have much more limited success and a much more extensive effort to reach clients through domiciliary services might be required. Similarly, in cultures where reproductive decision making is considered to be more a matter for the husband or other kin, concerns about the pain of childbearing and burdens of child rearing specific to women might not translate into latent demand and even less into an active effort to practice fertility control. In an unstable political environment, disruptions in policies or services could seriously impede the functioning of a family-planning program. At the same time, the extent of differences between Thailand and other developing countries in terms of latent demand, cultural features, and political stability is also variable. Thus, in some settings the operational lessons are likely to have considerably more relevance than in others.

With respect to understanding the process of fertility transition in the Third World, several implications can be drawn from the Thai experience. These are largely impressionistic and are offered more as hypotheses deserving further consideration than as firm conclusions based on the evidence presented in the present study.

1. Ideational change influencing reproductive behavior and changing perceptions of the socioeconomic environment encouraging small families can outpace the major socioeconomic structural shifts conventionally associated with development. A broad-based fertility transition is taking place in Thailand while the population is still predominantly rural and agricultural. To be sure, socioeconomic differentials in contraceptive use, family-size preferences, and fertility rates exist, and better-educated urban couples adopted modern fertility behavior somewhat earlier than the rest of the population. Nevertheless, a general receptivity to the changes in reproductive patterns that are now taking place is also evident among most major segments of the population. Indeed, minimally educated, low-income rural couples have been full participants in the fertility transition during the last decade and a half. Being urban, relatively wealthy, and better educated have clearly not been prerequisites for adopting modern reproductive behavior in Thailand. The broad-based nature of reproductive change and the temporary nature of many of the differences among socioeconomic groupings suggest that such differences may have little significance (Cleland, 1985).

As a result of the rapid expansion of the communications and transportation networks made possible by minibuses, transistor radios, and, more recently, television, and the rapid market penetration of the countryside, villagers are being exposed to a wide range of modern fashions, consumer goods, and life-styles. In response, aspirations, tastes, and attitudes, as well as perceptions of the socioeconomic environment, can change rapidly, without large proportions of the population moving to urban areas or moving out of the agricultural sector of the economy. As Freedman (1979) suggested, under modern conditions, ideas and aspirations for a different way of life can easily transcend actual changes in objective conditions and serve as an important motivating force to lower fertility. Consequently, changes in reproductive behavior may only be loosely linked to actual changes in socioeconomic structure and occur at a far more rapid pace. A similar conclusion has been reached by Cleland (1985) in an extensive review of results from a number of countries that participated in the World Fertility Survey program. Moreover, the socioeconomic changes that are taking place simultaneously help to reinforce the newly emerging attitudes and behavior regarding fertility. The processes of market penetration, monetization of daily life, and rising consumer aspirations are surely proceeding in Thailand and much of the rest of the Third World at a far more rapid pace than was true in the historical experience of the West. A combination of the far wider range and greater numbers of products to sell as well as the availability of modern mass communications and transportation networks largely accounts for the accelerated pace. Not only can the awareness and availability of the means of modern fertility control spread rapidly through these channels, but so can the perceptions of a changed socioeconomic environment that underlie increased motivation to use them.

2. Cultural factors may be important in facilitating or inhibiting the fertility decline largely independent of the level of socioeconomic development. Conventional statements of demographic transition theory have generally focused on the role of mortality and socioeconomic change as major causes of fertility decline. The importance of the cultural context has been largely ignored. This continues to be the case in much of the recent research on fertility change in developing countries, particularly by those studies that are primarily quantitative in nature. The Thai experience suggests that the cultural context may have important explanatory significance for fertility decline.

There is a similarity between many of the socioeconomic forces in Thailand and those that are thought to underlie the recent fertility decline in an area of South India being intensively studied by Caldwell and colleagues (Caldwell, Reddy, and Caldwell, 1982a,b, 1984b). In the Indian case, organized family-planning efforts also appear to have promoted awareness and increased availability of contraception (in this case, primarily sterilization). As in the case of Thailand, however, the Muslim minority is not fully participating in the reproductive changes, pointing again to the importance of culture as a mediating factor. Although there are considerable differences in social and cultural milieu among Hindus in South India and Buddhists in Thailand, these groups may have more in common with each other than with many societies in the Middle East, Africa, or Latin America. One of the challenging areas for future research on the fertility transition will be to determine more precisely which particular constellations of cultural traits promote and which hinder a fertility response to the common forces of socioeconomic change and the organized efforts to promote fertility control that are characterize most of the developing world.

3. The spread of family-limitation practices can precede and possibly influence declines in preferred family size. The Thai experience suggests that two related but nevertheless conceptually distinct processes are involved in the fertility transition as it is taking place in a number of developing countries. The predominant feature of the initial stage is a switch from a situation in which deliberate birth control within marriage is largely absent to one in which a critical minority of couples initiate family-limitation practices. Fertility begins to decline because of preexisting latent demand and does not require an accompanying attitudinal change in preferred family size. After a brief period, these increases in birth-control practice and changes in the views of couples about the possibility and appropriateness of family limitation may themselves stimulate reductions in desired family size, thereby contributing to further increases in contraceptive use and further declines in fertility. Such a sequence of events is consistent with the survey data presented for rural Thai women, which show attitudinal changes appear on average to lag behind behavioral changes. In urban areas, where contraceptive use was already moderate at the time of the first survey, this possible initial stage may have already been passed.

The fact that fertility desires in Thailand were lower than actual fertility prior to the onset of fertility declines is not exceptional. Surveys in a many other developing countries also revealed a similar situation at a time when contraceptive knowledge, accessibility to acceptable techniques of birth control, and probably even awareness of the concept of family limitation were often minimal among large proportions of the population (Mauldin, 1965). Under such circumstances, changes in the propensity to translate family-size preferences into appropriate behavior may be more important than changes in the preferences themselves (Cleland, 1985). Key determinants of this propensity could well be a spreading awareness of the possibility of effective family limitation and the introduction of the means of modern birth control to the population at large through family-planning organizations or informal channels.

At the initial stage of fertility decline, couples may be more interested in simply being able to exercise some effective control over fertility to keep family size moderate rather than to limit children to a small number. However, once the concept of deliberately controlling family size becomes more common and examples of couples who initially practice birth control become widespread, smaller family-size preferences may seem both realistic and desirable. This initiates the second process involved in the fertility transition: the crystallization and reduction of desired family size. Thus, in the early stage of the fertility transition, fertility desires may respond to, among other things, the spread of family-planning practices rather than just vice versa. As the transition proceeds, both processes occur concurrently and are probably mutually reinforcing. As long as the decline in desired fertility keeps ahead of the decline in actual fertility, increases in the demand for family-planning services will continue to be generated.

4. Deliberate intervention through organized family-planning programs can have a substantial impact on facilitating the fertility transition in a receptive setting. The development of a vigorous and innovative family-planning program in Thailand appears to have played an important role in bringing about rapid fertility decline. As discussed in connection with the programmatic lessons, this does not imply that family-planning programs will necessarily have important impacts in all settings. However, it is plausible in situations such as in Thailand, where latent demand already existed and where major cultural barriers to the practice of birth control or family limitation are lacking, that the introduction of a family-planning program resulting in publicity for the idea of family limitation and providing reasonably accessible services can be substantial and complement considerably the socioeconomic forces that change perceptions about the desirability of large families.

Assigning an important role to organized family-planning efforts in explaining the timing and pace of fertility decline is not contradictory to stressing the importance of socioeconomic change in creating or intensifying demand, including latent demand, for smaller family sizes. The types of socioeconomic change that have led the vast majority of Thai couples to perceive small families as the only reasonable choice in the present-day environment have been going on for some time. Although the pace and nature of such changes have undoubtedly altered over time, it seems unlikely that such alterations could explain in themselves the sudden discontinuity in reproductive behavior that marked the relatively abrupt onset of fertility decline, especially in rural areas. Thus, the instigation of organized efforts to promote and provide contraception can be viewed as a precipitating factor in a number of situations where socioeconomic change helped predispose the population toward fertility reduction and continued to reinforce and strengthen demand for smaller families after the process got underway.

There is sufficient reason to expect the continuation of fertility decline for at least some time to come in Thailand. Current fertility levels are above those that would yield reproductive levels consistent with the rapidly emerging consensus on a two- to three-child family. There is also little evidence to suggest that the forces of socioeconomic change underlying the decline in fertility are spent. Most of the changes discussed are continuing and many may well intensify in the future. For example, the penetration of the countryside by television, undoubtedly the most potent of all the mass media, is still only at an early stage but is proceeding rapidly. The family-planning program continues to be active and access to modern, effective means of birth control is increasing. Travel to existing outlets is easier and new outlets are being created or old ones upgraded to provide a wider variety of methods. Moreover, the almost universal desire for spacing births, evident from both focus-group and survey results, is only recently being realized to any substantial degree through contraceptive use. Thus, it is likely that sufficient momentum still exists to lead to further decreases in desired family size, increases in contraceptive practice, and reductions in fertility.[2] At the same time, the fact that very few Thais express a desired family size of fewer than two probably sets a reasonably well defined limit on the extent to which fertility will decline in the foreseeable future. The dominant preference for at least one child of each sex may also contribute to establishing a lower limit on how far fertility will fall. Nevertheless, if actual and desired fertility converge in the not too distant future at a level only moderately above two children per couple, Thailand will have achieved a remarkable transformation in reproductive behavior in a very short period of time. The substantial fertility reduction that has already taken place has occurred in the absence of coercive measures and without the need for introducing major incentives or disincentives into the family-planning program. Such a record is clearly an enviable one among Third World nations and underscores the importance of achieving an understanding of Thailand's reproductive revolution.

2. It is noteworthy, however, that the mean preferred family size did not decline further between 1981 and 1984, according to CPS2 and CPS3, the two most recent surveys. For example, among recently married women (i.e., married less than five years), preferred family size was 2.4 children in both surveys. This is consistent with the suggestion that the floor on fertility decline, at least in the intermediate run, may be somewhat above the replacement level.

Appendices

References

Index

Description of Sample Surveys

Much of the quantitative analysis presented in this book relies on results from a series of national sample surveys conducted between 1969 and 1984. In this appendix, a brief description is provided for the surveys that served most frequently as data sources.

The National Longitudinal Study of Social, Economic, and Demographic Change (LS1 and LS2)

The Longitudinal Study, as it is usually referred to, was conducted by the Institute of Population Studies, Chulalongkorn University. It actually consists of a total of four separate surveys done in two rounds. Interviews were conducted in a sample of rural households in April and May 1969 and in a sample of urban households a year later. These two surveys make up the first round of the study and are referred to jointly as LS1. The second round of the study consists of reinterviews as well as additional new interviews for the rural sample in April and May 1972 and for the urban sample a year later. Together they constitute LS2. Both ever-married women and household heads (predominantly male) were interviewed in both rounds.

In both LS1 and LS2, the urban population was defined as living within officially designated municipal areas and the rural population was defined as living outside these areas. The rural sample included 45 villages in 15 districts. The urban survey included 32 sample blocks in Bangkok-Thonburi (the capital and only metropolitan area) and 24 sample blocks in provincial towns. This reflects the fact that well over half of the urban population resides in the capital. The villages and city blocks covered were identical for both rounds with the exception of three villages that had to be dropped from the rural sample because of insurgency activities. In order to preserve the cross-sectional nature of the second round, these villages were replaced by three other villages in another district in the same province. For all other villages or blocks, houses selected in the first-round sample were retained in the second round. In addition, a selection of new respondents was also interviewed to compensate for loss to follow-up and growth in the number of households between the two rounds. Thus, the second-round samples were designed both to allow for longitudinal analysis and to preserve the cross-sectional nature of the samples.

Results for the country as a whole can be approximated by combining the results of the rural and urban phases of each round. Since different sampling fractions were used to select the rural and urban samples, it is necessary to appropriately weight the results of each sample when combining them. This is accomplished by assigning the urban sample a weight of 1 and the rural sample a weight of 7. No account is taken of the fact that for each round the rural and urban phases occurred one year apart, but this should be borne in mind when interpreting the results. Additional details about the Longitudinal Study are provided in several publications (Institute of Population Studies, 1971b; Prachuabmoh, Knodel, and Pitaktepsombati, 1973).

Survey of Fertility in Thailand (SOFT)

In 1975 the Survey of Fertility in Thailand (SOFT) was conducted under the auspices of the World Fertility Survey. Responsibility for the survey was shared jointly by the Institute of Population Studies at Chulalongkorn University and the National Statistical Office. Both ever-married women and household heads (mainly male) were interviewed. The bulk of the interviewing of SOFT took place during April and May 1975. The sample consisted of over 4,000 households in both rural (nonmunicipal) and urban (municipal) areas selected from 267 clusters (234 villages in 78 districts of 34 provinces, 4 rural districts that are part of the Bangkok metropolis, and 29 urban blocks, 14 of which were in Bangkok). The result was approximately an equal probability national sample. Some minor weighting of sample clusters is necessary when processing results from SOFT to compensate both for small original deviations from equal probability and for differential nonresponse. A detailed description of the sample design and survey is available from the first country report (Institute of Population Studies and National Statistical Office, 1977).

The National Survey of Family Planning Practices, Fertility, and Mortality (NS)

The National Survey was conducted in 1979 by the Institute of Population Studies, Chulalongkorn University, with interviewing concentrated in April and May. A description of the sample and methods is available in the summary report (Institute of Population Studies, 1981). Rural and urban in the NS was defined in terms of municipal and nonmunicipal areas. The sample was somewhat unusual in design as it attempted to draw some respondents from the villages or city blocks included in the earlier LS2 samples and other respondents from new sample areas. In those LS2 sample areas selected, an attempt was made to reinterview former respondents from the previous survey. Some, but not all, of the villages and blocks that had been part of the LS2 sample, as well as a number of new villages and blocks, were included. In the LS villages, lists of LS2 households were used in order to locate households with previous respondents. The sample design was such that in most LS villages all of the LS2 households were targeted for interview. However, attrition through death and migration reduced the number available. To make up for this loss, these households were replaced through a sampling of reserve LS villages in different districts or provinces. The NS sample design also called for interviewing a number of new households in some of the LS villages, plus new households in the new sample areas selected for the survey. In the urban LS areas, the sampling fraction was much smaller than that used in LS2. This resulted in the selection of only a relatively small proportion of the former LS households for reinterview. For this reason, there was no need to select new households in the urban LS areas and the small number recorded in this category was composed of new households living in houses formerly occupied by LS2 households.

As a substantial portion of the sample is made up of households purposely selected because they took part in LS2, the NS sample does not provide a representative cross section of the current national population. One result of the sampling procedure is a skewed age distribution, as members of LS2 households tended to be older than the average. Thus, among ever-married women in the reproductive ages, those toward the end of the childbearing span are somewhat overrepresented relative to younger women. Because of the unusual age distribution of the NS sample, when comparisons are made with results from other surveys for variables that are likely to be influenced by age, it is useful to control for age either directly or through age standardizations.

The total NS sample consisted of 2,579 households: 2,144 in rural areas and 435 in urban areas. The sample covers 60 rural villages in 21 districts of 18 provinces (8 villages, although officially rural, are within the boundaries of the Bangkok metropolis). The urban portion of the sample derives from 56 blocks, of which 32 are located in Bangkok and the remainder in 13 provincial towns. The rural and urban portions of the sample were self-weighting. Both household heads and ever-married women were interviewed.

The Contraceptive Prevalence Surveys (CPS1, CPS2, and CPS3)

The Research Center of the National Institute of Development Administration (NIDA) conducted the first two Contraceptive Prevalence Surveys under contract with Westinghouse Health Systems. The Institute for Population and Social Research (IPSR) at Mahidol University joined NIDA to conduct the third survey which was done independently of Westinghouse Health Systems. For all three rounds, the Family Health Division of the Ministry of Public Health in Thailand provided collaborative consultations. All Three Contraceptive Prevalence Surveys were designed to provide information that would assist family-planning program administrators in determining the progress of family-planning efforts. They thus differed in purpose and, to some extent, in content from the other surveys due to their more "applied" orientation.

CPS1

Fieldwork for the first survey, CPS1, took place from November 1978 through January 1979. A detailed description of the sample and methods is provided in the final report of the results (Suvanajata and Kamnuansilpa, 1979). Unlike the other surveys, single as well as ever-married women were interviewed for CPS1. The total sample consisted of 4,025 women (including 1,032 single women). The rural portion of the sample was selected by procedures parallel to those used to draw the SOFT sample. A major concern in drawing the rural sample was to increase comparability with SOFT. Thus, the provinces selected for the CPS1 sample were drawn from the list of 34 provinces included in the SOFT rural sample (excluding Bangkok). From each of the selected provinces, one district was drawn from those included in SOFT, whereas the other was independently and randomly selected from those not included in SOFT. The final sample consisted of women from 136 villages located in 34 districts of 17 provinces.

The urban portion of the CPS1 sample was drawn entirely from the Bangkok metropolis, treating it in its entirety as urban. Provincial urban areas were excluded entirely from the CPS1 sample. The proportion of the total CPS1 sample that comes from the Bangkok metropolis is approximately equal to the proportion of Thailand's population that lives in areas officially classified as urban (including provincial urban areas). Examination of results suggests that the use of a sample from the Bangkok metropolis in CPS1 to represent the entire urban population of Thailand has little effect on the representativeness of the sample on the national level. Comparison of results from the urban sample of CPS1 with those from the urban samples of the other surveys, however, is more hazardous; potential incomparability should be borne in mind when interpreting findings.

CPS2

The second Contraceptive Prevalence Survey (CPS2) was conducted in 1981 from March through June with interviewing concentrated in April and May. The sampling procedures employed in CPS2 were designed to yield a self-weighting nationally and regionally representative sample. Unlike CPS1, the sample of CPS2 covered only ever-married women. A detailed description of the sample and methods is provided in the country report (Kamnuansilpa and Chamratrithirong, 1982).

The total sample of CPS2 comprised 7,038 ever-married women aged 15–49. Multistage sample techniques were employed to select both rural and urban sample phases. The procedure used to select the rural portion of the CPS2 sample paralleled those in CPS1 (which in turn was drawn from the list of 34 sample provinces in SOFT). In addition to the 17 provinces covered in CPS1, seven more provinces were randomly selected, with probability proportional to size from the remaining provinces. Two districts were selected from each of the sample provinces. One of the two districts in each of the 17 provinces covered in CPS1 was randomly selected from the two districts covered in the first round; the other was randomly selected from the remaining districts. Next, in each selected district, two townships were drawn. In the districts that were also selected in CPS1, one of the two townships was the same as the first round. In the new provinces, each township was new. In the next step, two villages were randomly selected from each township drawn in the previous stage. In the township that was selected in the first round, the two villages were the same as in the first round. The final rural sample of CPS2 consisted of 5,823 ever-married women from 192 villages of 96 townships, 48 districts, and 24 provinces.

The urban sample of CPS2 was drawn from the Bangkok metropolis and provincial municipal areas separately. Thus,, the urban portion of CPS2, unlike that of CPS1, is representative of all of urban Thailand and not just the Bangkok metropolis. Interviewing yielded a total of 765 respondents in the Bangkok metropolis and 450 in provincial urban areas.

CPS3

Fieldwork for the third Contraceptive Prevalence Survey (CPS3) was carried out from April through July 1984. The sampling procedures employed were designed to yield both a nationally and regionally representative sample and followed a multistage sampling scheme similar in most respects to CPS2. Unlike the previous rounds, however, the design was based on a weighted sample scheme. To maximize comparability and for the purpose of trend analyses, all provinces selected in CPS2 were included in the sample. In addition, two purposively selected provinces with Muslim majorities were also included. The same total of 24 provinces, plus Bangkok, as in CPS2, were treated as the national sample in CPS3. The two specially selected Muslim provinces are excluded from analyses intended to be nationally representative.

The total size of sample in CPS3 was 7,576 ever-married women aged 15–49. Among these 7,576 sample cases, 317 were from the special purposively selected Muslim provinces, leaving only 7,259 cases to be employed as the national sample. The number of respondents is more or less equal for each of the four major regions and Bangkok. The sample design of CPS3 requires weighting of data in order to obtain nationally and regionally representative results. Details of both the sampling scheme and weighting procedures are provided in the country report (Kamnuansilpa and Chamratrithirong, 1985).

Concluding Comments on Surveys

There are several problems in involved when making comparisons across these series of surveys. Particular caution is required when comparing the urban portions of the samples. This is true for two reasons. First, the number of urban respondents is quite small in the cases of SOFT, NS, CPS1, and, to a lesser extent, CPS2, since these surveys were intended to be self-weighting with respect to the rural and urban sectors of the population. Second, the universes from which the urban samples were drawn were not uniform with respect to the inclusion of provincial urban areas and the Bangkok metropolis and, in case of the latter, the surveys differ with respect to whether all or only part of the area is treated as urban. In particular, the urban sample for CPS1 was drawn exclusively from the Bangkok metropolis and excluded provincial urban areas. Moreover, in all three rounds of CPS, the Bangkok metropolis is treated as urban in its entirety, whereas certain areas of it are defined as rural in LS1, LS2, SOFT, and NS. In cases where the rural and urban sectors of the sample were based on differing sample fractions, results for the total sample are appropriately weighted. Note should be made, however, that in the case of LS1 and LS2, there was a year's lag between the rural and urban phases. National estimates for LS2 are thus based on a combination of the 1969 rural sample with the 1970 urban sample, and LS2 on a combination of the 1972 rural sample with the 1973 urban sample.

Another problem relates to the unusual age distribution of NS. As pointed out above, the difficulties created by this can be minimized by controlling or standardizing by age when appropriate.

Finally, since the data from the surveys are derived from samples, the results necessarily incorporate some degree of sampling error and only approximate national parameters.

Study Design and Discussion Guide for Focus-Group Component

As indicated in chapter 2, our focus-group research was designed to facilitate a comparison between modal pre- and post-fertility-decline situations in Thailand. A total of twenty-three sessions were held in all major regions and Bangkok; the sessions consisted of six younger women's, six younger men's, six older women's, and five older men's groups. The number of participants and a summary of their characteristics are presented in table B.1 for each of the focus groups.

Three criteria were used to guide our recruitment of older-generation participants: preference was given to those who were over age 50, had at least five children surviving childhood, and had no more than an elementary-level education. Since there is little evidence of rural fertility declining before the second half of the 1960s (Retherford et al., 1979), persons over age 50 in late 1982 or early 1983, when the focus-group sessions were conducted, would either have been close to the end or already have passed out of their reproductive years by the start of the fertility transition. Concentrating on older persons with at least five children ensured a contrast with the reproductive experience typical of couples currently in the process of having families. Information from previous studies suggested that such older participants would be reasonably typical of the generation who bore their children just before the onset of the fertility transition in rural Thailand. For example, according to the rural round of LS1 in 1969, six to nine live births and five to eight living children were the most commonly reported numbers by rural women in their forties. About half of all such women reported numbers in these ranges. Furthermore, only a very small minority of older, or even younger, rural Thais has progressed past an elementary education.

In recruiting younger-generation participants, preference was given to married women under age 30 and married men under 35 who wanted no more than three children and had not exceeded that number, and who had no more than an elementary education. In addition, to ensure a personal reference point against which they could contrast their own low fertility goals, they

215

Table B.1. Number and Characteristics of Focus-Group Participants

| | | A. Older generation | | | | | | | | |
| | | Age | | | Years of schooling | | | Living children[a] | | |
Sex of group	Total N	45–54	55–64	65+	0–3	4–7	8+	2–4	5–7	8+
Central										
Men	7	0	1	6	5[b]	2	0	0	5	2
Women	8	1	6	1	3	5	0	1	4	3
Northeast										
Men	9	2	7	0	1	8	0	2	5	2
Women	8	3	5	0	2	6	0	1	4	3
North										
Men	8	3	2	3	5	3	0	1	5	2
Women	8	2	4	2	8	0	0	0	4	4
South, Buddhists										
Men	7	1	3	3	1	4	2	0	3	4
Women	7	4	2	1	2	5	0	1	0	6
South, Muslims										
Men	7	3	3	1	2	5	0	0	5	2
Women	8	4[c]	4	0	8	0	0	0	4	4
Bangkok[d]										
Women	6	4	2	0	4	2	0	0	4	2

themselves were to have come from families of typical pretransition size (five or more children).

Some deviations from the preferred criteria were accepted to facilitate formation of a group. Moreover, because of occasional misunderstandings on the part of persons helping with the screening process, older-generation participants were sometimes selected on the basis of the number of children born rather than the number of children surviving childhood.

Older-generation participants were on the average 59 years of age (58 for women and 60 for men). Younger-generation participants were 27 years old on average (26 for women and 28 for men). About three-fourths of the older-generation participants reported having between five and nine children. Although it is not possible to distinguish in all cases those who reported children ever born from those who reported surviving children, in either case the numbers would be within the modal range for the generation completing childbearing just prior to the fertility transition. Among the younger-generation participants, only one wanted more than three children and over half wanted no more than two. The groups for both generations were relatively homogeneous and typical in terms of educational background.

Sex of group	Total N	Age			Years of schooling			Desired number of children		
		0–24	25–29	30+	0–3	4–7	8+	1	2	3
Central										
Men	8	0	6	2	0	8	0	1	3	4
Women	7	2	4	1	0	6	1	1	4	2
Northeast										
Men	8	0	7	1	0	8	0	0	5	3
Women	8	2	5	1	0	8	0	0	5	3
North										
Men	7	0	4	3	1	6	0	2	5	0
Women	7	2	5	0	3[e]	4	0	3	4	0
South, Buddhists										
Men	8	0	3	5	0	8	0	0	2	6[f]
Women	9	1	7	1	0	9	0	0	3	6
South, Muslims										
Men	7	0	7	0	0	6	1	0	0	7[g]
Women	7	6	1	0	0	7	0	0	0	7
Bangkok[d]										
Men	6	4	2	0	0	6	0	2	4	0
Women	11	9	2	0	2	9	0	0	7	4

B. Younger generation

[a] In some cases, children ever born is all that is known. For the northeast, the number of children surviving until age 5 is given.

[b] Includes one participant with unknown education.

[c] Includes one woman under 45.

[d] Rural migrants in construction sites; no older-generation men's group was held.

[e] Includes one participant with unknown education.

[f] Includes one participant who has four children but wanted only three.

[g] Includes one participant who wants to have four children.

Since the selection criteria were not designed to yield groups representative of the entire spectrum of reproductive experience, our sample differs in certain ways from the overall population. Perhaps most important, older-generation Thais with fewer than five surviving children are largely excluded, and thus couples who experienced a high rate of child loss, those who may have practiced effective family limitation, and the subfecund are underrepresented. Nevertheless, since participants were all members of village communities for all or most of their lives, they were likely to have been aware of the attitudes and behavior of others in the community regarding many of the dimensions covered in the discussions and presumably were able to act as informants about their generation's situation in general. Given our interest in gaining qualitative insights into the fertility-transition process, we believe the advantages of a purposive design involving modal groups outweigh those of attempting to form a statistically representative sample.

All sessions followed more or less the same discussion guidelines, which encompassed topics gleaned from what we judged to be the most promising hypotheses about fertility transition as embodied in the current literature and in our own thinking. Some modifications in the topics discussed were made over the course of the project in accordance with the experience gained from prior sessions. In constructing the guidelines, we considered the ordering of questions to be important. For example, we first asked an open-ended question about the reasons for the intergenerational fertility differences and only asked about particular factors afterward to enable us to distinguish factors mentioned spontaneously from those cited after the moderator introduced them. We deliberately deferred the discussion of birth control until after the discussion of reasons for the change in family size, since we wished to determine whether availability of contraceptive methods spontaneously arose as a reason for the intergenerational fertility differences.

Discussion Guidelines for Focus-Group Sessions

Note: Unless otherwise indicated, an item was included in both the older- and younger-generation focus-group sessions. Items included only in the older-generation sessions are preceded by "O" while those included only in the younger-generation sessions are preceded by "Y".

A. *Introduction*

  Reason for session—to learn about family and children in Thailand
  Need your help
  Open expression of opinions encouraged
  Session will be tape-recorded
  Confirm names
  Warm-up questions (on topics unrelated to major concern)

B. *Marriage*

  Age at marriage of a randomly chosen respondent (or two)
  What is a good age at marriage for sons? Why?
  What is a good age at marriage for daughters? Why?

C. *Change in family size*

   O   Number of children of respondents

   O   Do respondents think their children will have fewer children than they had themselves?

   O   Why the difference? (Probe both why respondents had more and why younger-generations are having fewer.)

   O   Is this a general change? That is, do most younger couples want fewer children than their parents had?

   O   Is that good or bad?

   O   Will having fewer children improve the younger couple's chance to live better?

   O   Is the availability of consumer goods now greater than formerly?

   O   Do you think this affects the number of children younger people want today?

   O   Is more education necessary today than when you were growing up?

   O   Do you think this affects the number of children younger people want today?

   O   Do children nowadays help more or less around the house than in early days?

   O   Do you think this affects the number of children younger people want today?

   Y   How many children do you want? (ask about 2–3 persons)

   Y   How many brothers and sisters do you have? (ask about 2–3 persons)

   Y   Did the older-generation generally have larger families? Why?

   Y   Why did your parents have more children?

   Y   Why do respondents want fewer children than their parents had?

   Y   Do most young people want few (2–3) children only? Why?

   Y   Do some young people still want many children? Why?

   Y   What are the expenses involved in rearing children?

   Y   Are these expenses related to the number of children you want? In what way?

   Y   Do children today need more or less education than when you were growing up?

   Y   Does this affect how many children you want?

   Y   Do children today help with work more or less than before?

   Y   Does this affect how many children you want? Do you prefer sons or daughters? Why?

D. *Birth control*

       If a couple wants no more children, what can they do to prevent having more? (Probe for specific methods.)

Is birth control practiced widely today? How about in your village?
How can you have only the number of children you desire?
Who should decide about family planning? The husband or the wife?
What could couples do to stop having children twenty or so years ago
before modern methods were available?
Did couples ever practice abstinence? Withdrawal?

Y   Do younger couples still practice these two methods? (If no) Why not?

O   If you could have controlled the number of children, would you have
had fewer children or would you have wanted the same number you
had?

Y   Do you think that if your parents could have controlled the number of
children, they would still have had a large number of children? Why?
When did you first learn about birth control?
From what source of information? Which was the most important?

O   Did people in the past send out children to live with others? Why? To
whom?

O   Is this done today? Under what circumstances?

Y   Do some people send out children to live with others? Why? To
whom?
Do some people use abortion to prevent births?
Have you ever heard of anyone who ever had an abortion? Why did
they have it?
How widespread is abortion today? How about in your village?
Does the number of abortions differ from earlier times? How? Why?

E. *Child spacing and childbearing*

Is there anyone who got married and did not have a child immediately?
Why?
Is it better to have a child right after marriage or to wait? Why?
Is it better to space children or to have them in quick succession? Why?
Does breastfeeding a child help delay the next pregnancy? How?
After giving birth, how long should husband and wife wait before
resuming sex together?

Y   What is a good age for the wife to finish childbearing? Why?
Should married couples stop having sex together when they get old?
When should they stop? Why?

F. *Support in old age*

O   Expectations of respondents regarding support and help from children. In what ways (economic/noneconomic)?

O   What kind of help are you receiving?

Y Expectations of respondents' parents regarding support and help from children. In what ways (economic/noneconomic)?

Y What kind of help have you given your parents already?
   For children who are not residing in this village and are working elsewhere, do they help their parents? If so, in what way?

O Has the extent of help children give parents in old age changed? How so?

O Is the type of help changing? How?

Y Expectations of respondents regarding support and help from own children. In what ways (economic/noneconomic)?
   Is it important to have children to care for you in old age?

O Will the younger-generation receive less help since they will have fewer children? Why or why not?

Y How do respondents reconcile desire for few children with expectations of support in old age?

Y What do you expect your children to do when they grow up?
   If your land is not enough to give a sufficient amount to each of your children, how do you plan to divide it?

G. *Child survival*

Do many children or babies die today because of serious sickness? Comparison with earlier times.

O Did people in your village worry much about losing children?

Y Do people in your village worry much about losing children?
   Is it necessary to have more children than you want in case one dies?
   Did you ever have another child to replace one that died?

H. *Reproductive decision making*

Who has primary responsibility for deciding on number of children? (Husband/wife/others)? Why?
Have you ever discussed desired number of children with spouse?
Does he/she agree with you on desired number?
In case of disagreement who makes the final decision?
If husband and wife disagree about how soon to have a child after marriage or how many children to have, whose opinion should prevail? Why?
Have you ever discussed with anyone else (besides your spouse) about how many children you should have, or when to have children?

O Have you ever discussed with your children how many children they should have, or when they should have children?

O   Do your children agree with you? Do parents generally advise their children on this matter?

Y   In general do people consult others (such as parents, friends, relatives, etc.) about how many children you should have or when to start having children?

Supplementary Evidence on Fertility Trends and Levels

Since the collection of fertility data was restricted to married women in many of the sample surveys, they serve more appropriately as a basis for estimating marital fertility than total fertility. A convenient summary measure of marital fertility is provided by an age-standardized general marital-fertility rate. This measure expresses the number of births per year per 1,000 currently married women aged 15–44 after standardizing for age. More specifically, the age standardization is calculated by multiplying marital-fertility rates for each five-year age group of women by the national age distribution of currently married women as recorded in the 1970 census. Age standardization is useful in the present case because of substantial differences in the age distribution of currently married women included in the various samples. Results based on the major national sample surveys are presented in table C.1 by rural-urban residence. Rates based both on births occurring one-year and on births occurring two-years before the survey are shown whenever possible.

For unknown reasons, rates based on a two-year period before the survey are generally lower than those based on a one-year period. Trends, however, are quite similar. The results show a dramatic decline in the national level of marital fertility between the end of the 1960s and the end of the 1970s. However, the results do not indicate a continuation of the decline through the 1980s. In fact, the rates based on the 1981 and 1984 surveys are both higher than those based on the 1978 and 1979 surveys. Although a leveling off or even a genuine increase in marital fertility may actually have taken place, sampling error and differences in the questions and approaches used to derive these rates may mask a continuing downward trend. The increase between CPS1 and CPS2 appears to be an artifact of changes in sample coverage. The CPS2 sample incorporated all the sample provinces included in CPS1 plus an additional set of provinces to expand the sample. When fertility rates are calculated for CPS2 but limited only to those provinces covered in CPS1, fertility rates are virtually identical for the two surveys, with the CPS2 rate actually slightly lower. Evidence presented below on the percent pregnant and the open

Table C.1. Age-Standardized General Marital-Fertility Rates by Residence

Year of survey	Survey	Based on births one year prior to survey			Based on births two years prior to survey		
		National	Rural	Urban	National	Rural	Urban
1969/70	LS1	282	298	209	245	258	185
1972/73	LS2	251	260	200	217	224	179
1975	SOFT	223	227	193	206	211	179
1978	CPS1	172[a]	170	—	—	—	—
1979	NS	170	173	154	164	162	173
1981	CPS2	186	186	188	—	—	—
1984	CPS3	183	183	178	173	170	180

Sources: National Research Council (1980); Knodel et al. (1982); Kamnuansilpa and Chamratrithirong (1985); and original tabulations including some providing revisions to previously published figures.

Note: The national age distribution of currently married women as recorded in the 1970 census serves as the basis for the age standardization.

[a]Excluding provincial urban.

birth interval based on the same surveys as well as vital registration data all point to a continuing fertility decline. In addition, a substantial increase in contraceptive prevalence including a shift toward permanent methods, took place at the same time (see chapter 5). Regardless of whether or not fertility decline has slowed since the end of the 1970s, it is clear that the rates shown for CPS2 and CPS3 represent a major decline from the levels of fertility prevailing at the end of the 1960s.

A narrowing or even reversal of the rural-urban difference in marital fertility is clearly evident from the series of surveys. The first survey, LS1, indicated that rural marital fertility was substantially above urban levels. This difference generally declines with each successive survey and by the time of the 1984 CPS3, there is little difference. The two-year rates based on CPS3 actually show urban marital fertility to be higher than rural marital fertility. The fact that the total fertility rates for the equivalent period based on CPS3 (see table 4.1) show a difference in the opposite direction reflects the lower proportions married in urban than rural areas (see chapter 5). These nuptiality differences do not directly influence marital-fertility rates.

Additional information on recent fertility trends is provided by data on the percent currently pregnant and the mean interval since last birth. Since some women may not recognize or may hesitate to report an early pregnancy, the reported percent pregnant is undoubtedly underestimated. However, if the bias is relatively constant over time, it should reflect the trend in fertility. The

Table C.2. Percent Pregnant and Mean Open Interval by Residence, Currently Married Women
        Aged 15–44, Standardized for Age

Year of survey	Survey	Percent pregnant			Open interval		
		National	Rural	Urban	National	Rural	Urban
1969/70	LS1	15.3	16.2	12.2	31	28	49
1972/73	LS2	14.3	14.9	10.7	36	34	50
1975	SOFT	11.8	12.2	9.7	43	41	53
1978	CPS1	10.1[a]	10.0	—	49	49	—
1981	CPS2	9.1	8.5	11.9	51	52	50
1984	CPS3	8.6	8.6	8.8	56	57	55
Percent change 1969/70–1984		−44	−47	−28	+81	+104	+12

Note: The national age distribution of currently married women as reported in the 1970 census
serves as the basis for the age standardization.

nationally reported percent pregnant from the series of sample surveys for
which this measure is available decline steadily with each successive survey,
as shown in table C.2. The declines are substantial in both rural and urban
areas. Particularly noteworthy is the fact that nationally the percent of respondents reporting themselves as pregnant in CPS2 and CPS3, the two most
recent surveys, continues to fall, suggesting a continuation of the fertility decline rather than a cessation as implied by the marital-fertility rates reported
above.

The percent pregnant is less satisfactory for measuring rural-urban differences because urban women, who in general are better educated, may more
readily recognize pregnancy at an early stage and, in addition, have better access to medical facilities and drugstores and hence to pregnancy tests. The
higher percentage of urban as compared to rural women reporting themselves
pregnant in CPS2 and CPS3 may reflect such a difference rather than a genuine fertility differential. Nevertheless, it is noteworthy that if the CPS2 results
are ignored, the pronounced rural-urban differential in percent pregnant evident at the time of the earlier surveys contracts considerably over time, disap-
pearing by the time of CPS3. This probably reflects the more rapid fertility
decline among rural women and agrees with the disappearance of the rural-
urban difference in marital fertility.

The mean open interval, defined as the number of months since last birth, is
also shown in table C.2. Although a straightforward interpretation of the open
interval is not possible because of the series of biases to which it is subject, it
has been found on a cross-national basis to show very similar rank orders to
those of total fertility (Hanenberg, 1980). The fact that the open interval in-

creased steadily between each successive survey, including CPS2 and CPS3, the two most recent ones, is again consistent with a decline in marital fertility continuing through the early 1980s. Most of the increase in the open interval is attributable to the rural population with little change in the urban areas with the result that the rural-urban differential has disappeared. These findings, together with those on the percent pregnant, help support the conclusion that marital fertility has declined substantially in Thailand, and that this decline has been particularly pronounced among rural women. However, unlike the marital-fertility rates, they also suggest that fertility of married women has continued to decline since the end of the 1970s.

Additional evidence supporting a continuation of fertility decline into the 1980s is provided by vital registration data. The registration of births within Thailand is known to be incomplete but the degree of underregistration is uncertain. Various estimates have been made, including several based on the Surveys of Population Change which were designed to measure the degree of completeness. The estimates of the extent of underregistration during the 1960s and 1970s range from about 15 to close to 30 percent and show no consistent trend of improvement during this period (National Research Council, 1980).

Table C.3 presents total fertility rates based on birth-registration data from the Ministry of Public Health. General fertility rates (births per 1,000 women aged 15–49) are also shown for the country as a whole and the major regions. Results have been adjusted for 20 percent underregistration, a level consistent with several of the recent indirect estimates (National Research Council, 1980). No allowance has been made for either changes in the amount of underregistration or for regional differences, about which little is known. Given the uncertainty about the exact level of completeness, the levels shown should be considered only approximate. The major value of these results, however, lies in the trend they show. Of particular interest is the fact that they indicate a continuing fertility decline into the early 1980s at the national level, and in all regions except the south. Unless the degree of completeness of birth registration was deteriorating, which seems unlikely, the trends should be genuine even if the exact levels are uncertain. If the degree of underregistration was improving, the actual declines may have been greater than shown.

It should be noted that rises in the age of marriage during the period shown (see chapter 5) would contribute to declines in the total fertility and general fertility rates. Thus, the fact that total and general fertility declined does not strictly contradict a leveling off of marital fertility. It is extremely unlikely, however, that age-of-marriage changes would be sufficient to account for all or even most of the apparent declines.

Table C.3. Total Fertility Rate (TFR) and General Fertility Rate (GFR) Based on Birth-
Registration Data, Adjusted for 20 Percent Underregistration

Date	National		Regional GFR			
	TFR	GFR	Central[a]	North	Northeast	South
1977	4.26	143	132	115	163	158
1978	3.94	133	129	107	148	149
1979	3.89	133	125	107	148	153
1980	3.71	129	119	107	144	152
1981	3.51	121	116	98	135	147
1982	3.46	120	113	100	126	153
1983	3.30	114	109	93	118	152
Percent change 1977–83[b]	−23	−20	−18	−19	−28	−4

Note: Registration data are from the Division of Health Statistics, Ministry of Public Health.
Denominators are from the 1981 official population projections of the Working Group on
Population Program.

[a] Includes Bangkok.

[b] Based on rates calculated to more decimal points than shown and thus can differ slightly from
calculations based on rates as shown.

Estimating the Contribution of PDA to Contraceptive Prevalence

According to the published results of CPS3, only 0.5 percent of contraceptive users in Thailand in 1984 report that a Population and Development Association (PDA) outlet or distributor provided them with their current method (Kamnuansilpa and Chamratrithirong, 1985:56). More specifically, the following percentages of current users of specific methods reported a PDA office or distributor as their source; 0.9 percent of rural contraceptive pill users and 1.4 percent of urban pill users; 2.4 percent of rural condom users and 0.0 percent of urban condom users; 0.4 percent of rural injectable users and 0.0 percent of urban injectable users; and 0.2 percent of rural vasectomy users and 7.1 percent of urban vasectomy users. Results from surveys such as CPS3, however, are very likely to understate PDA's real share. PDA distribution points may sometimes be misreported in surveys as drugstores, since some PDA distributors operate out of small shops, or as township health stations, since the distinction between a government and private-sector source may have little relevance for the village client. In addition, because government outlets usually provide pills and condoms free and PDA distributors charge for supplies, some villagers may use PDA distributors only as a backup for government outlets rather than as a regular source. Under such circumstances, respondents would be unlikely to mention PDA as a source. Clients may also misreport the PDA mobile vasectomy unit as a government mobile unit. Thus, there are a number of compelling reasons for suspecting that CPS3 results seriously understate PDA's share.

Fortunately, there is another source of information that can serve as the basis of a more accurate assessment of PDA's contribution to overall prevalence. Since PDA activities in the area of contraceptive services are considered as part of the National Family Planning Program, with PDA obtaining most of its contraceptive supplies from the government, program-service statistics include data on the number of monthly pill cycles distributed through PDA as well as the number of male sterilizations performed by PDA. Information on the share of condoms or injectables provided by PDA are not available. However, condoms are rather insignificant as a method of contraception among married couples and the number of clients provided injectables by PDA is likely to be very small, as it is limited to only a few urban clinics.

PDA's share of pill cycles distributed and vasectomies performed is shown in table D.1. The data on pill cycles are shown from 1975, by which time the Community Based Family Planning Services network of village distributors was actively being established. Vasectomy activity is shown since 1979, the year PDA began its mobile-clinic program. From 1975 until 1980, it is possible to express PDA's contribution to the provision of pills in terms of the share of virtually all pill cycles distributed in Thailand, including most commercial distribution. The Ministry of Public Health, through an independent auditing firm, collected information on the commercial distribution of oral contraception from a number of leading drug companies. The data are not complete, since not all companies complied with the request for information. Moreover, the particular constellation of companies included in the statistics varies somewhat over time. Also, data refer to distribution to sales outlets rather actual sales. Nevertheless, the information probably includes the bulk of commercially distributed pills. More recent data is available only for cycles distributed by the government and private organizations associated with the National Family Planning Program.

Although both sets of figures show that PDA's importance as a source for oral contraceptives is considerably greater than indicated by CPS3 results, the contribution is still modest, generally under 15 percent of program cycles and under 10 percent of all cycles, including commercially sold ones. The PDA share of vasectomies is somewhat larger, especially since 1981, reaching almost 30 percent of all vasectomies reported to the program in 1983. Since the start of the PDA vasectomy program, the organization has been responsible for an average of 15 percent of all reported vasectomies. Given that private doctors who perform vasectomies are eligible for the government-sponsored bonuses referred to in chapter 9, the vast majority of all vasectomies are likely to be included in the program statistics.

Based on this information, in combination with prevalence data, it is possible to estimate roughly the contribution of PDA to overall prevalence. According to CPS3, 31 percent of married couples in which the wife was aged 15–44 relied on the pill in 1984 and 7 percent relied on male sterilization. If we assume that PDA was the source for about 10 percent of the pill users (allowing for the share of the unknown contribution of the commercial sector) and 15 percent of those relying on vasectomy, this would account for about 4 percent of all users [(0.10 • 31 percent) + (0.15 • 7 percent)]. Perhaps a maximum of another 1 percent of users obtained other methods, mainly condoms or injectables, from PDA. Adding this extra 1 percent to the 4 percent of users who obtain contraceptive pills or vasectomies from PDA results in a total of 5 percent as the share of all contraceptive users nationally who use PDA as their source of contraceptive supplies or services.

Table D.1. Percentage of Pill Cycles Distributed during 1975–84 and Percentage of Vasectomies Performed during 1980–84, by Source of Service

| | Pill cycles | | | | | | | Vasectomies | | |
| | As percent of all cycles distributed, including commercial sector | | | | As percent of NFPP cycles only | | | As percent of NFPP vasectomies | | |
	NFPP excluding PDA	PDA alone	Commercial	Total	NFPP excluding PDA	PDA alone	Total	NFPP excluding PDA	PDA alone	Total
1975	56	3	41	100	95	5	100	n.a.	n.a.	n.a.
1976	59	8	33	100	88	12	100	n.a.	n.a.	n.a.
1977	66	7	27	100	90	10	100	n.a.	n.a.	n.a.
1978	64	9	27	100	88	12	100	n.a.	n.a.	n.a.
1979	63	9	28	100	87	13	100	100	0[a]	100
1980	68	11	21	100	86	14	100	89	11	100
1981	n.a.	n.a.	n.a.	n.a.	86	14	100	82	18	100
1982	n.a.	n.a.	n.a.	n.a.	84	16	100	80	20	100
1983	n.a.	n.a.	n.a.	n.a.	86	14	100	71	29	100
1984	n.a.	n.a.	n.a.	n.a.	87	13	100	84	16	100
All years[b]	63	8	29	100	87	13	100	85	15	100

Source: National Family Planning Monthly Activity Reports and Price Waterhouse Audit of Commercial Pill Distributors.

Note: NFPP = National Family Planning Program; PDA = Population and Development Association.

[a] Less than 0.5 percent.
[b] Excludes years for which data are not available.

n.a. = not available.

230

References

Anderson, Peter. 1983. The reproductive role of the human breast. *Current Anthropology* 24(1):25–45.

Aneckvanich, Phasuk. 1979. Status of women in Thailand. M.A. thesis, American Univ., Washington, D.C.

Arnold, Fred et al. 1975. The value of children: A cross-national study. vol. 1. Honolulu: East-West Population Institute.

Arnold, Fred, Robert Retherford, and Anuri Wanglee. 1977. The demographic situation in Thailand. Paper no. 45. Honolulu: East-West Population Institute.

Arnold, Fred, and Chintana Pejaranonda. 1977. Economic factors in family size decisions in Thailand. World Fertility Survey, Survey of Fertility in Thailand. Report no. 2. Bangkok: Institute of Population Studies, Chulalongkorn Univ.

Arnold, Fred, Chintana Pejaranonda, and Minja Kim Choe. 1985. Provincial level fertility estimates, 1965–79: An application of the own children method. *Subject Report* no. 4. 1980 Population and Housing Census. Bangkok: National Statistical Office.

Arnold, Fred, and Nasra Shah. 1984. Asian labor migration to the Middle East. *International Migration Review* 18(2):294–318.

Back, K. W. 1967. New frontiers in demography and social psychology. *Demography* 4(1):90–97.

Baldwin, George. 1978. The McCormick Family Planning Program in Chiang Mai, Thailand. *Studies in Family Planning* 12:300–313.

Blanchard, W., ed. 1958. *Thailand: Its People, Its Society, Its Culture*. New Haven, Conn.: Human Relations Area File Press.

Bongaarts, J. 1978. A framework for the proximate determinants of fertility. *Population and Development Review* 4:105–32.

Bongaarts, J. 1982a. The fertility-inhibiting effects of the intermediate fertility variables. *Studies in Family Planning* 13:179–89.

Bongaarts, J. 1982b. Fertility determinants: 1. Proximate determinants. In John Ross, ed., *International Encyclopedia of Population*. vol. 1. New York: Free Press, 275–79.

Bongaarts, J. 1983. The proximate determinants of natural marital fertility. In R. A. Bulatao and R. D. Lee, eds., *Determinants of Fertility in Developing Countries*, vol. 1. New York: Academic Press.

Bongaarts, J., and Jane Menken. 1983. The supply of children: A critical essay. In R. A. Bulatao and R. D. Lee, eds., *Determinants of Fertility in Developing Countries*, vol. 1. New York: Academic Press.

231

Bongaarts, J., and R. Potter. 1983. *Biology and Fertility Behavior: An Analysis of the Proximate Determinants*. New York: Academic Press.

Bunge, F., ed. 1981. *Thailand: A Country Study*. Washington, D.C.: U.S. Government Printing Office.

Bunnag, Jane. 1971. Loose structure: Fact or fancy? Thai society reexamined. *Journal of the Siam Society* 59(1):23.

Calder, Bobby. 1977. Focus groups and the nature of qualitative marketing research. *Journal of Marketing Research* 14:353–64.

Caldwell, John C. 1980. Mass education as a determinant of the timing of fertility decline. *Population and Development Review* 6:225–55.

Caldwell, John C. 1982. *Theory of Fertility Decline*. New York: Academic Press.

Caldwell, John C. 1985a. Micro approaches: similarities and differences; strengths and weaknesses. Mimeographed paper.

Caldwell, John C. 1985b. Strengths and limitations of the survey approach for measuring and understanding fertility change: Alternative possibilities. In John Cleland and John Hobcraft, eds., *Reproductive Change in Developing Countries*. Oxford: Oxford Univ. Press, 45–63.

Caldwell, John C., P. H. Reddy, and P. Caldwell. 1982a. Demographic change in rural south India. *Population Development Review* 8:689–727.

Caldwell, John C., P. H. Reddy, and P. Caldwell. 1982b. The determinants of fertility decline in India. Unpublished manuscript.

Caldwell, John, P. H. Reddy, and Pat Caldwell. 1984a. The micro approach in demographic investigation: Toward a methodology. Paper presented at the IUSSP Seminar on Micro-Approaches to Demographic Research, Canberra, Australia, 3–7 September 1984.

Caldwell, John, P. H. Reddy, and Pat Caldwell. 1984b. Investigating the nature of population change in south India. Paper presented at the IUSSP Seminar on Micro-Approaches to Demographic Research, Canberra, Australia, 3–7 September 1984.

Caldwell, John, P. H. Reddy, and Pat Caldwell. 1986. Periodic high risk as a cause of fertility decline in a changing rural environment: Survival strategies in the 1980–1983 South Indian drought. *Economic Development and Cultural Change* 34:677–702.

Chamratrithirong, A. 1980. Nuptiality in Thailand: A cross-sectional analysis of the 1970 census. Paper no. 69. Honolulu: East-West Population Institute.

Chamratrithirong, Aphichat, and Chintana Pejaranonda. 1984. Levels, trends and differentials in mortality in Thailand. Paper presented at the National Seminar on ASEAN Morbidity and Mortality Differentials Studies in Thailand. Bangkok, 1–3 November, 1984.

Chao, Dennis N. W., and Karen B. Allen. 1984. A cost-benefit analysis of Thailand's family planning program. *International Family Planning Perspectives* 10(3):75–81.

Chayovan, Napaporn, Albert Hermalin, and John Knodel. 1984a. The impact of accessibility on contraceptive use in rural Thailand. Paper no. 51. Bangkok: Institute of Population Studies, Chulalongkorn Univ.

Chayovan, Napaporn, Albert Hermalin, and John Knodel. 1984b. Measuring accessibility to family planning services in rural Thailand. *Studies in Family Planning* 15(5):201–21.

Chayovan, Napaporn, and John Knodel. 1985. Improving the collection of village-level data: An experience from Thailand. In John Casterline, ed., *The Collection and Analysis of Community Data*. Voorburg, The Netherlands: International Statistical Institute.

Cho, L. J. 1973. The own-children approach to fertility estimation: An elaboration. International Population Conference, Liége, 1973. vol. 2:263–78. Liége, Belgium: International Union for the Scientific Study of Population.

Cleland, John. 1985. Marital fertility decline in developing countries: Theories and the evidence. In John Cleland and John Hobcraft, eds., *Reproductive Change in Developing Countries*. Oxford: Oxford Univ. Press.

Cleland, John, Jane Verral, and Martin Vaessen. 1983. Preferences for the sex of children and their influence on reproductive behavior. *WFS Comparative Studies*, no. 27. Voorburg, The Netherlands: International Statistical Institute.

Coale, Ansley J. 1969. The decline of fertility in Europe from the French Revolution to World War II. In S. J. Behrman, L. Corsa, Jr., and R. Freedman, eds., *Fertility and Family Planning*. Ann Arbor, Mich.: Univ. of Michigan Press.

Coale, Ansley J. 1983. Recent trends in fertility in less developed countries. *Science* 221(4613):828–32.

Cook, Michael, and Boonlert Leoprapai. 1974. Some observations on abortion in Thailand. Paper presented at the Asian Regional Research Seminar on Psychosocial Aspects of Abortion. Katmandu, Nepal. November 1974.

Coombs, L. C., and Te-Hsiung Sun. 1981. Familial values in a developing society: A decade of change in Taiwan. *Social Forces* 59:1229–55.

Curtin, Leslie B. 1982. Status of women: A comparative analysis of twenty developing countries. *Reports on the World Fertility Survey*, no. 5. Washington, D.C.: Population Reference Bureau.

Davis, K. 1955. Institutional patterns favoring high fertility in underdeveloped areas. *Eugenics Quarterly* 2:33–39.

Davis, K., and J. Blake. 1956. Social structure and fertility: An analytic framework. *Economic Development and Cultural Change* 4:211–35.

Davis, Kingsley. 1967. Population policy: Will current programs succeed? *Science* 158:730–39.

Debavalya, Nibhon. 1983. *Economic Activities of Thai Women: As Assessed in the 1980 Population Census*. ASEAN-Australia Population Programme. Bangkok: Institute of Population Studies, Chulalongkorn Univ.

Deemar Company, Ltd. 1975. *Rural Population Survey, Thailand 1975*, vol. 1. Prepared for Westinghouse Population Center, Westinghouse Health Systems. Bangkok: Deemar Company, Ltd.

Demeny, Paul. 1975. Letter to the editor. *Scientific American* 232(5):6.

de Young, J. 1955. *Village Life in Modern Thailand*. Berkeley and Los Angeles: Univ. of California Press.

Dixon, Ruth. 1976. The roles of rural women: Female seclusion, economic production, and reproductive choice. In Ronald Ridker, ed., *Population and Development*. Baltimore: Johns Hopkins Press.

Duhl, Leonard. 1984. Social communication, organization and community development: Family planning in Thailand. *Assignment Children* 65/68:117–36.

Durch, J. 1980. Nuptiality patterns in developing countries: implications for fertility. *Reports on the World Fertility Survey*, no. 1. Washington, D.C.: Population Reference Bureau.

Dusitsin, Nikorn, and Suvanee Satayapan. 1984. Sterilization of women by nurse-midwives in Thailand. *World Health Forum* 5:259–62.

Dyck, John H. 1979. Expected schooling for children in rural Thailand and its relationship to fertility. Unpublished M.A. thesis. Department of Agricultural Economics and Rural Sociology, Pennsylvania State Univ.

Dyson, Tim, and Mick Moore. 1983. Kinship structure, female autonomy and demographic behavior in India. *Population and Development Review* 9:35–60.

Easterlin, Richard A. 1980. *Birth and Fortune*. New York: Basic Books.

Easterlin, Richard A., and Eileen Crimmins. 1985. *The Fertility Revolution: A Supply-Demand Analysis*. Chicago: Univ. of Chicago Press.

Economic and Social Commission for Asia and the Pacific. 1976. *Population of Thailand*. ESCAP Country Monograph Series no. 3. Bangkok: Economic and Social Commission for Asia and the Pacific.

Economic and Social Commission for Asia and the Pacific. 1982. *Migration, Urbanization and Development in Thailand*. Comparative study in migration, urbanization and development in the ESCAP region. Country report V. Bangkok: Economic and Social Commission for Asia and the Pacific.

Economic and Social Commission for Asia and the Pacific. 1984. Urbanization in Thailand and its implications for the family planning program. *Population Research Leads*, no. 77. Bangkok: Population Division, ESCAP.

Economic and Social Commission for Asia and the Pacific. 1985a. *Declines in Fertility by Districts in Thailand: An Analysis of the 1980 Census*. Asian Population Studies Series, no. 62-A. Bangkok: Economic and Social Commission for Asia and the Pacific.

Economic and Social Commission for Asia and the Pacific. 1985b. The use of contraception in the Asian and Pacific Regions. *Population Research Leads*.

Embree, J. F. 1950. Thailand—a loosely structured social system. *American Anthropologist* 52:181–93.

Evers, H. D., ed. 1969. *Loosely Structured Social Systems: Thailand in Comparative Perspective*. Southeast Asian Studies, Cultural Report Series 17. New Haven: Yale Univ.

Fagley, R. M. 1967. Doctrines and attitudes of major religions in regard to fertility. In United Nations, *World Population Conference, 1965, vol. 2*. New York, 78–84.

Fawcett, J. T., A. Somboonsuk, and S. Khaisang. 1967. Thailand: An analysis of time and distance factors at an IUD clinic in Bangkok. *Studies in Family Planning* 1(19):8–12.

Ferry, Benoit, and David Smith. 1983. Breastfeeding differentials. *WFS Comparative Studies* no. 23. Voorburg, The Netherlands: International Statistical Institute.

Foster, B. L. 1975. Continuity and change in rural Thai family structure. *Journal of Anthropological Research* 31:34–50.

Foster, B. L. 1977. Adaptation to changing economic conditions in four Thai villages. In William Wood, ed., *Cultural-Ecological Perspectives on Southeast Asia*. Athens, Ohio: International Studies Series, Ohio Univ., no. 41, pp. 113–26.

Foster, B. L. 1978. Socioeconomic consequences of stem family composition in a Thai village. *Ethnology* 17:139–56.

Freedman, Ronald. 1979. Theories of fertility decline: A reappraisal. *Social Forces* 58(1):1–17.

Freedman, Ronald, Ming-Cheng Chang, and Te-Hsiung Sun. 1982. Household composition, extended kinship and reproduction in Taiwan: 1973–80. *Population Studies* 36(3):395–411.

Freedman, Ronald, L. C. Coombs, Ming-Cheng Chang, and Te-Hsiung Sun. 1974. Trends in fertility, family size preferences and practice of family planning: Taiwan, 1965–1973. *Studies in Family Planning* 5:270–88.

Friedlander, D., Z. Eisenbach, and C. Goldscheider. 1980. Family size limitation and birth spacing: The fertility transition of African and Asian immigrants in Israel. *Population and Development Review* 6:581–93.

Goldsen, Rose, and Max Rales. 1957. Factors related to acceptance of innovations in Bang Chang, Thailand. Data paper no. 25, Ithaca: East Asia Program, Cornell Univ.

Goldstein, S. 1970. Religious fertility differentials in Thailand, 1960. *Population Studies* 24:325–37.

Goldstein, S., and A. Goldstein. 1978. Thailand's urban population reconsidered. *Demography* 15(August):235–58.

Goldstein, S., A. Goldstein, and Sauvaluck Piampiti. 1973. The effect of broken marriage on fertility levels in Thailand. Paper no. 4. Bangkok: Institute of Population Studies, Chulalongkorn Univ.

Gupte, Pranay. 1984. *The Crowded Earth: People and the Politics of Population*. New York: W. W. Norton.

Hajnal, J. 1965. European marriage patterns in perspective. In D. V. Glass and D. E. C. Eversley, eds., *Population in History*. London: Edward Arnold.

Hanenberg, Robert. 1980. Current fertility. *WFS Comparative Studies*, no. 11. Voorburg, The Netherlands: International Statistical Institute.

Hanks, Jane Richardson. 1963. Maternity and its rituals in Bang Chang. Data Paper no. 51. Ithaca: Southeast Asia Program, Cornell Univ.

Hanks, L., Jr., and J. R. Hanks. 1963. Thailand: Equality between the sexes. In B. Ward, ed., *Women in New Asia*. Paris: UNESCO.

Hashimoto, Masanori, and Chira Hongladarom. 1981. Effects of child mortality on fertility in Thailand. *Economic Development and Cultural Change* 29:781–94.

Hawley, A. H., and Visid Prachuabmoh. 1971a. Eight-month program effects: 1965. Chapter V in Institute of Population Studies, *The Potharam Study*. Research Report no. 4. Bangkok: Institute of Population Studies, Chulalongkorn Univ.

Hawley, A. H., and Visid Prachuabmoh. 1971b. Fertility before the program began: 1964. Chapter II in Institute of Population Studies, *The Potharam Study*. Research Report no. 4. Bangkok: Institute of Population Studies, Chulalongkorn Univ.

Henderson, J., et al. 1971. *Area Handbook for Thailand*. Washington, D.C.: U.S. Government Printing Office.

Hull, Terence H., and Riningsih Saladi. 1977. The application of Hutterite fertility-weighted indexes to studies of changing marriage patterns. Working Paper Series no. 13. Yogyakarta: Population Institute, Gadjah Mada Univ.

Ingersoll, Jasper, and Fern Ingersoll. 1984. Change in energy uses in village Thailand: A review of experience. Background paper prepared for the World Bank.

Ingersoll, Jasper, and Fern Ingersoll. 1985. A case study: changes in energy uses in village Thailand. In World Bank, *Thailand: Rural Energy Issues and Options.* Washington, D.C.: World Bank.

Institute of Population Studies. 1971a. The Potharam Study. Research Report no. 4. Bangkok: Institute of Population Studies, Chulalongkorn Univ.

Institute of Population Studies. 1971b. *The Methodology of the Longitudinal Study of Social, Economic and Demographic Change.* Research Report no. 6. Bangkok: Institute of Population Studies, Chulalongkorn Univ.

Institute of Population Studies. 1981. A preliminary report of the National Survey of Fertility, Mortality and Family Planning in Thailand, 1979. Paper no. 39. Bangkok: Institute of Population Studies, Chulalongkorn Univ.

Institute of Population Studies. 1982. Knowledge and attitudes concerning abortion practice in urban and rural areas of Thailand. Paper no. 43. Bangkok: Institute of Population Studies, Chulalongkorn Univ.

Institute of Population Studies and National Statistical Office. 1977. *The Survey of Fertility in Thailand: County Report.* Volumes I and II. Bangkok: Allied Printers.

Jones, G., and Yanee Soonthornthum. 1971. *Fertility and Contraception in the Rural South of Thailand.* Bangkok: Manpower Planning Division, National Economic Development Board.

Kamnuansilpa, Peerasit, and Aphichat Chamratrithirong. 1982. *A New Decade of Fertility and Family Planning in Thailand: 1981 Contraceptive Prevalence Survey.* Bangkok: Research Center, National Institute of Development Administration.

Kamnuansilpa, Peerasit, and Aphichat Chamratrithirong. 1985. *Contraceptive Use and Fertility in Thailand: Results from the 1984 Contraceptive Prevalence Survey.* Bangkok: NIDA and IPSR.

Kamnuansilpa, Peerasit, Aphichat Chamratrithirong, and John Knodel. 1983. Family planning and fertility in the south of Thailand with a special emphasis on religious differentials: an analysis of data from the 1981 Contraceptive Prevalence Survey. *Contraceptive Prevalence Surveys Further Analysis Report,* Westinghouse Health Systems.

Kanchanasinith, Kanchana, Wanne Kolasartsenee, and Anthony Bennett. 1980. *Attitudes of Religious Leaders Toward Family Planning and Abortion.* Bangkok: National Family Planning Program, Ministry of Public Health.

Kaplan, Irving. 1981. The society and its environment. Chapter 2 in Frederico Bunge, ed., *Thailand: A Country Study.* Washington, D.C.: U.S. Government Printing Office.

Kemp, J. H. 1970. Initial marriage reidence in rural Thailand. In T. Bunnag and M. Smilkies, eds., *Memorian Phya Anuman Rajdhon.* Bangkok: Siam Society.

Keyes, Charles F. 1984. Mother or mistress but never a monk: Buddhist notions of female gender in rural Thailand. *American Ethnologist* 11(2):223–41.

Khoo, S. E. 1979. Measuring the Thai family planning program's impact on fertility rates: A comparison of computer models. *Studies in Family Planning* 10:137–45.

Kingshill, K. 1960. *Ku Daeng, The Red Tomb: A Village Study in Northern Thailand.* Chiang Mai: The Prince Royal College.

Kirsch, A. T. 1977. Complexity in the Thai religious system: An interpretation. *Journal of Asian Studies* 36(2):241–65.

Knodel, John. 1979. From natural fertility to family limitation: The onset of fertility transition in a sample of German villages. *Demography* 16:493–521.

Knodel, John. 1981. Espacement des naissances et planification familiale: une critique de la mèthode Dupâquier-Lachiver. *Annales Economies Sociétés Civilisations* 36(3):479–94.

Knodel, John. 1982. Child mortality and reproductive behavior in German village populations in the past: A micro-level analysis of the replacement effect. *Population Studies* 36(2):177–200.

Knodel, John. 1983. Natural fertility: Age patterns, levels and trends. In R. A. Bulatao and R. D. Lee, eds., *Determinants of Fertility in Developing Countries*, vol. 1. New York: Academic Press.

Knodel, John, Tony Bennett, and Suthon Panyadilok. 1984. Do free pills make a difference? Thailand's experience. *International Family Planning Perspectives* 10(3): 93–97.

Knodel, John, and Aphichat Chamratrithirong. 1978. Infant and child mortality in Thailand: Levels, trends, and differentials as derived through indirect estimation techniques. Paper no. 57. Honolulu: East-West Population Institute.

Knodel, John, and Etienne van de Walle. 1979. Lessons from the past: Policy implications of historical fertility studies. *Population and Development Review* 5:217–45.

Knodel, John, and Nibhon Debavalya. 1980. Breastfeeding in Thailand: Trends and differentials 1969–79. *Studies in Family Planning* 11(12):355–77.

Knodel, John, Aphichat Chamratrithirong, Napaporn Chayovan, and Nibhon Debavalya. 1982. *Fertility in Thailand: Trends, Differentials, and Proximate Determinants*. Washington, D.C.: National Academy of Sciences.

Knodel, John, and Anthony Pramualratana. 1984. Focus group research as a means of demographic inquiry. Paper presented at the IUSSP Seminar on Micro-approaches to Demographic Research, Canberra, Australia, 3–7 September 1984.

Knodel, John, Nibhon Debavalya, Napaporn Chayovan, and Aphichat Chamratrithirong. 1984. Marriage patterns in Thailand: A review of demographic evidence. In Aphichat Chamratrithirong, ed., *Perspectives on the Thai Marriage*. IPSR Publication no. 81. Bangkok: Institute of Population and Social Research, Mahidol Univ.

Knodel, John, and Gary Lewis. 1984. Postpartum amenorrhea in selected developed countries: Estimates from Contraceptive Prevalence Surveys. *Social Biology* 31(3–4):308–20.

Knodel, John, Peerasit Kamnuansilpa, and Aphichat Chamratrithirong. 1985. Infant feeding practices and postpartum amenorrhea in Thailand: Results from the 1984 Contraceptive Prevalence Survey. *Studies in Family Planning* 16(6/1):302–11.

Koetsawang, Suporn, ed. 1980. *Facts about Abortion in Thailand*. (In Thai). Bangkok: Thira. Karn Pim.

Krannich, Ronald, and Carlyl Rae Krannich. 1980. *The Politics of Family Planning Policy: Thailand—A Case of Successful Implementation*. Monograph series no. 19. Berkeley: Center for South and Southeast Asia Studies, Univ. of California.

Lapham, Robert J., and W. Parker Mauldin. 1984. Family planning program effort and birth rate declines in developing countries. *International Family Planning Perspectives* 10(4): 109–18.

Lapham, Robert J., and W. Parker Mauldin. 1985. Contraceptive prevalence: The influence of organized family planning programs. *Studies in Family Planning* 16(3): 117–37.

Lauro, Don. 1977. A village perspective from two countries: Some implications for differential fertility behavior. In John Caldwell, ed., *The Persistence of High Fertility*. Canberra: The Australian National Univ.

Lauro, Don. 1979. The demography of a Thai village. Unpublished Ph.D. dissertation. Research School of Social Sciences, Australian National Univ., Canberra.

Lee, L., B. Winikoff, V. Laukaran, and J. Bongaarts. 1984. Explaining the differential effects of breastfeeding on duration of amenorrhea: Frequency and patterns of breastfeeding. Paper presented at the Population Association of America Annual Meetings, Minneapolis, May 1984.

Leoprapai, Boonlert, and Sauvaluck Piampiti. 1982. Application of methods of measuring the impact of family planning programmes on fertility: the case of Thailand. In United Nations, *Evaluation of the Impact of Family Planning Programmes on Fertility: Sources of Variance, Population Studies* 76. New York: United Nations.

Leridon, Henri. 1981. Fertility and contraception in 12 developed countries. *International Family Planning Perspectives* 7(2): 70–78.

Limanonda, Bhassorn. 1979. Mate selection and post-nuptial residence in Thailand. Paper no. 28. Bangkok: Institute for Population Studies, Chulalongkorn Univ.

Limanonda, Bhassorn. 1983. Marriage patterns in Thailand: Rural-urban differentials. Paper no. 44. Bangkok: Institute of Population Studies, Chulalongkorn Univ.

Ling, T. O. 1969. Buddhist factors in population growth and control: A survey based on Thailand and Ceylon. *Population Studies* 23(1): 53–60.

London, Bruce. 1980. *Metropolis and Nation in Thailand*. Boulder: Westview Press.

Mauldin, W. P. 1965. Fertility studies: Knowledge, attitude and practice. *Studies in Family Planning* 7: 1–10.

McBeth, John. 1984. A condom a day keeps the doctor away. . . . *Far Eastern Economic Review* 126(41): 49–50.

McCann, M. F., L. S. Liskin, P. T. Piotrow, W. Rinehart, and G. Fox. 1981. Breastfeeding, fertility, and family planning. *Population Reports* I(24).

McDaniel, E. B., and Tieng Pardthaisong. 1973. Evaluating the effectiveness of a two-year family planning action program at Ban Pong village, in North Thailand. Institute of Population Studies, Paper no. 5. Bangkok: Chulalongkorn Univ.

Meesook, Kanitta. 1980. The economic role of Thai women. In Thailand National Commission on Women's Affairs. *Aspects of Thai Women Today*. Bangkok: Arcadia Ltd.

Mizuno, Koichi. 1978a. Change and development of two rice-growing villages in Thailand. *South East Asian Studies* 16(3): 353–77.

Mizuno, Koichi. 1978b. The social organization of rice-growing villages. In Y. Ishii, ed., *Thailand: A Rice-Growing Society*. Translated by Peter and Stephenie Hawkes. Honolulu: Univ. of Hawaii Press.

Mole, Robert L. 1973. *Thai Values and Behavior Patterns*. Rutland, Vt: Charles E. Tuttle.

Morgan, David, and Margret Spanish. 1984. Focus groups: A new tool for qualitative research. *Qualitative Sociology* 7(3):253–70.

Mougne, Christine. 1978. An ethnography of reproduction—changing pattern of fertility in a northern Thai village. In P. A. Scott, ed., *Nature and Man in South East Asia*. London: School of Oriental African Studies, Univ. of London, 68–106.

Mougne, Christine. 1982. The social and economic correlates of demographic change in a northern Thai community. Unpublished Ph.D. dissertation. School of Oriental and African Studies, Univ. of London.

Mougne, Christine. 1984. Women, fertility and power in northern Thailand. Paper presented at the International Conference of Thai Studies, 22–24 August 1984, Bangkok: Chulalongkorn Univ.

Muangman, Debhanom, and Anek Hirunraks. 1980. *Report on a Study on Knowledge, Attitudes and Practices on Family Planning of Buddhist Monks in Thailand*. UNFPA Grant no. THA/76/P05. Bangkok: Faculty of Public Health, Mahidol Univ.

Muecke, Marjorie. 1984. Make money, not babies. *Asian Survey* 24(4):459–70.

Nag, Moni. 1983. Factors affecting natural fertility components: Socio-cultural determinants. In R. A. Bulatao and R. D. Lee, eds., *Determinants of Fertility in Developing Countries*, vol. 1. New York: Academic Press.

Nag, Moni, and Neeraj Kak. 1985. Demographic transition in a Punjab village. *Population and Development Review* 10(4):661–78.

Nagi, Mostafa. 1983. Trends in Moslem fertility and the application of the demographic transition model. *Social Biology* 30(3):245–67.

Narkavonnakit, Tongplaew, and A. Bennett. 1981. Health consequences of induced abortion in rural northeast Thailand. *Studies in Family Planning* 12(2):58–65.

National Council of Women of Thailand. 1977. *The Status of Thai Women in Two Rural Areas*. Survey Report. Bangkok.

National Research Council. 1980. *Fertility and Mortality Changes in Thailand, 1950–1975*. Panel on Thailand, Committee on Population and Demography. Washington, D.C.: National Academy of Sciences.

Ness, Gayl, and Hirofumi Ando. 1984. *The Land Is Shrinking: Population Planning in Asia*. Baltimore: Johns Hopkins Press.

Nortman, D. L. 1985. *Population and Family Planning Programs*, 12th ed. New York: Population Council.

Page, H. J., R. J. Lesthaeghe, and I. H. Shah. 1982. Illustrative analysis: Breastfeeding in Pakistan. *WFS Scientific Reports*, no. 37.

Palmer, Ingrid, Sukaesinee Subhadhira, and Wilaiwat Grisanaput. 1983. The Northeast rainfed agricultural development project in Thailand: A baseline survey of women's roles and household resource allocation for a farming systems approach. Population Council, International Programs, Series for Planners, Study no. 3. New York: Population Council.

Pardthaisong, Tieng. 1978. The recent fertility decline in the Chiang Mai area of Thailand. Paper no. 47. Honolulu: East-West Population Institute.

Pardthaisong, Tieng. 1986. Factors in achievement of below-replacement fertility in Chiang Mai, Thailand. Paper no. 96. Honolulu: East-West Population Institute.

Pejaranonda, Chintana, and Fred Arnold. 1983. Economic characteristics. *Subject Re-*

port no. 1. 1980 Population and Housing Census. Bangkok: National Statistical Office.

Pejaranonda, Chintana, Fred Arnold, and Philip Hauser. 1983. *Revised Estimates of the 1980 Population of Thailand.* Bangkok: National Statistical Office.

Pejaranonda, Chintana, and Aphichat Chamratrithirong. 1984. Fertility and family planning. *Subject Report* no. 3. 1980 Population and Housing Census. Bangkok: National Statistical Office.

Pejaranonda, Chintana, and Aphichat Chamratrithirong. 1985. Nuptiality. *Subject Report* no. 5. 1980 Population and Housing Census. Bangkok: National Statistical Office.

Pfanner, David, and Jasper Ingersoll. 1962. Theravada Buddhism and village economic behavior. *Journal of Asian Studies* 3:341–61.

Phillips, Herbert P. 1965. *Thai Peasant Personality.* Berkeley: Univ. of California Press.

Phillips, Herbert P. 1967. Social contact vs. social promise in a Siamese village. In J. M. Potter, M. N. Diaz, and G. M. Foster, eds., *Peasant Society.* Boston: Little Brown, 346–67.

Phongpaichit, Pasuk. 1982. *From Peasant Girls to Bangkok Masseuses.* Women, Work and Development, no. 2. Geneva: International Labor Office.

Pitayanon, Sumalee. 1983. The impact of short-term contract overseas employment of Thai workers on the economy of rural households and communities: A case study of northeastern villages. In Suchart Prasithrathsint, ed., *Population and Development Interactions in Thailand.* Bangkok.

Podhisita, Chai. 1985a. Peasant household strategies: A study of production and reproduction in a northeastern Thai village. Unpublished Ph.D. dissertation. Univ. of Hawaii.

Podhisita, Chai. 1985b. Buddhism and the Thai world view. In Amara Pongsapich, et al., *Traditional and Changing Thai World View.* Bangkok: Social Science Research Institute, Chulalongkorn Univ.

Population Council. 1981. *Abortion in Thailand: A Review of the Literature.* Bangkok: Population Council, Regional Office for South and East Asia.

Porapakkham, Yawarat, and Anthony Bennett. 1978. *Family Planning/Health and Hygiene Project: A Report on the Baseline Survey.* Bangkok.

Porapakkham, Yawarat, Somjai Pramanpol, and John Knodel. 1983. Maternal and child health and family planning: Comparative study of Thai Buddhists and Thai Moslems, Jana district, Songkla. UNFPA Symposium on Fertility, Family Planning and Development Issues of Population in the South of Thailand, Hat Yai, 16–18 March, 1983.

Porapakkham, Yawarat, Thavatchai Vorapongsathorn, and Somjai Pramanpol. 1986. *Review of Population/Family Planning Needs of Adolescents in Thailand.* IPSR Publication no. 93. Bangkok: Institute for Population and Social Research, Mahidol Univ.

Potter, J. M. 1976. *The Peasant Social Structure.* Chicago: Univ. of Chicago Press.

Prachuabmoh, Chavivun. 1980. The role of women in maintaining ethnic identity and boundaries: A case study of Thai-Muslims [the Malay-speaking group] in southern Thailand. Unpublished Ph.D. dissertation. Univ. of Hawaii.

Prachuabmoh, Chavivun. 1986. The role of religion and economics in decision making: The case of Thai/Malay women. In Ronald Renard, ed., *Anuson Walter Vella.* Honolulu: Univ. of Hawaii Press.

Prachuabmoh, Visid, John Knodel, Suchart Prasithrathsin, and Nibhon Debavalya. 1972. *The Rural and Urban Population of Thailand: Comparative Profiles.* Research Report no. 8. Bangkok: Institute of Population Studies, Chulalongkorn Univ.

Prachuabmoh, Visid, John Knodel, and Pichit Pitaktepsombati. 1973. *The Longitudinal Study of Social, Economic, and Demographic Change in Thailand: The Second Rounds.* Paper no. 3. Bangkok: Institute of Population Studies, Chulalongkorn Univ.

Prasithrathsin, Suchart. 1976. Trends and differentials in fertility. Chapter 5 in Economic and Social Commission for Asia and the Pacific, *Population of Thailand.* Country Monograph Series, no. 3:62–80.

Rabibhadana, Akin. 1984. Kinship, marriage, and the Thai social system. In Aphichat Chamratrithirong, ed., *Perspectives on the Thai Marriage.* IPSR Publication no. 81. Bangkok: Institute for Population and Social Research, Mahidol Univ.

Rachapaetayakom, Jawalaksana. 1983. The demography of the Thai Muslims with special reference to nuptiality and fertility. Ph.D. dissertation. Research School of Social Sciences, Australian National Univ., Canberra.

Rauyajin, Oratai. 1979. Induced abortion: Facts and prospects in Thailand. Mimeographed manuscript. Bangkok: Faculty of Social Sciences and Humanities, Mahidol Univ.

Research and Evaluation Unit, National Family Planning Program, Thailand. 1978. *Second Report: 1977 Continuation Rate Survey for Pill and IUD Acceptors during 1974 to 1976.* Bangkok: Ministry of Public Health.

Research and Evaluation Unit, National Family Planning Program, Thailand. 1979. *Rural Abortion in Thailand: A National Survey of Practitioners.* Bangkok: Ministry of Public Health.

Retherford, R., Chintana Pejaranonda, Lee-Jay Cho, Aphichat Chamratrithirong, and Fred Arnold. 1979. Own children estimates of fertility for Thailand based on the 1970 Census. Papers of the East-West Population Institute, no. 63. Honolulu: East-West Center.

Retherford, R., and J. Palmore. 1983. Diffusion processes affecting fertility regulation. In R. A. Bulatao and R. D. Lee, eds., *Determinants of Fertility in Developing Countries,* vol. 2. New York: Academic Press.

Riley, J. N. 1972. Family organization and population dynamics in a central Thai village. Unpublished Ph.D. dissertation, Department of Anthropology, Univ. of North Carolina, Chapel Hill.

Riley, James, and Santhat Sermsri. 1974. *The Variegated Thai Medical System as a Context for Birth Control Services.* Bangkok: Institute for Population and Social Research, Mahidol Univ.

Robinson, W. C., and Chupensri Wongbuddha. 1980. A revised set of urban population estimates for Thailand. In W. C. Robinson, ed., *Studies in Thai Demographic-Economic Planning.* Bangkok: Population and Manpower Division, National Economic and Social Development Board.

Ron, Zvi. 1980. Agricultural variation and household behavior: A microeconomic analysis of human fertility among Thai rice farm families. Unpublished M.A.

thesis, Department of Agricultural Economics and Rural Sociology, Pennsylvania State Univ.

Rosenfield, A. G., Winich Asavasena, and Jumroon Mikhonorn. 1973. Person-to-person communication in Thailand. *Studies in Family Planning* 4:145.

Rosenfield, A. G., Anthony Bennett, Somsak Varakamin, and D. Lauro. (1982) Thailand's family planning program: An Asian success story. *International Family Planning Perspectives* 8(2):43–51.

Ross, J. A., and K. S. Koh. 1977. Transition to the small family: A comparison of 1964–1975 time trends in Korea and Taiwan. In Y. Chang and P. J. Donaldson, eds., *Population Change in the Pacific Region.* Thirteenth Pacific Science Congress, Vancouver.

Rungpitarangsi, B. 1974. Mortality trends in Thailand: Estimates for the period 1937–1970. Paper no. 10. Bangkok: Institute of Population Studies, Chulalongkorn Univ.

Sadik, Nafis. 1985. Muslim women today. *Populi* 12(1):36–51.

Safilios-Rothschild, Constantina. 1985. The status of women and fertility in the Third World in the 1970–80 decade. *Working Papers* no. 118, Center for Policy Studies. New York: Population Council.

Satayapan, Suvanee, Kanchana Kanchanasinith, and Somsak Varakamin. 1983. Perceptions and acceptability of Norplant implants in Thailand. *Studies in Family Planning* 14(6/7):170–76.

Schneider, Jane, and Peter Schneider. 1984. Demographic transitions in a Sicilian rural town. *Journal of Family History* 9:245–72.

Sermsri, Santhat. 1980. Differentials in urban-rural demographic behavior and events in Thailand. Unpublished Ph.D. dissertation, Department of Sociology, Brown Univ.

Sharp, Lauriston. 1970–71. Neglected entrepreneurs in Thailand. *The Social Science Review Quarterly* 8(3):58–63.

Shevasunt, Somphong, and D. Hogan. 1979. *Fertility and Family Planning in Rural Northern Thailand.* Chicago: Community and Family Study Center, Univ. of Chicago.

Siddiqui, Mohammed. 1979. The initiation of contraception in Taiwan. Unpublished Ph.D. dissertation, Department of Sociology, Univ. of Michigan.

Simmons, George, and Ghazi Farooq. 1985. Introduction. In Ghazi Farooq and George Simmons, eds., *Fertility in Developing Countries.* Hong Kong: MacMillan.

Siripirom, Chavalit. 1982. *Role of Women in Family Decision Making.* Hat Yai, Thailand: Prince of Songkla Univ.

Siripirom, Chavalit. 1983. Social, economic and political characteristics of Thai Buddhists and Moslems in the South. UNFPA Symposium on Fertility, Family Planning and Development Issues of Population in the South of Thailand, Hat Yai, 16–18 March, 1983.

Smith, D. P. 1981. Illustrative analysis: Marriage dissolution and remarriage in Sri Lanka and Thailand. *WFS Scientific Reports,* no. 7. Voorburg, The Netherlands: International Statistical Institute.

Smith, H. E. 1979. The Thai rural family. In M. Singh and P. D. Bardis, eds., *The Family in Asia.* London: George Allen and Unwin.

Smith, H., D. Bernier, F. Bunge, F. Rintnz, R.-S. Shinn, and S. Teleki. 1968. *Area Handbook for Thailand.* Washington, D.C.: U.S. Government Printing Office.

Smith, P. C. 1978. Indexes of nuptiality: Asian and the Pacific. *Asian and Pacific Census Forum* 5(2):9–12.

Smith, P. C. 1980. Asian marriage patterns in transition. *Journal of Family History* 5:58–97.

Stix, Regine, and Frank Notestein. 1940. *Controlled Fertility.* Baltimore: Williams and Wilkens.

Sudaprasert, Kamol, Vichai Tunsiri, and Ta Ngoc Chau. 1980. Regional disparities in the development of education in Thailand. In Gabriel Carron and Ta Ngoc Chau, eds., *Regional Disparities in Educational Development: Diagnosis and Policies for Reduction.* Paris: UNESCO, International Institute for Educational Planning.

Sudham, Pira. 1980. Life in a Buddhist temple. *Sawadee,* July-August.

Suebsonthi, Krich. 1980. The influence of Buddhism and Islam on family planning in Thailand: Communication implication. Unpublished Ph.D. dissertation. Univ. of Minnesota.

Suthasasna, Arong. 1985. The Muslims in Thai polity. Paper presented at the Regional Workshop in Ethnic Minorities in Buddhist Polities: Burma, Sri Lanka and Thailand. 25–28 June 1985. Bangkok: Chulalongkorn Univ.

Suvanajata, Titaya, and Peerasit Kamnuansilpa. 1979. *Thailand Contraceptive Prevalence Survey: Country Report 1979.* Bangkok: Research Center, National Institute of Development Administration.

Szaz, Z. Michael. 1983. *Southeast Asia.* Washington, D.C.: Council for Social and Economic Studies.

Textor, Robert B. 1961. *From Peasant to Pedicab Driver: A Social Study of Northeastern Thai Farmers Who Periodically Migrated to Bangkok and Became Pedicab Drivers.* Cultural Report Series no. 9:43. New Haven: Yale Univ., Southeast Asian Studies.

Thailand, Department of Labor. 1984. *Yearbook of Labor Statistics, 1983.* Bangkok.

Thailand National Commission on Women's Affairs. 1980. *Aspects of Thai Women Today.* Bangkok: Arcadia Ltd.

Thailand National Statistical Office. 1978. *The Survey of Population Change: 1974–1976.* Bangkok: National Statistical Office.

Thai/U.S. Evaluation Team. 1980. *Third Evaluation of the Thailand National Family Planning Program.* A.I.D. Program Evaluation Report no. 3. Washington: Agency for International Development.

Thai/U.S. Evaluation Team. 1984. *Thailand's Population Planning Project II (1982–1987): Mid-term Project Evaluation.* Washington: Agency for International Development.

Thitsa, Khin. 1980. *Providence and Prostitution: Image and Reality for Women in Buddhist Thailand.* London: Change International Reports (Women and Society).

Thomlinson, R. 1971. *Thailand's Population: Facts, Trends, Problems, and Policies.* Bangkok: Thai Watana Panich Press.

Turton, A. 1978. The current situation in the Thai countryside. In A. Turton, J. Fast, and M. Caldwell, eds., *Thailand: Roots of Conflict.* London: Russell Press, 104–42.

Turton, A. 1982. Poverty, reform and class struggle in rural Thailand. In S. Jones, P. C. Joshi, and M. Murmis, eds., *Rural Poverty and Agrarian Reform*. New Delhi: Allied Publishers Private Limited.

United Nations. 1973. *The Determinants and Consequences of Population Trends*, vol. I. New York: United Nations.

United Nations. 1979. *National Experience in the Formulation and Implementation of Population Policy, 1960–1978: Thailand*. ST/ESA/SER.R/31.0 New York: United Nations.

United Nations. 1983. *Indirect Techniques for Demographic Estimation*. New York: United Nations.

United Nations. 1984. *Recent Levels and Trends of Contraceptive Use as Assessed in 1983*. New York: United Nations.

United Nations. 1985. *World Population Prospects: Estimates and the Projections as Assessed in 1982*. Population Studies 86. New York: United Nations.

United States Bureau of the Census. 1983. *World Population 1983*. Washington, D.C.: Department of Commerce.

Vaessen, Martin. 1984. Childlessness and infecundity. *WFS Comparative Studies*, no. 31, Voorburg, The Netherlands: International Statistical Institute.

van de Walle, E., and John Knodel. 1980. Europe's fertility transition: New evidence and lessons for today's developing world. *Population Bulletin* 34, no. 6.

Van Ginneken, J. K. 1974. Prolonged breastfeeding as a birth spacing method. *Studies in Family Planning* 5:201–205.

Warwick, D. 1982. *Bitter Pills*. Cambridge: Cambridge Univ. Press.

Wells, William. 1974. Group interviewing. In Robert Ferber, ed., *Handbook of Marketing Research*. New York: McGraw-Hill, 133–46.

Whitaker, Donald P. 1981. The economy. Chapter 3 in Frederico Bunge, ed., *Thailand: A Country Study*. Washington, D.C.: U.S. Government Printing Office.

Wijeyewardene, G. 1967. Some aspects of rural life in Thailand. In T. H. Silcock, ed., *Thailand: Social and Economic Studies in Development*. Canberra: Australian National Univ. Press, 65–83.

Williamson, N. E. 1976. *Sons or Daughters: a Cross-Cultural Survey of Parental Preferences*. Beverley Hills, California: Sage.

Wirtz, Irma. 1981. Family planning—the Thai way. *Development and Cooperation* 5 (October/November): 21–22.

World Bank. 1980. *Thailand: Toward a Development Strategy of Full Participation*. Washington, D.C.: World Bank.

World Bank. 1985. *World Development Report*. New York: Oxford Univ. Press.

Wyatt, David. 1984. *Thailand: A Short History*. New Haven: Yale Univ. Press.

Yoddumnern, Bencha. 1983. Preliminary report on fertility behavior in a northern Thai village: Determinants and consequences. Unpublished manuscript prepared for the World Health Organization.

Zimmerman, C. C. 1931. *Siam: Rural Economic Survey 1930–31*. Bangkok: Bangkok Times Press.

Index